THE
DAWN
OF
AVIATION

Cover image: Pilots Travers and Noel with their Farman at Eastbourne in 1912.

THE
DAWN
OF
AVIATION

THE PIVOTAL ROLE OF SUSSEX, PEOPLE AND PLACES
IN THE DEVELOPMENT OF FLIGHT

JOSH SPOOR

With compliments to Roy Brooks

AIR WORLD

AIR WORLD

THE DAWN OF AVIATION

First published in Great Britain in 2021 by
Air World
An imprint of
Pen & Sword Books Ltd
Yorkshire – Philadelphia

ISBN 978 1 52678 634 0

Typeset by SJmagic DESIGN SERVICES, India.

Printed and bound in the UK by CPI Group (UK) Ltd, Croydon, CR0 4YY.

Pen & Sword Books Limited incorporates the imprints of Atlas, Archaeology, Aviation, Discovery, Family History, Fiction, History, Maritime, Military, Military Classics, Politics, Select, Transport, True Crime, Air World, Frontline Publishing, Leo Cooper, Remember When, Seaforth Publishing, The Praetorian Press, Wharncliffe Local History, Wharncliffe Transport, Wharncliffe True Crime and White Owl.

For a complete list of Pen & Sword titles please contact

PEN & SWORD BOOKS LIMITED
47 Church Street, Barnsley, South Yorkshire, S70 2AS, England
E-mail: enquiries@pen-and-sword.co.uk
Website: www.pen-and-sword.co.uk

Or
PEN AND SWORD BOOKS
1950 Lawrence Rd, Havertown, PA 19083, USA
E-mail: Uspen-and-sword@casematepublishers.com
Website: www.penandswordbooks.com

Contents

Foreword

I had the privilege over twenty-five years ago of meeting, and becoming friends with, one of this country's unknown aviation authors.

Roy Brooks would always have time (and patience) with me in my endeavours to learn about the history of aviation in Sussex.

The first part of this story of Sussex aviation was researched and written by Roy at a time when the internet had not been born. Thus, this story was conceived and executed by hand. His tenacity and determination with local libraries and historical sources was a remarkable and unmatched feat, to his external credit.

Why it was never published in anything other than microfiche form I'm not sure, but it is possible that Roy did not have access to supporting material such as postcards and pictures etc. This story has now been enhanced to show the history of aviation in Sussex.

My wish that this book will stand as a tribute to Roy and all his hard work.

I wish to thank Roy's widow Betty and her family for allowing me to have this published and never losing faith.

Josh Spoor,
Southwick, 2020

Introduction

Here is a story to be read, enjoyed and cherished. It recounts, in vivid style, the way in which successive generations of Sussex men – and women – carved out, within this ancient and delightful county, a memorable place in the history of British aviation.

Through long, patient and perceptive research, Roy Brooks has vividly brought to life much of the remarkable, but largely forgotten, story of Sussex flights and flyers. From Roman times onwards, Sussex has been immersed in British history. But what has not been properly understood – nor previously recorded in any depth – has been the way in which Sussex responded to mankind's restless quest to fly.

The story goes back to 1785 when one of the first cross-country flights in Britain alighted at Horsham – by balloon.

There followed a steady stream of Sussex adventures into aeronautics – from cross-Channel balloon flights to early aircraft manufacture at Shoreham, through flying instruction there, and the operation of coastal patrol airships from Polegate, to the founding of two of the most historic – and one of them now, the busiest – airports in Britain: Shoreham and Gatwick.

Shoreham Airport indeed – with Brooklands and Farnborough – ranks among the earliest of airfields in the United Kingdom. All three have been continuously in use for more than eighty years, in peace and throughout the two world wars.

Alongside came the busy Sussex airship station at Polegate, the aerodromes at Eastbourne and at Ladies Mile, Brighton, the seaplane station at Newhaven and from the 1920s onwards, Tangmere, near Chichester, which became one of the front-line fighter stations during the Battle of Britain.

The pleasant Sussex countryside, especially along the Channel coast, is full of the sometimes brief, but always gallant, history of Royal Air Force fighter stations. Some of them were set up during the 1920s but all have historic links with the Second World War. A few of them – such as Bognor and Goodwood – usefully remain for civil use today.

Those wartime airfields have names that are redolent of Sussex lore – many of them close around Chichester. Lest they should be forgotten, let us place on record Apuldram, Chailey, Coolham, Deanland, Funtingdon, Merston, Selsey, Westhampnett and Wilmington.

And then there are also those dedicated men and women whose names will be remembered with pride and affection wherever flying is enjoyed.

Roy Brooks has assembled, with skill, devotion and understanding, the story of 'Sussex Flights and Flyers', and, with it, he recalls those Sussex places where doughty aeronautical deeds were done. Now thanks to his industrious efforts, they will not be forgotten.

Chapter 1

The Balloonatics

At about 5pm on Wednesday, 23 March 1785 the first aerial passengers descended by balloon in Sussex at Kingsfold near Horsham, having left London one hour earlier. Two hundred years later on a Saturday, some 8 miles away, 48,000 passengers passed through Gatwick Airport (transferred from Surrey to West Sussex under the 1974 County Boundary changes), and 434 aircraft took off or landed on its runway that day. The first successful hot air balloon flights had taken place in France some three years earlier than the one that ended in Sussex as a result of experiments by the Montgolfier brothers, Joseph and Etienne. As an aviation historian put it, the balloon was born 'and most unexpectedly born, so to say out of a clear blue sky; and born without any prophecy or preamble'.

The news of the first manned flight by balloon appeared in the *Sussex Weekly Advertiser* for Wednesday, 15 December 1783 and gave the following details of this momentous occasion:

> The following account of the late remarkable experiment made by Monsieur Montgolfier, is taken from a Verbal Process, that is, an Affidavit of several persons of distinction November 21 1783.
>
> This afternoon Monsieur Montgolfier exhibited a new trial of his aerostatic machine at the Castle de La Mutte. The sky being clouded in some parts, and clear in others, the wind north-west, precisely eight minutes after midday, a mortar was fired as a signal that the machine was going to be filled. In eight minutes notwithstanding the wind it appeared unfolded at every point, and ready to go off, the Marquis d'Arlandes and M Pilâtre de Rozier, both being

in the gallery annexed to it. The first intention was to make the machine rise, and at the same time hold with the ropes, for the purpose of examining the exact weight it was able to carry, and whether everything was properly contrived and arranged for the grand trial. But the machine being pushed off by the wind, far from rising vertically, took its own direction over one of the walks in the garden, and the several ropes that held it acting with too much resistance, occasioned several rents, one of which was more than six foot in length. Being brought back, they repaired it in less than two hours. It was filled a second time and set off fifty-four minutes after one, carrying the same persons. The machine was then seen to rise in quite a majestic manner, and when it reached an elevation of 250ft, the intrepid travellers, shaking their hats, saluted the spectators.

Our aerial navigators were soon out of sight, but the machine hovering on the horizon and displaying the noblest spectacle attained 3,000ft at least, where it remained in view. It crossed the Seine under the field gate of La Conference, and passed between the Ecole Militaire and the Hotel of the Invalids, so all of Paris had the opportunity of viewing it. The travellers, being satisfied with their experiment and unwilling to take a longer course, agreed amongst themselves to descend. But perceiving that the wind was carrying them on the houses of the street de Seve, in the suburb of Saint-Germain, with great presence of mind immediately unfolded more gas and rose again, pursuing their way, until they found themselves past the metropolis, in open fields. With the utmost tranquillity they came down, beyond the new bulwark, facing the mill of Coultebarbe, without having felt the slightest inconvenience and having still in their gallery, two thirds of their provisions. It is, therefore, evident, that it was in their power to go over a space three times greater than they did, their progress was from four to five thousand fathoms, that is 30,000ft and the time they employed from twenty to twenty-five minutes. The machine was 70ft high and 46ft in diameter; it contained 60,000 cubic feet and the weight it lifted amounted to sixteen or seventeen hundred pounds or thereabouts.

Done at the Castle de la Muttee at five o'clock in the afternoon.

(Signed) the Duke of Polignac, the Duke of Guinês, Count of Polastorn, Count of Vaudreuil, d'Hunand, Benjamin Franklin, Faujas de Saint Fond, Delisle and Lercy of the Academy of Sciences.

The signature of Benjamin Franklin, the American statesman, philosopher and scientist, who was touring Europe at the time, undoubtedly lent an air of verisimilitude to the whole affair. What the report did not mention was that the balloon had a large brazier suspended underneath, which the two aeronauts fed with straw throughout the voyage to keep the balloon aloft. The two had also providentially provided themselves with buckets of water and sponges on sticks to enable them to damp down the sparks that burnt holes in the balloon envelope and which had to be extinguished without delay.

This successful ascent was swiftly emulated by Jacques Alexander Cesar Charles, a promising young physicist from the French Academy of Science, with a companion on the first day of December. Their balloon was 28ft in diameter and filled with hydrogen, produced by the action of sulphuric acid on iron filings. The balloon was designed by Charles and had been given a great deal of thought. Its features were copied and became common to all balloons for many years. There was an open neck at the bottom of the envelope for filling and to allow the gas to escape in the reduced atmospheric pressure of high altitudes, or when the sun heated the envelope. The upper part of the balloon was held within cord netting and attached to a hoop from which the passenger car, made of wickerwork, was suspended. A valve was also fitted to the top of the balloon that could be operated from the basket to allow the aeronaut to release gas rapidly for a speedy return to earth.

Meanwhile in Britain, two Italians were following these events with keen interest – intent on repeating these French successes here. The first was Vincente Lunardi, who had already been in London for two years as the private and confidential secretary to the Prince of

Caraminico, the Neapolitan Ambassador to the Court of St James. Lunardi was a handsome and personable figure, very vain with a mercurial temperament. He was a great favourite with the ladies and, with all his faults, an honest and brave man. His rival was Count Francesco Zambeccari, an indigent nobleman and sailor of fortune. Earlier he had been a lieutenant in the Spanish Navy, serving off the American coast and taking part in the capture of Pensacola. After some ill-advised remarks about the Spanish clergy, he roused the antagonism of the Inquisition. Given advice from friends to flee the country, he decamped on a French frigate from Havana sailing to the Cape. From there he made his way to France and then moved on to Britain to seek sanctuary. It was when he was passing through Paris that he became aware of the ballooning fever that was sweeping the capital and took the opportunity to learn something of the latest ballooning techniques.

On arrival in London, the Count stayed at the house of a fellow Italian, Michael Biaggini, who made and sold artificial flowers from his house in Noble Street, Cheapside. It was there that the pair made their first balloon of some 5ft diameter and attached a small box underneath with a note to the finder to return it and claim a reward of three guineas. Released on 1 November, it was found by a farmer near Waltham Abbey, Essex, and Zambeccari wrote to his father at the end of the month about the incident and the subsequent balloon that was released later, as follows:

> The news of the extraordinary experiments being carried out with the sphere of M. Montgolfier prompted me to set about building one myself, and this I accomplished without difficulty. On the first of this month I succeeded in sending up a sphere, five feet in diameter, from the roof of a certain Biaggini, a trader in artificial flowers, who made a financial contribution to the experiment. Although this sphere was sent into the air with no witnesses to the event, and from a purely private location, some amazed person spotted it in the sky and by the next day the news had run through London. Spurred on by this interest I then built another sphere 10ft in diameter, in order to satisfy the curiosity of the public. I took great pains in

4

the accomplishment of this task, and this unusual display took place at the Artillery Ground on 25 November attended by a dense crowd. The satisfaction gained on my part from this experiment was multiple … I first studied the fortifications which enable one to resist a powerful enemy and then applied them to aerial spheres; at the moment I am in the process of making one which has a diameter of 30ft. I hope this will be of assistance to me in carrying out what I am sure will be some extremely productive experiments; I would like to navigate it horizontally and steer in any direction I wish. For me, the most intense pleasure is the thought that this news will bring some measure of consolation and should alleviate the disappointments of the past.

It would seem Biaggini soon saw that ballooning had commercial possibilities because the second balloon was put on exhibition at the Lyceum in the Strand before its ascent, a charge of sixpence (2½p) being made to view it. Tickets were also sold from half-a-crown (12½p) upwards to view the filling of the balloon and its ascent.

The first public launching of the 10ft diameter balloon took place at one o'clock on Tuesday, 25 November 1783 before a large multitude, most of whom were non-paying spectators. Caught in a northerly air stream, it came down at Graffham, near Petworth, Sussex, after travelling some 48 miles. There is a story, probably apocryphal, that a Sussex farmer who found the balloon put it on display in his barn and charged his neighbours a penny each to satisfy their curiosity. No local account seems to have survived but a London paper reporting the event said that the balloon was carried the following morning, Wednesday, to Petworth. The only Sussex paper at the time, the *Sussex Weekly Advertiser*, reported in its issue of 8 December as follows:

The descent of the air balloon near Petworth, in this county, mentioned in the London papers, we presume needs confirmation, as one of the carriers of this paper was at that place on Wednesday morning last and did not hear a syllable on the matter.

By January 1784 Zambeccari was talking of building a man-carrying balloon of some 50ft diameter that would ascend from Hyde Park, but his attempts to raise the estimated £800 for its construction by public subscription failed. Zambeccari, realising that the project was impossible without incurring debts that he could not possibly repay, decided to return to France.

In the meantime, his arch rival Lunardi, who moved in more affluent circles and had also set up a public subscription to build a balloon, was having a great deal more success. By August his balloon was on show at the Lyceum. It was 34ft in diameter and made from 500 yards of oiled silk in alternate stripes of red and white. It was while at the Lyceum that he met his patron, George Biggen, a well-to-do amateur chemist and inventor of the coffee percolator, who, Lunardi agreed, should accompany him on his proposed balloon ascents. He had permission originally to make his first ascent from the grounds of Chelsea Hospital. This was cancelled because a certain mountebank, Chevalier de Moret, announced an earlier balloon ascent, which turned out to be a fiasco and led to a riot and much damage to nearby property.

As it turned out, ballooning proved to be a pursuit involving a great deal of risk, of which the actual ascent and subsequent descent could be the least of an aeronaut's worries. In the first place, balloon ascents, whether advertised or not, attracted vast crowds, the great majority of whom paid nothing to view the balloon or the ascent. The authorities had little or no control over such large assemblies, and such crowds were not slow to show their displeasure. The generation of hydrogen gas, for example, was more often than not very much a hit and miss affair, and balloons were rarely ready for departure at the stated time. By then the spectators' patience could have been worn thin amid mayhem, and the destruction of nearby property as well as the balloon with bodily violence against the balloonist was by no means unusual. So even in adverse weather, which could not always be anticipated, the aeronaut would often prefer to take his chance in the air rather than risk the displeasure of the crowd. These large gatherings also provided a field day for thieves and pickpockets, and a letter said to be from one of them was published in the *Universal Register* of 1785 (later to be retitled *The Times*). The following is an extract:

To the Worshipful Company of Balloon managers and High Flyers Etc., We the ancient and numerous society of pickpockets, freebooters etc., should be wanting in gratitude, did we not take an early opportunity of thankfully addressing you, our best friends, for the many benefits received from the weekly exertions you have made for your own profit and the public amusement. While thousands are looking up in astonishment at your cloud capped aerial vehicles, we are actively diving into their pockets for what is called the root of all evil, yet devoutly wished and prayed for by men of every descriptions. Your station, Gentlemen, enables you to look down on mankind, while gaping with admiration at the elevated extensive sphere in which you move. For the additions almost daily making to all balloon proprietors and adventurers in both kingdoms, we presage a happy increase in business of golden opportunities, for frequent filching, which shall be properly applied. Signed Legion for we are many.

An example of this was reported in the *General Evening Post* for 25–27 November 1783, when Zambeccari's unmanned balloon ascended at Moorfields. A foreigner of distinction had his pocket picked of a purse containing a valuable diamond ring and some 40 guineas. The robbery was thought to have been committed by a genteel lady who spoken French fluently and asked the gentleman about the balloon.

However, the setback to Lunardi's plans as to the place of his ascent turned out ultimately to his advantage. Some friends arranged for him to use the Artillery Ground at Moorfield, at a much-reduced fee to that payable to the Chelsea Hospital. The Lunardi ascent was made on 15 September, and he met all of the usual problems. Although his balloon was supposed to have been filled overnight, by one o'clock in the afternoon it was still not fully inflated. By then the Prince of Wales and his entourage had arrived to view the ascent, and the authorities, fearful for the safety of the Royal Personage in view of the vast multitude that had gathered, insisted that Lunardi ascend without further delay. So, at two o'clock, with the balloon only two-thirds full, Lunardi had to abandon Biggen and, taking his place in the basket, rose into the air somewhat to the surprise of most of the crowd, who had been looking forward to a fiasco and a riot. They comforted themselves, however, with the thought that Lunardi was unlikely to ever be seen again, and cheered lustily as the balloon climbed into the sky. The Prince of Wales and the gentlemen present also removed their hats as a sign of respect.

In fact, of course, the Lunardi voyage was a great success and one hour later he came down at South Mimms. Lighting the balloon, he re-ascended to land later at Standen, near Ware. He had a triumphal return to London, was presented to the Prince of Wales and was lionised as the first man to fly in England. His balloon was again exhibited in Oxford Street and had a constant flow of visitors. With this money and various testimonials, Lunardi was able to meet all his debts and still make a handsome profit, said to be between £2,000 to £4,000, a not inconsiderable sum at that time.

The news of the ascent seems to have lured Zambeccari to return to England and resume his attempt to build his own balloon, even if Lunardi had stolen his thunder. By now interest in ballooning was blossoming, with Lunardi bonnets and even, for the daring, Lunardi garters. This time Zambeccari was successful in obtaining the funds he needed, mainly from noble patronage. He built a 34ft diameter balloon with an 11ft car to hold three passengers, and gave it the name of the 'British Air Balloon'. It was completed before the New Year and in January the Count inserted a notice in the London press, saying it was his intention to ascend with a 'Gentleman of the first distinction' and if such a daring creature could be found, a lady. This was also the month that the French balloonist Blanchard and his patron, the American Dr Jefferies, crossed the Channel from Dover. They only finally succeeded in the enterprise by throwing all loose items overboard to keep above the waves. At the end they had to cast their clothes on the waters before finally making landfall near Calais.

In the following month the 'British Balloon' was exhibited in the Lyceum from 9am to 10pm, with an admission charge of one shilling (5p). The gentleman who was originally supposed to accompany the Count, according to the press was a General Vaughan but this was later changed to Rear Admiral Edward Vernon. A non-returnable fee of 300 guineas was paid by the admiral for the privilege of being the first naval man to ascend in a balloon. Said to suffer, from one newspaper account, from a 'weakness of the nerves', the admiral was sixty-two years old and perhaps not an ideal companion for such an enterprise. The Count's scheme for squiring a lady aloft produced no applicant until the eve of the ascent, when a Miss Grist, who had worked for a tambour maker in Fleet Street, applied and was accepted. The ascent had been fixed for 23 March from what was described as a cheap bread warehouse on Tottenham Court Road. The weather was abominable, with sleet, snow and rain. Nevertheless, the streets around the building were soon jammed with sightseers and although Zambeccari had extolled his new apparatus for producing hydrogen, inflation was still painfully slow. It started at eleven o'clock, and four hours later the balloon was still less than half full. During this time the strong winds had damaged the balloon netting, and many spectators were convinced that the ascent would have to be postponed.

There, is, however, another letter from Zambeccari to his father dated 10 April 1785 telling him about the voyage:

> On the 23 of last March, the public was informed my balloon would be leaving in one hour after midday. It was thirty-four feet in diameter and made of painted taffeta covered with a large net of silk cord which hung from an extremely light gondola, eleven feet long by four feet at its widest point and richly decorated with silk trimmings and gold bows. This gondola was to carry Admiral Vernon and myself. But that day a very strong wind combined with the cold weather split some of the fabric and the net was partly torn, so at 4pm the balloon was only half inflated. However, it had enough force to resolve me to leave, so as to avoid the impatient mob, and restore a source of boredom for the numerous noble spectators. It was then that I entered the gondola, the Admiral followed me as well as a young Englishwoman who was very keen to fly. But my balloon, being overloaded by a few pounds, lifted and lowered itself successively, much

to the regret of the pretty lady who was obliged to leave. Then, to the cheers of the many thousands of people, the machine lightened by some 100lbs and a further ten I threw from the sandbag, we rose rapidly with the force of the same weight, almost vertically in spite of the wind. In a few minutes it disappeared from the spectators' view and they searched for me with telescopes to no avail as we had risen, according to the barometer, to an altitude of about two and half miles. The view of the horizon from that isolated spot is as pleasing as it is novel and majestic. We encountered no problems with cold, lack of breath etc., but as three of the cords that held the gondola to the net had broken and remembering the strength of the wind close to the ground, I advised my companion that the machine should start to descend. This was accomplished by releasing some of the inflammable air. We touched down in a ploughed field, which softened the landing after having covered 35 miles in a space of 54 minutes. Having caught the coach at the next village, we returned to London in perfect health by ten o'clock that night.

This account seems rather at odds with the details given by the press, one paper indeed, calling it the most hazardous balloon voyage yet. Miss Grist, for example, described as the darling of the watching crowd, was extremely reluctant to give up her place in the balloon and made every effort, including copious tears, to persuade the admiral to yield his place to her. He was unmoved, no doubt reflecting on the amount he had paid for the ascent, and she had to leave the balloon, assisted, it was said, by the Count with 'gentle force'. One reporter, carried away by the scene, described what followed:

Being divorced of its loveliest burden, the balloon ascended with great rapidity conveying the Admiral to an element, which neither he or any of his naval predecessors had ever before navigated, if sailing an ocean of air may be allowed this term.

When the three cords parted from the gondola, the car had a decided list and the balloon went into a rotary motion that continued for the rest of the voyage. By now, the admiral it seemed, not unnaturally, expressed a strong desire to descend. It was at this point that Zambeccari discovered, to his consternation, that the cord that operated the valve at the top of the balloon to vent the gas for a controlled descent had been pushed, inadvertently inside the envelope. The admiral then decided to take matters in his own hands and tried to cut a hole in the bottom of the envelope, but found he was not tall enough to reach it. Zambeccari then made two holes in the envelope and at the same time threw out the last bag of ballast, reasoning that although the balloon would rise, the pressure would force the gas out more quickly. In the event the balloon did rise above the clouds, which precipitated snow over the pair and they were frozen before the balloon started on its descent.

No local account of their landing at Kingsfold near Horsham seems to have survived, as no known copies of the *Sussex Weekly Advertiser* for 1785 exist. The next month the Count apologised in the *Universal Register* for the 'mortifying' circumstances of his March ascent, blaming it on the weather and assuring its readers of a second and more successful ascent. This time it was conjectured that a 'Field Officer' would accompany the Count, which may have referred to Major Money, the only Army officer who seemed to show any interest in the use of balloons in war. However, nothing seemed to come of this and Zambeccari reverted to his original intention of squiring the first English lady into the air to upstage Lunardi.

The second ascent of the 'British Balloon' was due on 2 May with a Miss Hall, who was doomed, like Miss Grist, to disappointment. During the inflation a hole appeared at the top of the balloon and the gas started to escape. Upset by the stench of the gas, the crowd tore down the scaffolding erected for viewing the ascent and also reduced a nearby wall to rubble. Fourteen of the ringleaders were taken into custody before the rest of the mob could be dispersed. This seems to have been the final blow as far as Zambeccari's ballooning in England was concerned; he disposed of his balloon and continued his travels. Joining the Russian Navy, he was captured by the Turks, spending two years as a prisoner of war. On release he returned to

Italy and resumed his ballooning career, making nearly fifty ascents before being killed in Bologna in 1812 when his balloon caught fire and he leapt from the burning gondola to be dashed to his death on the ground below.

As a footnote, Lunardi's second proposed ascent with Biggen and Mrs Letitia Sage was also a fiasco, the balloon not having sufficient 'lift' to rise with three passengers. Lunardi went up alone but was forced down after half an hour with a rent in the balloon envelope. The press were unsympathetic, suggesting that Lunardi should both weigh and measure any future lady aeronaut, as it turned out that Mrs Sage actually weighed 14st. However, on the next ascent Lunardi stood down and Biggen and Mrs Sage did achieve a two-hour flight, so he did, in the end, put the first English lady in the air.

Although Zambeccari did not achieve the fame of Lunardi, he still holds two 'Firsts' for Sussex aviation in that his was the first unmanned balloon in Sussex and he made the first balloon flight with a passenger to the county. It has also been said that a popular boy's book called *The Travels of Count Zambeccari* caught the imagination of a youthful Otto Lilienthal and stimulated his interest in flying. As he was undoubtedly the foremost pioneer of the hang glider and made a significant contribution to the development of the aeroplane, perhaps Count Francesco Zambeccari rests content in the balloonist's Valhalla.

Chapter 2

The Showmen and a Woman

With the passage of time, the novelty of ballooning subsided and degenerated into public spectacle, while balloonists had been reduced to dreaming up bizarre stunts to attract more people to their ascents.

In 1785, two years after the first launches, Charles Green was born, to become, in due course, the premier British balloonist. It is said he first became interested in the properties of coal gas for ballooning when he experimented with its use for the illumination of the family fruiterer's at Goswell Street, Cheapside, in London. At the time coal gas was only just coming into use, almost solely for lighting. Before the advent of the incandescent gas mantle it was the heavier hydrocarbons in coal gas that contributed most to its illuminating power. Each charge of gas in the retorts produced a greater release of hydrocarbons at the beginning, which tailed off towards the end of the process. Thus, when the charge was 'burnt off' it was then producing gas that had little in the way of hydrocarbons but was ideal for inflating balloons, and giving the maximum 'lift' that Green discovered, when he inflated a number of small balloons and released them in experiments.

Very little seems to be known about Green's career before, at the age of forty-six, he emerged as a professional balloonist, with the assistance of his wife, his son Charles George and his three brothers William, James and Henry. It seems from the start of this enterprise, Green had managed to convince the newly emerging gas, light and coke companies that coal gas produced at the end of their distillation process was ideal for inflating balloons. The new companies were not slow to realise that balloon flights, which still attracted big crowds, were good publicity for their increasingly popular product. Thus balloonists, for a while, were even subsidised or at least supplied with gas at much below its commercial price. The gas for ballooning was, where possible, put into separate gas holders where the company had spare capacity. Since most ascents took place in the summer months when the demand for lighting was reduced, this worked out very well. The use of separate gas holders also enabled the balloon to be filled more quickly, a prolonged filling period meant much of the gas would escape through the envelope, leaving only the heavier components behind with a consequent loss of 'lift'. The comparative ease of now being able to fill balloons with coal gas undoubtedly gave a fillip to ballooning as the use of coal gas spread around Britain.

Green's first balloon was given the name of George IV Royal Coronation Balloon to celebrate the royal event. It had a diameter of 31ft and a lifting capacity of 8cwt and was decorated with the Royal Arms to honour the new monarch. Green's first public ascent was on 19 July 1821, but it was not until 3 October that he came to Brighton, which would be his fifth ascent, from the recently opened gasworks at Black Rock in East Brighton and the first balloon ascent from what was then a town. As it turned out, it was an experience he did not forget for many years, which served as a warning to other balloonists of the folly of making ascents near the coast unless their balloon had sufficient capacity and ballast for a Channel crossing. Although the ascent had been fixed for midday, Green was persuaded to delay the inflation to ensure that the maximum number of people could be present to watch the ascent. After an hour or so the balloon was filled up under the supervision of Mr Ingledew, the gas company engineer. When this was completed, Green attached the car, by which time the strength of the wind had risen. The release of a pilot balloon showed the wind to be south-east by east, and Green realised that he would almost certainly be forced out over the Channel. By now the number of spectators assembled at Black Rock and the surrounding hills was about 30,000 and he had little alternative but to go through with the voyage. His subsequent account of the ascent was as follows:

I took my leave amid the plaudits and anxious good wishes of the surrounding company, and ascended slowly but majestically towards the celestial region. I rose about 800ft when the gas, which before had been expanded by the heat of the sun, became condensed by the change in temperature, and the balloon consequently descended, this I could easily have prevented by the discharge of ballast, but I felt confident I was affording to the spectators a gratification unprecedented in the history of aeronautics; I therefore chose to take advantage of the circumstances. I eventually threw out two bags of ballast and re-ascended, the balloon taking a direction southeast by south; it appeared to be floating for a considerable time at the land's edge.

The appearance of earthly objects gradually diminishing, I still ascended, so as to afford the spectators a diminished view of my aerostatic machine. The balloon here took a more southerly direction, and finding myself going rapidly to sea, at an altitude of about two miles, I espied two vessels, the only assistance in sight at that elevation. I immediately opened the valve, and the balloon began to descend with great velocity, and in the end, was plunged by the force of the wind into a tremendously heaving sea. It then drifted rapidly, assuming the appearance of an immense umbrella before me; the car striking the water on its side, its ornaments and covering were presently destroyed, and it instantly filled with water. I had previously put on my life preserver, but unfortunately it became entangled with the cords. I was here in a perilous situation, the life preserver useless, and the car repeatedly turning over, so I was alternately under water. In this distress I continued for some minutes, when, almost exhausted, the propriety occurred to me of separating the cords which entangled the preserver, and which, after much difficulty, I accomplished with a knife. After this, I had the consolation of being raised considerably above the water, which enabled me to hail a boat humanely sent to my assistance by Captain Clear of the Unity packet, whose humane and active exertions I shall ever feel proud to acknowledge. I was at the time so much exhausted that it would have been utterly impossible for me to have continued my hold five minutes longer. I remained in the water, according to the opinion of Captain Clear about twenty minutes; but it appeared to me much longer. The balloon dragged me about two miles through heavy surf, until, with great difficulty, I got on board. My distress was so great as to render it absolutely necessary to strip me. I continued for some hours insensible and must refer the public to Captain Clear for particulars during that period. After my recovery, I anxiously enquired of the Captain if my property was safe on board; when he informed me that the balloon was literally torn to ribbons and my philosophical instruments, and my apparatus, all lost or destroyed. Upon examination I found the balloon impossible to repair. I landed safely on Wednesday morning at one o'clock at Newhaven and reached the gas establishment at Brighton at ten o'clock.

On Thursday morning the 'Inhabitants and visitors' in Brighton held a meeting at the Old Ship Tavern and agreed to open a public subscription to reward the 'Intrepidity of the gallant aeronaut, Mr Green', forming a Committee for the purpose. It is not known exactly how much was actually collected and given to Green, but it seems that he did not resume ballooning until the August of the following year.

In 1824, two other aeronauts, a husband and wife team, George and Margaret Graham, appeared in Sussex. George Graham had made his first ascent only in August of the previous year. A notice in the local press informed the public that Mr Graham's fourteenth ascent would be made from the Ireland Royal Gardens, near the Level in Brighton, on Tuesday, 5 October. An admission charge of two shillings and sixpence (12½p) was to be made to view the inflation and ascent and a salon was fitted up expressly for the accommodation of Mrs Fitzherbert, spouse of the Prince of Wales. For three days before this there was a charge of one shilling (5p) to view the balloon, its car and all its associated equipment. There were echoes of Green's early immersion when a notice issued finally added, 'Should the balloon be driven to sea a reward of £10 will be given to the first boat which comes to Mr Graham's assistance.' Unfortunately, the weather on the Tuesday was very wet and windy and the ascent had to be postponed. On Wednesday, Graham started to make his balloon ready for the voyage despite the increasing wind and driving rain. Many people in the Gardens thought the attempt would be foolish, and should be postponed again. One group asked Graham if the conditions were dangerous for flight and Graham admitted they were. After one of the group said, 'God forbid that a man should risk his life for our amusement!' Graham was persuaded to abandon the flight until the weather improved. It seems the non-paying spectators outside the enclosure were the loudest in the protestations on hearing of this decision, and threatened to wreck the balloon, though they later dispersed peacefully.

On Friday the weather improved greatly and Graham, together with a Mr Slee Junior, took off at three o'clock and remained in the air for forty minutes, finally descending near the Earl of Chichester's Park, some 5 miles outside Brighton. Slee related he asked Graham as they neared the end of the ascent and were preparing to land, 'How was he to act?' The aeronaut told him, 'When we get to within a few yards of the ground, leap from it when you think you are near enough,' which he did without injury.

Charles Green also made a return visit to Sussex in October 1824 to make his twenty-fifth ascent from the Chichester gasworks near the Barns, South Gate. The large yard in the gasworks was set out with wagons and a platform to enable the ladies to sit and listen to the band of the Sussex Militia, who played while the balloon was being inflated. Some 500 people paid for admission, who the local paper described as 'highly respectable', while even the non-paying crowd outside were said to have preserved a 'most orderly decorum'.

By noon the wind was favourable, having veered to the south-west, and the fine clear sky with warm sunshine made it ideal for an ascent. This took place after three o'clock, again being delayed slightly to ensure that nobody would be disappointed, and as the balloon rose into the air the band played 'God Save the King', The voyage proved uneventful, and the balloon was in the sight of spectators for nearly three-quarters of an hour before disappearing in the direction of Henfield. Green made a safe landing near the village and got back to Chichester at ten o'clock that evening in a chaise and four, sleeping the night in the Swan Inn before leaving next day for London.

In 1828 the Grahams reappeared in Sussex at Chichester, while Henry Green, the lesser-known brother of Charles, arranged for ascents in Lewes and Brighton. Both of the ascents made by the Grahams were marred by lack of lift, perhaps due to the quality of the gas or even to the deterioration of the varnish coating on their balloon envelope, common problems with travelling balloonists. On the first occasion, on 9 October Graham had to ask his passenger, a Mr Pickering, to leave the car to enable him to ascend. He then made a 5-mile flight, landing at Colworth, and from there his balloon, still inflated, was towed back to town. A few days later Mrs Graham succeeded in ascending with Pickering, but only by abandoning all the ballast and the grapnel. Their flight lasted only eleven minutes, and as the balloon came down the car struck a walnut tree, nearly throwing them out. Fortunately, several people appeared on the scene and managed to secure the balloon so that they could disembark. The balloon was again walked back to the gasworks and the gas discharged. That evening the wagon containing the deflated balloon was driven around Chichester Market Cross but the balloon netting caught in one of its pinnacles and tore it off. To the Grahams' relief, the Corporation agreed to pay for its replacement, as the Grahams had made very little profit from their visit.

Henry Green seems to have been the only one of the Green brothers who attempted to take up ballooning on his own, with as it turned out, indifferent success. His two ascents from Lewes went reasonably well, the first one, on 22 September, taking place on the town's Fair Day, thus assuring him of a captive audience. There were some 15,000 people present, of which about two-thirds were assembled on Cliffe Hill. His passenger had to step down to allow

Henry to ascend at all, but he eventually made a trip of three-quarters of an hour, covering 10 miles before landing in a field at Deanlands Wood, near Ripe. On his return to Lewes he made an appearance at the local theatre, the 'Public Temple', describing his voyage in suitably grandiloquent terms, and was warmly cheered by his audience for his poetic description of his ascent.

On 29 September he managed to ascend with a Mr H.W. Gardiner of East Hoathley, and flew over the latter's house. His passenger was highly amused to see a horse-drawn wagon end up in a ditch when the driver lost control of the horse after staring up at the balloon. The descent was made in a clover field, the grapnel securing a good purchase, and labourers appeared from all over the surrounding area to help them control and deflate the balloon. The local farmers made no secret of their wish that the balloon had ended up in Pevensey Bay in view of the time lost by their labourers.

His two scheduled ascents from the Royal Pavilion Gardens at Brighton were less successful. During the first, fog came swirling in during the afternoon, and when the balloon was finally released it only just cleared some nearby trees, although Henry released two bags of ballast. It then seems that he tried to cut loose the grapnel in an attempt to lighten the balloon further, but caught hold of the gas valve by mistake and tore the valve away, releasing all the gas before sinking back on the ground. Henry inserted a notice in the *Brighton Herald*, apologising for the debacle and assuring the public that his next ascent on the following Monday at 2pm would not be a disappointment. A substantial crowd, estimated to be over 15,000 people, gathered outside the Royal Gardens before the actual ascent. Amongst them were Dr Gideon Mantell, a medical practitioner in Brighton, famed for his discovery of dinosaur remains in the Sussex area. He, together with William Lee, the Lewes editor of the *Sussex Weekly Advertiser*, made an ascent in the balloon on the tethered line, before the main event.

At four o'clock the balloon was topped up with more gas and Henry got ready for the voyage. A number of people in the Gardens were, however, worried that the wind direction could result in him being blown out to sea and managed to persuade him to abandon the ascent. So, a compromise was reached; he was towed up the Lewes Road for a mile or more and then released. The balloon did reach about 600ft but was blown back to the Gardens in a few minutes and the crowds dispersed homewards.

In 1836 Charles Green had the opportunity to leave his personal mark on ballooning history. It started when Robert Holland, who was to become a barrister and MP for Hastings (1837–52), made his first balloon flight with Green's son, Charles George. They ascended from Cambridge, where Holland was a student, on 8 May 1830; he was then 26 years old. This appears to have fired an interest in ballooning, and, since he was quite affluent, his support for the sport.

Green had for some time wanted to build a very large balloon, which would carry more passengers and also enable scientific observations to be made at a greater altitude. Unable to meet the cost himself, he persuaded the proprietors of the Vauxhall Gardens in London, where he made most of his ascents, to fund the project. The balloon when completed was 137ft in circumference, and 80ft high when inflated and the car attached. It was christened the Royal Vauxhall balloon. Before its trial flight on 9 September 1836 in pouring rain (which added another 300lb to its all up weight) it needed thirty-six policemen with their staves through the cordage, over forty weights of 56lb each and finally another twenty groundsmen to even keep it on the ground. With 400lb of ballast aboard it was said to have shot up to 13,000ft in five minutes, with nine passengers aboard including Robert Holland.

A spectator at the event was Henry Coxwell, then seventeen years old, who had seen his first balloon ascent when Charles Green went up from Rochester gasworks in 1828. When his father died, the family moved to London, increasing Coxwell's opportunities for watching ballooning. He idolised Green and had dreamed of a flight in a balloon.

On 7 November 1836 the Royal Vauxhall balloon with Green, Robert Holland and Monck Mason on board took off on their record voyage, all expenses having been met by Holland. In eighteen hours, they flew to Weiburg in Nassau, Germany, a distance of about 480 miles. This long-distance record was not eclipsed until 1907, and the balloon was afterwards renamed the 'Great Nassau' in honour of this famous flight.

This exploit made Green a celebrity in the first rank of international balloonists and he was subsequently to be immortalised by Charles Dickens in *Sketches by Boz* in the chapter 'Vauxhall by Day'. It was not clear whether Holland made any further balloon ascents, but there was a comment in the Sussex press that he was not averse to securing his election at the hustings by drawing electors into 'habits of drunkenness'.

Two years later in 1838, by which time Green had made over 250 ascents, he was approached by Charles Rush, described as a gentleman of means, who wished to make scientific observations from a balloon. Several voyages were made from Vauxhall, one of which resulted in a descent near Lewes. The ascent took place at 6.30pm on 16 September after Green had carefully calculated the lifting power of the gas and decided to attach a much smaller car. The flight lasted an hour, during which the balloon covered 50 miles; the maximum altitude attained being just over 5 miles. Rush said he suffered no discomfort at this height but Green said his hands and feet were very cold and he had difficulty in breathing, but he was now over sixty years old. They landed in a field at Southover near Lewes by a house belonging to the Reverend West. The earlier sight of the balloon over Lewes had aroused great interest and a large crowd had followed it over hedges, ditches, streams and walls to its eventual landing place. The two aeronauts were met by a local farmer, Mr Morris and his son, Mr Shoesmith, a carrier, and other local worthies. They adjourned to Mr Shoesmith's house, where Green and Rush refreshed themselves and their new found friends from a flask of brandy, which they always carried on such trips. A toast to the success of their next ascent was drunk and at nine o'clock the balloonists took the chaise to Brighton, where Mr Rush's father was staying. The *Sussex Express* reported on the following day, an amusing story about the occupier of the field, who unaware of the arrival of the balloon until coming past the spot, saw this huge monster still inflated with hundreds of people surrounding it. Hurrying forward, he spoke to Charles Green in great excitement saying 'How'd ye come here? Why didn't you send word? I'd have left the gate open rather than ye should broke down the hedges. How'd ye come here eh!' It seems Green answered all these questions satisfactorily by presenting the aggrieved peasant with a half sovereign.

On 18 August 1843 Charles George, son of Charles Green, ascended with a companion, a Mr Bradley, from the Stepney Green gasworks in his balloon Albion, which had a capacity of 27,000 cubic feet, for a trip across the Channel. Unfortunately, in arriving over Cuckfield, near Haywards Heath, the wind changed and the voyage had to be abandoned, but the balloon was sent on to Brighton for another attempt. Next day the balloon was re-inflated at the Hove gasworks and by 8.30am was towed by many willing helpers to the beach at a height of 40ft with the two aeronauts in the balloon car. Although the proposed voyage had received very little publicity there were well over a thousand people assembled on the beach to wish the aeronauts bon voyage. It soon became plain, however, that frequent changes in the direction of the wind were occurring and when the balloon was released, although it did drift out to sea for 2 or 3 miles, another change in direction led the balloon to curve back to the shore and end up near the Hove Coastguard Station. The younger Green then decided to abandon the proposed sea voyage and fly inland to satisfy the curiosity of the locals. They descended near the Patcham railway station, a railway engine was passing at the time and the driver, seeing it come down, reported it to the Superintendent of Traffic at Brighton station. A train and a coach were therefore sent to Patcham to pick up the balloon and the aeronauts and bring them back to Brighton. Before returning to London, the balloonists said they would return to Brighton when the weather was more suitable for another attempt, but as far as is known, nothing happened.

The first crossing of the Channel by balloon from the Sussex coast appears to have been accomplished in 1850 by Lieutenant George Gale, formerly of the Royal Navy. Gale, originally an actor, had played to audiences in the United States and had been a passenger on several balloon ascents with a professional aeronaut when in America. On his return to this country he served with the Royal Navy until leaving to take up a third career as a professional balloonist.

His balloon was 90ft high and 50ft in diameter, and was inflated in the early morning of 8 July 1850 at the Hove gasworks under his supervision. The balloon was then towed by some one hundred willing helpers to the Swiss Cottage Amusement Gardens at Shoreham-by-Sea, the car being sent on by train to be taken off at Shoreham railway station. It was then conveyed to the Gardens and attached to the balloon to await the ascent at seven o'clock that evening, while Lieutenant Gale attempted to get some sleep.

Up and ready by 6pm, Gale refused all offers to accompany him on his voyage, which was felt to be quite a risky undertaking at night by many of his friends, and the spectators. At 7pm he rose from the Gardens to the sound of a band playing and the cheers of the assembled crowd. In a matter of minutes, he was setting out on a north-west wind above numerous small sailing craft on the Channel below. After a while he came abreast of Beachy Head, which was to be his last sight of land for some time. As the sky darkened, he came down to about 200ft above the water to gauge his speed and height and released his grapnel as a guide. He hailed a passing schooner, but was unable to distinguish their response. Discharging ballast, he climbed again and soon lost sight of the sea, reaching an altitude of 3 miles, sliding along under the stars, with lightning flashes in the distance. It was very cold and Gale, exhausted after his early start, found he was dozing off over the edge of the basket. Shaking off his tiredness, he brought the balloon down until he could hear the waves and his grapnel splashing the water below. Knowing the grapnel rope was 120ft long, he discharged some ballast and rose again. Then he saw a light that vanished and he realised it was a revolving lamp, which he kept in sight for nearly an hour and a half while peering into the blackness to try and identify his position. Suddenly he heard the sound of breakers and then the grapnel dashed against some rocks and then held fast, the car coming to the ground above the surf having passed over a ledge of rock without going into the water. Gale then realised he had landed under a large cliff, and set to discharging the gas and folding up the balloon envelope as best he could and weighing it down with rocks until he could retrieve it.

It was now midnight, and he had been five hours in the balloon after travelling around 100 miles, and it had taken another two hours to secure the balloon. By now he was almost totally exhausted and parched with thirst, and he set off along the beach to look for help. He walked 6 miles along the beach before he found a small dwelling on a slope at the end of the cliffs. He knocked on the door and an elderly lady in strange garb appeared who was much alarmed at his appearance and gabbled away in French. Gale's knowledge of French was rudimentary, but he did manage by signs to tell her he was thirsty and she gave him some water, about a quart, which he drank greedily. Seeing his distraught condition, the woman then produced some brandy and food, but his throat was still so dry he could not eat anything. Then the woman called to a man who was passing by in uniform and he came up to Gale and demanded to see his papers. The only thing Gale had on him was a British newspaper, which he showed to the official and tried to explain that he had landed from a balloon. The official was very suspicious and called out, whereupon another five armed men appeared and Gale realised he had been arrested as a spy or conspirator from nearby Boulogne. His position worsened when they told him to undo his coat and they found the Union Jack flag tied round his waist. It appeared this rather histrionic gesture was made because Gale thought that if he was lost over the Channel, his body would at least be recognised as that of an Englishman.

Gale insisted that he be taken to a higher authority, and he was marched another 3 miles to the nearest town at Creal in Normandy, which was another 14 miles from Dieppe. The local mayor could see he was totally exhausted and sat him down and gave him some excellent wine and bread and butter, agreeing to take him to the British Consul in Dieppe. After the meal and rest, Gale recovered somewhat and he, the mayor, and an armed guard set off in a horse and cart for Dieppe. On the way the mayor stopped off at several houses of people he knew, where it was explained that Gale had come from England in a balloon, which few of them seemed to believe. As they were given more food and wine at each of these stopping places, Gale eventually reached Dieppe full of food and more than a little tipsy. The British

Consul soon arranged for his release from custody and arrangements were made to collect the balloon and forward it without delay to England. Gale left Dieppe on the Wednesday morning after thanking the mayor and the Consul for their help, landing at Newhaven at two o'clock that afternoon.

It seems Gale went back to France shortly after this to make a number of balloon ascents, but he had now started to drink heavily. After one descent, the French helpers saw he was drunk and waving a knife about, and they let go of the balloon with him clinging to the basket. It seems he lost his hold and fell but his body was not found until the following day.

Chapter 3

More Channel Crossings and the New Aero Club

On Tuesday, 4 March 1851, Charles Frederic William, the Duke of Brunswick, arrived at ten o'clock at the gardens of the hostelry, the Golden Property at Vauxhall, London. He was to accompany Charles Green on a voyage by the balloon 'Victoria' to Germany. Preparations for the ascent had been made on the previous Sunday under the direction of Mr Lumm, the principal engineer of the London Gas Company, to lay a 9in pipe from the gasworks to the balloon inflation bay. By 7am on the Monday everything was ready for the inflation, and by eleven the balloon was fully inflated and ready for the voyage.

The Duke was accompanied to the ascent site by a party of friends and a large supply of provender, which included hams, fowls, pheasants, partridges, breadstuffs, chocolate and coffee etc. He also brought a Sayer portable cooking stove and thirteen carrier pigeons, the last named not being to eat, but for the Duke to communicate details of the flight to his anxious friends below. At midday the Duke and Green stepped into the balloon car and ascended. There was 13cwt of ballast in the balloon, plus of course the piles of food, and equipment designed by Green for the Channel crossing. This included gutta percha line, water drags and air vessels. The balloon set off on a south-easterly course, passing over Surrey and Kent in the direction of the Continent, and knowledgeable spectators felt the voyage had started well. This optimism was not justified as the voyage only lasted two hours, the balloon having to come down at Gravesend due to a change in wind direction. The Duke was not put off by this disappointment, and insisted Green should make another attempt when the weather was favourable.

The Duke had been the subject of adverse press comments in an earlier ascent with Mrs Graham in 1836 when their balloon came down somewhat precipitately at a farm near Brentwood, Essex. The Duke's version of the incident was that he had been thrown out but eyewitnesses declared he had leapt from the balloon when it neared the ground. As a result, the balloon had risen and Mrs Graham had fallen from a height of some 100ft and had been seriously injured. It was later put with some delicacy by one paper that Mrs Graham, who was pregnant at the time, had lost her child. Fortunately, Mrs Graham recovered to resume her ballooning career and have many more narrow escapes from injury.

Green decided that the next attempt to cross the Channel would be made from Hastings and the pair arrived there on 22 March for the ascent, but the wind was in the south-west until the last day of the month. It then shifted to the north-west and at a quarter to eight in the morning the inflation of the balloon began in the Priory Brook meadow near the Hastings gasworks. The engineer, Mr Ginner, and the foreman, Mr Inkpen, were fortunate in having three gasholders available and were therefore able to supply gas with the minimum carbon content most suitable for ballooning. As a strong wind was blowing, a shield of canvas was erected to the windward to protect the balloon. Fortunately, the wind moderated as the day wore on.

At nine in the morning the town crier went around announcing that the Royal Victoria balloon would ascend on its journey at ten o'clock. It seems the authority for this announcement was the landlord of a nearby hostelry, although the Greens reckoned it would take to noon or one o'clock before the envelope could be fully inflated. As a result of this premature announcement, crowds of people flocked to the scene, the thirstier making for the inns to quench their thirst. A multitude of spectators assembled at Castle Hill and lined the front of St Andrews Terrace, and there were more in the road and the meadow near the gasworks. By midday the crowd had increased to 5,000 plus onlookers from the houses overlooking the meadow.

At ten minutes to one the inflation was completed and Henry Green started to attach the car. This was described by one reporter as a 'frail and rickety piece of plain basketwork of small dimension affording just about room for two persons … providing they did not fall asleep, so they might avoid falling out'. The balloon also had the special apparatus including 200ft of gutta percha line, at one end of which was a wooden log, with two more logs above each a few feet above the other. The theory was that the line would be lowered so the first log lay in the water, thus reducing the weight, and this would be reduced still further as the other two logs floated. Green felt by this means he could dispense with some ballast and also keep the balloon at a fixed height above the water. In addition, the grapnel was used as an anchor, being fitted with two airtight containers and air bladders so it contributed to the drag.

It seems that on this occasion there was no intention of contemplating a voyage to Germany, as, apart from the 5 or 6cwt of ballast, the only food aboard was a small supply of biscuits. Several tests were then conducted to test the buoyancy of the balloon, and when Green pronounced himself satisfied the Duke of Brunswick appeared, who until then had been hiding under the anonymity of the name 'Mr Smith' and ran down the bank of the gasworks. He was followed more sedately by his friends G.T. Smith, Baron Audlau and Mr Pereda. The Duke wore an oilskin suit covering him from head to toe, with a travelling cap, and was obviously prepared for all known emergencies. He jumped into the car and a speaking trumpet and a walking stick were placed in the car with him. Then Green clambered into the car and at a word the balloon was set free. Green waved his hat and the crowds cheered but the Duke sat stoically in his seat ignoring the tumult. The balloon rose steadily and cleared Castle Hill, although at one point some of the crowd thought it was drifting their way and stepped back from the ridge, some falling or rolling to the 'Ladies Parlour' below.

The balloon followed a course nearly south-east for some 12 miles or so, then more southerly or south-westerly before becoming becalmed in mid-Channel. At this point there was some alarm among spectators, who could still make out the balloon, that something had gone wrong, particularly as several fishing boats came up under the balloon. However, it seems Green was merely letting the balloon descend so the logs went in the water and acted as a counterbalance. The Duke then resorted to the speaking trumpet to warn fisherman to stay clear of the apparatus. A wind rose to the south-east again and the balloon ascended to a height of 4,000ft, its highest point of the voyage. This forced the excess gas out of the safety valve and the balloon started to descend again. Eventually the logs re-entered the water and the balloon sailed over the water, much to the delight of the Duke, who, Green said later, thoroughly enjoyed the trip. There were splendid views of the English coast from Beachy Head to Dungeness, and when the balloon was 20 miles out the French coast was visible, terminating in a port that Green identified as Cherbourg.

Remaining on their south-easterly course, the aeronauts came to the French coast with sands extending for a mile or a mile and a half from the sea. The tide was low and the grapnel was lowered and drawn behind the balloon with the guide line. Suddenly two men appeared and made an attempt to grab the trailing lines. As a result, one man was violently smashed to the ground while his companion performed a complete somersault in the air, much to the amusement of the Duke. Green was worried that they might have been seriously injured, but was relieved to see them get back on their feet before they disappeared out of sight of the balloon. In the meantime, the balloon was approaching a steep hill, over which they flew, clearing it by some 50 feet. The sight of a village immediately below decided Green to land as the grapnel descended the slope almost before the balloon. As they reached the bottom of the valley, the Duke shouted directions to the villagers, who came out to render assistance. The balloon initially touched the ground quite gently but then shot up some 30 feet, bounced twice and then was almost stopped by the villagers, enabling the Duke to alight in a field. The vessel then rose again before being finally secured so that Green could disembark. It was then only a few minutes after 6pm, the journey having taken five hours. The aeronauts had travelled some 60 miles to their landfall at Neufchatel, 7½ miles south of Boulogne. As the railway was only a mile away, the Duke was taken to the station and soon ensconced in the next train for

Paris. After discharging the gas, Green had the balloon folded and put on a cart for Boulogne, where he arrived at ten o'clock that evening and stayed overnight. The following morning, he took the steamer to Folkestone, and on arrival purchased a railway ticket for Hastings. Unfortunately, he did not hear the call to change at Ashford for Hastings and went on to Tunbridge Wells. Despite this delay, he did reach Hastings by eight o'clock in the evening, where his wife and family and a welcoming party waited for him on the railway platform. This seems to have been Green's last ascent from Sussex, his final ascent being in September 1852, at the age of seventy-seven. He died eight years later in March 1870.

Charles Green has been described as a John Bull-like character. Although he had little education, he had great physical courage and like all successful balloonists did not indulge in unnecessary risks. When in the air he was often taciturn to the point of being brusque and brooked no opposition to his orders. On returning to earth, he was a different person. Impressive, with a likeable personality, he had a vast fund of stories of his adventures and the famous people he had met on his voyages. These he would relate to his passengers once they were safely on the ground, to their vast entertainment.

As Green gradually withdrew from ballooning, Henry Coxwell took over his mantle as the leading British balloonist. Green had, of course, known Coxwell, since as a young boy he had haunted the site of Green's balloon ascents in London. He had never, however, taken Coxwell up in his balloon, even when space was available. Green is said to have confided in a friend that there was something in Coxwell's eyes that told him he would take anything he told him about ballooning and use it to his advantage. When Coxwell got his own balloon, the Green family cold shouldered him. Hurt at the time, he later realised they saw him as a rival.

Coxwell undoubtedly advanced the scientific use of ballooning, and was convinced balloons had a significant role to play in warfare for observation and even bombing. He later built a larger balloon at his own expense, to enable Professor James Glaisher to make a number of ascents to increase knowledge of meteorology. In 1863 he made two descents in Sussex, the first on 18 April, which proved to be the most nerve-racking.

The balloon had been filled the previous evening at Crystal Palace to enable an early start next morning, but the wind direction was unsuitable. At one o'clock, the wind dropped and Coxwell told Glaisher and his assistant, Mr Inglehow, that it could only be a short trip, the balloon being filled for an altitude ascent. If they were then to be blown out to sea, they would not be able to make a Channel crossing. Taking their places in the basket, they were discussing the situation when the anchor rope snapped in the high wind, the balloon lurched and ascended, flinging Glaisher and his assistant on to their scientific instruments and breaking a number of them. Within three minutes, the balloon rose to 3,000ft and twenty-three minutes later they were at 7,000ft in thick mist. At 10,000ft the towers of Crystal Palace were still visible. By a quarter past two they had ascended to 24,000ft. By now Coxwell was seriously worried that they were drifting towards the coast, and he started to open the venting valve. They fell a mile in a minute and then broke through the clouds. When Coxwell realised that Beachy Head lay below them he shouted to Glaisher, 'There is not a moment to spare; we must save the land at all risks. Leave the instruments.' So, both he and Glaisher hung on the valve release and gas flooded out while Inglehow threw out all the remaining ballast. The envelope quickly emptied and became in effect a parachute. In four minutes, the basket struck the beach at Newhaven with a violent crash. Few of the precious instruments survived but the aeronauts, despite a severe shaking, were uninjured by the impact. The sight of the balloon falling out of the sky caused a great commotion in Newhaven, and large crowds were soon flocking to the beach to see the crumbled vessel and its occupants.

In a later voyage, on 12 July, again from Crystal Palace, Coxwell and Glaisher were accompanied by two fare-paying passengers, a Mr Norris of the Conservative Club and Lieutenant Hatton Turner of the Rifle Brigade. The latter was to make many more balloon ascents and write a history of ballooning, *Astra Castra*, in 1865. The intention was to combine an altitude flight with a voyage to Devonshire but when they took off at 5pm it was soon clear neither of these plans were feasible as they were caught in another current that took them towards the coast. There they met another current, which put the balloon on a course for Brighton, Shoreham and eventually Chichester. The inhabitants en route were much excited at the sight of the balloon as it sped along the coast and shouted to them to land. By eight o'clock in the evening they came upon Goodwood House outside Chichester, where cricket was being played in the park. The cricketers seized a rope thrown down from the balloon and it landed lightly with no impact at all. It was then walked around the front of the house for the benefit of all the guests staying at Goodwood. Thereafter the balloon was deflated and the aeronauts were afforded hospitality for the night by the Earl of Richmond's steward, Captain Valentine. They left the next day by train with the balloon in the guards van.

It seems that the somewhat abrupt arrival on the beach at Newhaven mentioned earlier led Coxwell to visit the nearby seaside town of Seaford, which he found very congenial. In any event, he set up a balloon factory in the town in the 1870s, and later retired there. He died on 5 January 1900 and has a plaque in the church of St Peter, East Blatchington, Seaford.

It was on Thursday, 13 September 1883, the hundredth anniversary of the first balloon flight, and some thirty years after the ascent by the Duke of Brunswick and Charles Green from Priory Green meadow, that another Channel crossing was to be attempted from Hastings.

The aeronaut, a professional, was Joseph Simmons, his passenger was a local photographer named C.J. Small, and the venue this time was the Central Recreation Ground at Hastings. Their balloon was the 'Colonel', which was 68ft high and 38ft in circumference, and held 40,000 cubic feet of coal gas when full. The car, some 5ft by 3ft, held four seats that were subsequently described as very uncomfortable. Simmons had by then made over four hundred ascents, and had crossed the Channel a month before. Small was a partner in the photographic firm of Boning and Small of Hastings and London, he had constructed an apparatus with an automatic shutter that he thought would improve the quality of aerial photography from a balloon, and hoped to test it during the flight.

Early that morning the balloon envelope was conveyed to the Recreation Ground, where a 6in gas pipe had already been laid from the main gas supply in South Terrace for the inflation. The pure

India rubber envelope was laid in a railed off area, covered with balloon netting and surrounded by a circle of sandbags to hold it down while inflation took place. The envelope was filled in four hours, by which time a strong wind arose, making the envelope flap and dragging the sandbags all over the place as the balloon tried to escape from the netting. Finally, fully inflated the car was attached and adjusted to hang properly, the car having a cork bolster on the outside to enable it to float. Two portmanteaux, some instruments, provisions and some twelve bags of ballast were then loaded into the car.

The men charged with holding down the balloon found it difficult in the strong wind, and Simmons, who had become apprehensive about the wind direction, said they might have to postpone the ascent until the following day unless the wind direction changed. Half an hour later the wind did veer, and after some discussion with Small it was decided to attempt an ascent in the hope of reaching Paris or at least Cherbourg in some six or seven hours. The crowd, which Simmons later said was 40,000, but which a local reporter said consisted of 4,000 inside the ground and 8,000 outside, silently awaited the ascent. Small lashed his camera to the side of the car while the helpers removed the rest of the retaining sandbags. The balloon was now only held by the helpers until a rope was passed around the car line and then secured to a large iron grass roller. The wind was such that the balloon occasionally lifted some of the helpers off their feet. A local reporter wrote in dramatic style:

> Simmons stood with erect figure and blazing eye, his lips forming the final word, 'Now!' roared the excited aeronaut, and the balloon relieved of the weight of the men who clung to it rose a few feet, and then hesitated to either rise or fall. The aeronaut waved his hand and two or three men bounded into the air, and brought the car down to earth again, when two bags were dropped. For a second time Simmons roared 'Now!' and this time the balloon rose as far as the rope fastened to the grass roller would allow, and then stopped. Swaying slightly in the wind, his countenance seemed cast in bronze as he

thundered 'Let Go!'… and the balloon shook itself free rapidly and then bore to the southeast, to the cheers of the multitude below.

Small was so amazed at seeing the panorama of Hastings spread before him that Simmons had to remind him to start taking photographs of the ascent, although one of Small's own photographers also took pictures, which sold very readily in the town. In fifteen minutes, the balloon was over Beachy Head, and Simmons later confessed that he was tempted to descend but felt it would have been rather ignominious and decided to keep to their course. In another hour Beachy Head receded northwards and they were high above a magnificent cloudscape. Smith now wanted to test his automatic camera, but found the shutter mechanism had frozen up so he had to operate it manually.

At five-thirty the aeronauts had a snack, Simmons refusing a second sandwich as 'it would not do to be too lavish'. He was still worried about their course and anxious to make landfall. By now they were beginning to feel the cold. Simmons borrowed a pair of thick homespun 'Scotch' drawers from the spare clothes brought by Small, which he put over the top of his trousers, while Small donned an extra flannel shirt and thick socks. By nine o'clock Small was feeling drowsy and wanted to take a nap, but Simmons would not allow him to do so. Meanwhile, condensation was forming on the balloon envelope, and it seemed highly doubtful whether the balloon could stay up all night, although Simmons released small amounts of ballast to try and maintain height. Small noticed one of the beer tins they had brought with them was starting to bulge. In another hour a flashing light was seen, and the pair debated whether to descend, but the balloon took matters into its own hands and dropped. Below them they could see the sea and a ship. Small hailed it in French until he was hoarse, whereupon Simmons took over. They finally heard a voice in broken English saying, 'Vot you want?' They shouted again in French, asking for their position, but this only elicited the same response and as they were now quite low, they had to drop more ballast to climb.

A little later they heard the sound of surf in the distance, but it was another hour before Simmons saw what he thought was a low bank, and became convinced they were over land. Seizing the valve cord and pulling hard, they went down like a stone and Simmons flung out the grapnel. Suddenly there was a very heavy bump and they rose briefly before crashing down as the grapnel got a hold. Small then realised they had scudded over a cliff and the grapnel had lodged in some rocks only about 12ft from the sea. The only casualty was the beer tin, which exploded as they hit the ground, the cork hitting Simmons in the eye, fortunately without any lasting damage. As Small related in a subsequent lecture, he had been very impressed with the cool courage shown by Simmons and his judgement in making such a speedy descent, since if he had left it a few minutes later they would have landed in the sea.

Two people appeared on the beach, but were initially reluctant to approach, but then realising the situation came up to help, proving to be Auguste Laven and his wife of Canton de Beaumont, near Cape de la Hägue. It took the quartet another three hours to empty and repack the balloon before they were taken back to their host's small stone cottage and enjoyed a supper of eggs and coffee.

Small woke early and dressed, going to the beach to take photographs of their point of landing and general views of the area. Returning, he offered to photograph the Laven family. As this involved all of them putting on their Sunday best, it took some time to accomplish. By this time Simmons awoke and they all had breakfast, after which a horse and cart was hired to take the balloon to Cherbourg and the pair bade farewell to their kind hosts. They reached the town by four o'clock and Small boarded a steamer for Southampton after they sent telegrams announcing their safe arrival. Simmons stayed behind to dry out the balloon and returned the next day.

The next crossing of the Channel from Sussex appears to have taken place on 12 October 1897. The aeronaut was Charles F. Pollack, a London solicitor who was among the first of a new breed of amateur balloonists. Described by an associate as a huge fellow, he was the soul of kindness and wonderfully efficient. His ballooning tutor had been Percival Spencer, a member of the famous ballooning family from Highbury. The ascent took place from Devonshire Park at Eastbourne and was the first cross-Channel flight from that town. The balloon, which cost £150 to build, was inflated with 35,000 cubic feet of gas from a 6in main under the direction of a Mr Hammond, the manager of the town's gasworks, in two and a half hours. By nine-thirty all was ready and weather conditions were ideal for the ascent, the sun shining in a cloudless sky. Pollack, then said to be in his thirties, had made several previous ascents with Percival Spencer, and it was thought that Spencer would accompany him on the voyage, but in the event, Pollack went on his own. A local reporter described the ascent as being one of a series to test certain apparatus similar to that used by Herr Andree on his aerial voyage to the Arctic region. Other reports only listed the equipment carried as land and sea anchors and a lifebelt. Although it was unknown at the time, the Andree expedition to the North Pole by balloon had already made a forced landing on an ice floe after ice had formed in their balloon envelope. The bodies of the members of the expedition were not discovered until a Norwegian sealing expedition came across them in 1930.

The *Eastbourne Chronicle* gave a rather grudging account of the Pollack ascent, saying that due to the short notice only a limited number of spectators witnessed the event. The few people on the front at that time were astonished to see the balloon glide over the parade and out to sea. The local reporter seemed to have few details of the flight, so it would appear he was one of the late risers. Pollack landed at Domart, south-east of Abbeville, at four thirty in the afternoon and despatched a telegram to Eastbourne apprising them of his safe arrival. By 1909 Pollack had made more than a dozen Channel crossings, more than twice that of any other aeronaut of the time.

On the afternoon of Thursday, 24 May 1900, Horace Short was watching from the balcony of the Menlo Laboratories at Hove waiting to see his younger brother Eustace ascend in his balloon. This ascent was to be the grand finale to the local celebrations on the opening of the Aldrington Recreation Ground, near Portslade, by the Mayoress of Hove. The balloon had been bought in a sale by Eustace and his younger brother Oswald in about 1898 and had seen better days. Despite their repairs to the envelope, there was a perceptible loss of gas on inflation. Thus, would be passengers at the Ground were disappointed and Eustace himself was forced to ascend with only a partially inflated balloon. Consequently, the balloon only managed to drift seawards before it reached the Old Shoreham Road and eventually settled in the garden of St George's Home. This was not, however, the end of the family troubles, Horace, upon sighting the balloon, leant heavily on the wooden balcony rail, which collapsed and precipitated him some 20ft to the ground below. He broke both arms and suffered other injuries before being rushed to Hove Hospital. This incident only confirmed Horace's already deep aversion to ballooning in general.

Horace was born in 1872, followed by Eustace in 1875 and Oswald in 1883. It was Horace who suffered a head injury that resulted in an attack of meningitis in early childhood and caused abnormal brain development and a grotesquely large head. In compensation he was intellectually brilliant, had great physical strength and an impressive presence, a truly larger than life character. At the age of eighteen he left his home town of Chesterfield on a working voyage to visit an uncle in Australia, and travelled to Samoa and Shanghai, before moving on to South America and ending up in Mexico. His adventures it was said would have thrilled schoolboys throughout the Empire and made many superior persons incredulous.

In the meantime, his father had died and the family were living in penury, so Eustace decided he would have to go out and find Horace and get him to come home. By now Horace had taken a job as the manager of the Panuco silver mine in Mexico and had so impressed the bandits with his fierce mien none of them ever attempted to attack the silver convoys that took the precious metal to the coast. So, after a 300-mile journey by mule, the two brothers met and Horace agreed to return home without delay, in the meantime giving his brother £500 for the family coffers. He seems to have come back to England in around 1896 with one of his new inventions, the Auxetophone, which was an amplification system to amplify pre-recorded sound and could be used as a loud hailer.

On Horace's return the family moved to London and it was then that Eustace and Oswald became interested in ballooning. Their first ascent in their own balloon was at a village gala, and Horace, against his better judgement, was persuaded to join Eustace and a companion for the trip. There was a strong wind blowing and their 47-mile journey was completed in forty minutes, ending with a very heavy landing, confirming Horace's conviction that ballooning was unsafe, not to say dangerous. Having patented his invention, Horace was offered the opportunity to continue his research by Thomas Edison, who set him up in a laboratory in Hove.

Despite his dislike of ballooning, Horace did allow his brothers to use one of the lofts in the building to make their first balloon. Of 41ft circumference, it held 38,000 cubic feet of gas, and was completed in May 1901. On 22 June 1901, Eustace made a balloon ascent from St Ann's Well Gardens in Hove. Inflation was not completed until half past seven in the evening, when Eustace and two passengers, a Mr Ben Parker and a Mr George Brown, embarked. After releasing a half bag of ballast, the balloon soared into the air. Caught by the breeze, it flew over Preston Park on the outskirts of Brighton, and then passed over Falmer, Lewes, Plumpton and Chailey. During the course of the voyage, Eustace passed the time by dropping leaflets advertising balloon trips over the more populated areas.

As it was getting dark, they came down close to Violet Cottage at Horsted Keynes. The sight of the balloon caused great excitement in the area and numerous cyclists and walkers appeared on its descent. The farmers William and George Noble from nearby Tanyard Farm helped to deflate the balloon and they agreed to pack it up and return it by goods train next day before the balloonists caught the train back to Hove. After their departure, William Noble took his horse and cart back to the field where the balloon lay. As his brother George said later, it seemed that the smell of the gas and the sight of the balloon unsettled the horse, which was of a nervous nature, and it bolted, the cart going over the farmer's body. Taken back to the farm in great pain, the doctor was called but the farmer died next morning, the coroner's jury returning a verdict of accidental death.

In 1902 Eustace and Oswald issued their first catalogue from Hove offering to build flying machines, kites etc., from plans. But the following year Horace sold his amplification patents and was offered a job up north to work on steam turbine development, and the two brothers moved back to London to build their second balloon.

Eventually they built up a thriving business and became appointed aeronauts to the Aero Club. In late 1908 the brothers agreed to form a partnership to construct aircraft and thus started on their way, their Short Brothers company becoming one of the first and biggest aircraft manufacturers in this country.

In the 1880s, the days of free ballooning had seemed to be over, the old showmen balloonists were a dwindling race, and the public appetite for aerial stunts had been satiated. The invention of the steam engine and petrol engine, and the possibility of large-scale production of aluminium, led to the development of airships with the ability to be steered. However, the emergence of a well-to-do middle class both in Britain and on the Continent, who were already keen motorists and were seeking even more exciting pursuits, led to an Indian summer for the free balloon, which lasted almost up to the First World War. The almost universal availability of coal gas for filling balloons with a growing transport network of cars, trains and ships meant that it was possible to make a balloon voyage and return with your balloon in the train luggage van, the boot of a car or even the hold of a ship. Initially, the new breed of balloonists employed professional aeronauts, but it was not long before they gained the necessary expertise to undertake their own ascents with relatives and friends without any serious risk to life or limb. The cancellation of a motor tour of Scotland planned by Miss Vera Butler with her father, Frank Hedges Butler, led her to arrange for their first balloon ascent, in which the Honourable Charles S. Rolls (later of Rolls-Royce fame) participated. It took place on 24 September 1901 in the balloon 'City of York' from Crystal Palace, with aeronaut Sidney Spencer in charge. While they were over the Kent countryside, the three agreed they should form an aero club, similar to that already existing in France, to encourage ballooning. Landing in Sidcup Park, they entrained for London and called at Somerset House to register the new title 'The Aero Club'. The new club and its members were to exert considerable influence having, it was said, the social and political backing of some 80 per cent of the members of Debrett.

Frank Hedges Butler, short, rotund and thick-set, was then in his mid-forties, a genial man and a good mixer as befitted his trade as a wine merchant. A restless soul, he had travelled widely for trade and pleasure in Europe, Russia, Asia and North and South America. Already a keen golfer and yachtsman, he bought his first car in 1896. He possessed great energy and drive and saw the Aero Club as very much his own creature, but as it expanded, his influence tended to decline. From 1901 onwards he made over one hundred balloon flights, a number of which resulted in descents in Sussex. A bon viveur, his balloon trips were always noted for their excellent cuisine, with good champagne being a standard requirement.

On one of his early flights with an aeronaut pilot, Hedges Butler took up Sir Vincent Hunton Barrington-Kennett, brother of the then Lieutenant Colonel Brackley Herbert Barrington-Kennett, who resided in Petworth. Sir Vincent, it appeared was on his eighth ascent on 10 June 1903 when he forgot to flex his knees on the final descent and jarred and sprained his ankle, dying a month later. Hedges Butler told the coroner that Sir Vincent had written to him after the flight asking for a place on his next ascent. He had last seen him putting the Prince of Wales's children in a balloon basket on 7 July and he had seemed perfectly well at that time. There was some dispute between the medical profession about the cause of death. His doctor thought he had probably died from a skull injury suffered in the descent. On the other hand, the pathologist gave the cause of death as blood poisoning from the suppuration of the ankle, while a verdict of accidental death was returned by the coroner's jury.

On the day following his last sight of the late knight, Hedges Butler took part in a balloon race arranged by the Aero Club with Percival Spencer in the Aero club balloon. It carried viands including soup, ham, tongue and petit fours with coffee, brandy and champagne and even Perrier, which invoked memories of the Duke of Brunswick, who considered food and drink an essential part of ballooning. Pollack had ascended an hour earlier with a companion. Meeting adverse winds, Butler and Spencer were forced down in a brickfield at Roffey near Horsham, after midnight. After finding accommodation for the night, they returned to town next day by train with their balloon in the luggage van. Butler was also unsuccessful on 6 April 1905 when he was in another cross-Channel balloon race from London to Paris. Again, he was accompanied by Percival Spencer and they had come down at Hollington, near Hastings, while two other competitors made forced landings at Robertsbridge and Westfield in Sussex. A local report said that the two aeronauts Hedges Butler and Spencer, smoking cigars, were very cool and collected about the landing. They told the farmer who gave them hospitality they had to abandon the flight because they only had one bag of ballast left from their original fifteen and dared not risk a Channel crossing.

One of the most amusing flights occurred in May 1906. Butler, with C.F. Pollock and a Mr Martin Dale, ascended from Wandsworth gasworks in the former's balloon 'Dolce far Niente'. After passing over the Ideal Home Exhibition, they travelled southwards. At two o'clock in the morning they dropped a trail rope, which caught in a tree, in which there was a rookery, thereby rousing the birds. To add to the noise, the aeronauts shouted down to try and find out where they were. In the midst of all this din a nearby window was flung up and the face of an irate gentleman in his pyjamas appeared. Seeing the balloon towering over the trees, he was somewhat taken aback and said 'Good Gracious! Who are you?' The aeronauts explained, tongue in cheek, that they were resting and asked where they were. The householders replied that they were about 12 miles from Brighton and asked if they were stuck? 'No' said Butler, 'we are happy here; you don't mind us sitting on top of your trees, do you?' The householder replied 'Not at all' and with a 'Goodnight' shut the window and went back to bed. As the birds settled down, peace again descended, and the aeronauts opened their capacious hamper and partook in true Butler style of a supper of chicken, cold meat and champagne, toasting their host, the householder. Then they released some ballast to land at Portslade early next morning.

On 30 December 1906 the first International Balloon Race started from the Tuileries in Paris, with a strong team from the Aero Club, which included Hedges Butler and Griffith Brewer, C.S. Rolls and Colonel Capper and C.F. Pollack and Professor Huntingdon. Each balloon had a barograph, food for three days and envelopes addressed to the Aero Club of France, which had to be completed and dropped every two hours over land to report progress. A printed list of phrases translated into French, German, English and Russian were supplied to all contestants. These were adjudged suitable for all occasions.

The longest, and probably the most vital, said, 'Will you take me to the house of the Mayor or Chief Officer of this place, as I wish to have a certificate of descent verified and signed by him in accordance with the rules of the race?' However, it was soon apparent that the winds were unfavourable for any record-breaking voyages, and half the balloons came down somewhere in northern France, Hedges Butler and Brewer accomplishing 120 miles before descending at Blonville-sur-Mer. The other two pairs did make it across the Channel, upon which the Rolls/Capper balloon 'Britannia' passed over Hastings Old Town, and Rolls dropped a message attached to a parachute. This floated over several streets pursued by a crowd of people to eventually land in the backyard of a house in the High Street belonging to a Miss Fisher, where it was seized by her dog. This escaped to be chased by the crowd, finally being cornered in a cul-de-sac. It was found to contain two telegrams and half-a-crown (12½p) to cover the cost of their despatch. The 'Britannia' finally came down at Sandringham in the late evening, a total distance of some 287 miles that earned them fourth place, the winner being an American Lieutenant F.P. Lahm who reached Whitby, Yorkshire.

There was considerable mystification when a balloon appeared over Newhaven on 19 October 1911 in the early morning and sailed over Lewes at 7am. Its trailing rope then became entangled with some bushes and it finally landed across the main Brighton to London Road near Danny Park. Examination of the balloon showed it had recently been immersed in seawater and fear was expressed as to the fate of the occupants. It was identified as a French balloon from a flag and some name tags on coats in the car. The following day the mystery was solved; it was identified as the 'Helene', which had been taken out on a night voyage by three French aeronauts. It seems it was blown out to sea and was hovering above the sea when the three occupants were rescued by a fishing trawler. As they scrambled aboard the boat, the empty balloon ascended and crossed the Channel to England.

A not dissimilar situation arose on 21 November 1912 after two members of the Royal Aero Club hired a balloon and left Battersea for a Channel crossing. Conditions were ideal initially and they came down at Buxted in Sussex to enquire where they were, then re-ascending to 3,000ft. They were then forced down by fine fog and rain until they were only about 6ft above the waves and were extremely apprehensive as they thought it would not be long before the balloon went into the water. Then they saw a light half a mile away and glimpsed some fishermen putting out their nets. Fortunately, they were seen by the fishermen, who did not initially realise they were in a balloon. When they reached them after abandoning their nets, they managed to seize the trailing rope and hauled down the balloon so it landed on the boat deck. All agreed they had to puncture the balloon, the fumes from the gas nearly overcoming them. They eventually reached the shore to find they were at Eastbourne and wearily made their way to a hotel for the night. The fishermen managed to recover their net and found it contained over 1,000 herrings, so when they also received a reward from the two aeronauts for rescuing them, it turned out to be quite a profitable night.

Chapter 4

Early Military Flights

The French, the inventors of the balloon, not unnaturally, were the first nation to use it for the observation of the enemy, at the battle of Fleurus in June 1794 and at Ourthê near Liege in the following year, when they defeated the Austrians. It seemed, however, that Napoleon felt the use of balloons to gather information on the disposition of the enemy reflected adversely on his military tactical genius, and they were eventually abandoned.

In 1803 Major John Money, whose name had been mentioned as a possible companion with Count Zambeccari on one of his ascents, did make two ascents in Zambeccari's balloon after the Count left England. Later he wrote a pamphlet on the use of balloons entitled *A Short Treatise on the use of Balloons and Field Observers in Military Operations*. It was dedicated to the then Secretary of War, Charles York. Money, who seemed to have a nice sense of humour, ended his treatise with a Parthian shot that 'old Generals who had opposed light artillery and telegraphy were unlikely to accept balloons'. As he was later promoted to general, it seems even the brass hats at the War Office did not appear to hold it against him.

It was some sixty years later that two Army officers, Lieutenant G.E. Grover and Captain F. Beaumont, members of the Royal Engineers Ordnance Select Committee, persuaded the War Office to make funds available to undertake a series of experimental ascents with a balloon and equipment hired from Henry Coxwell. Although the ascents were judged to have been successful, it was thought by senior officers that the cumbersome nature of the equipment and the lack of an impermeable balloon fabric were serious stumbling blocks to its use for military purposes. When Captain Templer, already an experienced balloonist, became a member of the Committee, he and Lieutenant Watson made a number of ascents in Templer's balloon, the 'Crusader', including one when they came down at Ardingly near Haywards Heath on 3 July 1878. A year later, the Army balloon 'Pioneer' was built at the cost of £71, and this led to the setting up of the Balloon Equipment Store. By now Captain Elsdale had joined the select band of enthusiasts for Army ballooning, and on 4 November 1879 made an ascent from Greenwich at 1.30pm, in the balloon 'Saracen'. As the wind was carrying him towards the coast on a southerly path to the Cadborough Cliffs near Rye, he decided he would have to descend. Attracting the attention of some fishermen, he threw down some ropes and carefully guided his helpers to tow the balloon to the Crown fields near Rye railway station. He let some local boys make some short-tethered ascents before lowering the balloon to open the gas valve and deflating the balloon. The envelope was then packed into the car basket and labelled for return to Greenwich via the next goods train. As the removal of the balloon from the cliffs to the Crown fields had involved crossing telegraph wires and a footbridge, then skirting several houses, the good captain invited his helpers to a nearby taproom for some liquid refreshment. Here his health was toasted several times by the now somewhat inebriated fishermen before he took the next passenger train back to Greenwich.

The first use of the military balloon in exercises in Great Britain seems to have been at the Easter Volunteer Review at Dover in 1879. The following year the Review moved to Brighton, starting on 29 March, with the 'Crusader' attached to the attacking force. The total number of men in these Reviews varied, but probably some 20,000 took part, including contingents from Hampshire, Surrey, Middlesex, Kent, Essex and London, with of course, volunteers from Sussex. The War Office organization to bring all these troops together, with their horses, artillery and equipment was quite impressive. Volunteers from outside the county marched to their nearest railway station and there entrained for their destination.

The participants from Sussex were the 1st Sussex (Brighton) Rifle Volunteers and the 1st Sussex (Brighton) Artillery Volunteers, with seven 40-pounders, rifle breech loaders and an 18lb small bore. These numbers were increased by No. 12 (Shoreham) Battery.

Each infantryman had thirty-five rounds of blank ammunition, and the same number of blank rounds were also allocated to each artillery piece. Opposing troops were not to approach to within 100 yards of each other or fire their muskets at a range of less than 600 yards. The defending forces held a line between Falmer and Rottingdean on Newmarket Hill, Balsdean and Bostel, with some 12,000 volunteers and fourteen guns. The Commander of the Brighton forces was General Radcliffe CB, and the attacking force approached from Kingston, Iford and Swanborough Hills.

One local reporter, seemingly anxious to be in the thick of things, reached the Newmarket Plantation to find a detachment of the Sussex Artillery under the command of Captain Wood at breakfast. In the adjacent hollow was the main body of the Corps awaiting action under Colonel Tester. By now the sun had partially dissipated the mist on the top of the Downs, although it still lay thickly in the valleys. Soon the sound of martial music could be heard as the invaders advanced towards the defenders. A shift of wind started to disperse the valley mists, so the head of the attacking columns could be seen, with one large and two small balloons in front. On the left of the defenders, the officers of the 10th Kent (Cinque Ports) were still enjoying a champagne breakfast with every delicacy, which now had to be abandoned to range their guns and repulse the enemy. The battle started round about 11.30am but lasted only two hours, mainly because at the end of the conflict all troops had to march some 3 miles to the Brighton Race Course for the march past the Commander-in-Chief, Prince Edward of Saxe Weimar.

A report of the review was subsequently made by Captain Elsdale and is reproduced below:

In accordance with authority received by telegram from the War Office on Thursday March 25th, the ballooning party, consisting of two officers, nine non-commissioned officers and sappers proceeded to Brighton with two balloons and all necessary equipment. The balloon Crusader containing 25,000 cubic feet was inflated with carburetted hydrogen obtained from the Lewes gasworks early on the morning of the Review, and was conveyed in safety across a difficult piece of ground to the position under the brow of the hill occupied by the outposts of the Lewes force, indicated by the General Officer commanding the force. The position was reached by 10am, the distance being traversed being about two miles and a half, including the crossing of a tidal river and a railway with telegraph wires adjoining, besides enclosures and other obstacles. Two small balloons contained 1,500 cubic feet of gas each accompanied the large one as a reserve supply of gas. On the signal gun announcing the commencement of action the balloon, in accordance with instructions, was immediately sent up to about 1,100ft. Captain Norton, Aide-de-Camp, accompanied me in the car. We were provided with maps of the ground on which it was proposed to make rough sketches of the enemy dispositions for the information of the officer commanding the Lewes forces. But owing to the prevailing fog and mist we found at no elevation could a sufficiently good view be procured to enable us to forward any useful information. While we were occupied at this elevation, Captain Templer succeeded in moving the wagon below, with the balloon attached, at a very rapid pace through the intervals between the advancing battalions, to a forward position immediately behind the front line. Had the weather been only fairly fine the whole of the operations of both sides would have been clearly visible; but in addition to the haziness of the atmosphere, the dense clouds of smoke arising from firing, as well as the burning fuses lit by the artillery, prevented any good view being obtained from any elevation. Later in the day the weather cleared, and then a most excellent view of every man and movement was obtained. At the final march past, the balloon, in accordance with instructions went past the saluting point immediately in the rear of the last infantry volunteer battalion, with a squadron of Lancers closely following. No difficultly was experienced keeping the balloon on a steady course at an elevation of about 250ft. When the troops were dismissed, the wagon was retired at a gallop, with the balloon attached, so as to clear the crowds, and returned to Lewes without difficulty. Captain Templer's conduct of the operation for moving the whole equipment from place to place required was most successful throughout the day. I remained in the car all day, up to and including the march past. In summing up the results of the valuable experience gained on this occasion, I would respectfully submit for consideration that the following points would have appeared to be established: A balloon in fairly favourable weather could be conveyed captive over any ground accessible to the infantry to the required position for observations. It can be moved from time to time, as required in the course of operations, to any other suitable point. The loss of gas is trifling, and can easily be replenished, if required, as was done on these occasions with great facility, from a reserve supply which can be carried to any required point with utmost ease. Under more favourable circumstances of weather than obtained on this occasion, it seems probable that valuable observations might from time to time be made at periods of the operation.

Balloon units were later raised for expeditions to Bechuanaland and the Sudan, and later detachments were used in the Boer War. By then balloon detachments had become highly efficient, had their own transport and were trained in mobility and the effective handling of balloons. An envelope could be filled and the balloon be on the line of march in twenty minutes using a six-horse team.

From 1901 to 1908 the Army took an interest in the possible use of kites to lift observers when the wind conditions precluded the use of a balloon. The expert on kites at this time was Samuel Franklin Cody, who had been a cowboy in his home state of Texas, USA. He had been a buffalo hunter, 'bronco' buster and gold prospector.

A crack shot and an expert with the lasso, he had spent some time in Wild West shows demonstrating his various skills. While in England, he conceived and produced a melodrama *The Klondyke Nugget*, in which he played the villain.

This was a great financial success, and as Cody had long been interested in kites, he used some of this new-found wealth to finance more ambitious kite trials and acquired considerable expertise in this field. On 25 June 1903 he and one of his sons, Leon, entered two of their kites in an International Competition held by the Aeronautical Society on the Sussex Downs, being Muntham Court at Findon near Worthing. Over 2,000 spectators were present, including at least 1,000 from the International Kite Flying Groups. The rules called for the winning kites to fly at a height of 3,000ft for a duration of at least one hour. In the event no one reached this standard, although one of the Cody kites came second, and consequently the Society's Silver Medal was not awarded. The poor results were attributed to the weather, it being thundery and overcast with only light winds, insufficient to raise the very large kites Cody had brought. Further experiments by Cody resulted in the production of practicable man-carrying kites, which were tested by both the Royal Navy and the Army.

Cody's solution was to create an 'Aerial Ropeway' that was first sent aloft with a pilot kite. This was then followed by the 'lifter kites', which slotted into holders as they climbed up the rope at certain allotted points. The number used depended on the wind and lifting power needed. Then the final kite with a car for the observer was hauled up the rope until the occupant reached the height required. It was claimed that, despite using the system in very high winds, no serious injury had ever occurred.

As a result of these successes, Cody was engaged as the Chief Kite Instructor to the Balloon Factory in 1906. On a more personal note, one RFC officer confessed that he found going up in a man-carrying kite was absolutely terrifying, describing it as being suspended in a waste paper basket on a steel cord no thicker than a light flex. With the wind shrieking and the kite snatching madly at the wire, he insisted that the motion was such that no serious observation was possible. In September 1906 the Aldershot Army Corps moved into the Chichester area for manoeuvres, the bulk of the Corps being designated the Blue Force under the Commander-in-Chief of the British Army, Sir John French. The defenders, the Red Force, were commanded by Lieutenant Colonel R. Scott Kelly. The Corps were accompanied by the 1st Balloon Company of the Royal Engineers with their complements of balloons. One was inflated while on the march down and caused some difficulties when the Company encountered telegraph and telephone wires. The problems were overcome by fastening extra trail ropes to the balloon car. The balloon was then walked up to the overhead wires where one of the ropes was thrown over while the balloon was secured by the other end and the process repeated.

The Royal Engineers were housed at the back of the Goodwood Race stand with their equipment and compressed gas cylinders. Unfortunately, throughout the exercise the wind proved too strong for any balloon ascents. However, the Cody man-lifting kites were available and did succeed somehow in supplying some information on enemy movements to a large glass-sided wagon in a nearby paddock where Sir John French's staff officers were receiving and sending out messages and orders during the course of the mock battle.

On 18 September, Lieutenant Wright, RE was making an observation from a man-lifting kite near the Goodwood racecourse when his kite suddenly swung and caught a large clump of trees. As a consequence, the car tipped and the officer was thrown into the treetops. There he lodged until a rescue operation could be mounted. No ladders were tall enough to reach him, and climbing irons and ropes had to be procured to use in his rescue. Eventually both rescuer and the rescued were lowered to the ground, Wright escaping with a few scratches. Many onlookers watched the rescue, among them Councillor Turnbull JP and a Mr Hopper, who took photographs of the officer when he finally reached the ground.

This was also the year that the Balloon Factory moved to Farnborough, and Colonel Capper took command. He lost no time in getting authority to recruit a Lieutenant J.W. Dunne of the Wiltshire Regiment, who was on sick leave after service in South Africa. Dunne was interested in building a tailless aeroplane with V-shaped wings, which he hoped would achieve automatic stability. His dedication had impressed Capper, who saw great advantages in such an aircraft since a pilot could not only observe while in the air, but also have the machine under control. His experiments were carried out in some secrecy while Cody moved on to experiments with a powered kite and a glider as a prototype for an eventual powered aircraft of his own design.

Meanwhile, Frank Hedges Butler had suggested that the War Office should consider a Volunteer Corps of balloonists but it came to nothing. Nevertheless, the Ballooning Branch of the Royal Engineers was grateful for the free use of the Aero Club facilities and on one occasion Hedges Butler was taken on a night run in a balloon from Aldershot. In view of the weight of their guest and his food hamper, it was necessary to use their largest balloon. With a drop in the temperature when aloft, there was a heavy dew on the balloon envelope, and the balloon only just kept above the surface of the lake while awaiting the arrival of a rescue boat. However, the occupants were able to enjoy an excellent meal of superb ham and veal pie, with a vintage champagne that had thoughtfully been provided by Hedges Butler, so there were no complaints.

The Zeppelins now being produced and flown in Germany were being seen as a major threat to the security of the British Isles and on 25 April 1909 the Parliamentary Air Defence Committee was formed by likeminded MPs, who were alarmed at what they saw as a lack of any real air defence in the country. Their intention was to exert pressure on the Government to improve this state of affairs as soon as possible. The Secretary to the Committee was the Hastings MP Arthur du Clos (1908–18) and the Committee, in association with the *Daily Mail*, arranged for a French airship manufacturer to send one of their airships, a Clement Bayard, on approval, for possible purchase by the War Office. It was also about this time that the *Morning Post* issued an appeal for the public to contribute to buy a French semi-rigid Lebaudy airship for use by the nation. In the interim, of course, Blériot flew across the Channel and landed at Dover to public acclaim, sparking the realisation that the Royal Navy was no longer the impregnable bulwark it had been in the past.

The Clement Bayard airship was flown across the Channel on 22 October 1910 but the War Office found when they inspected the envelope that it was so porous it was almost continuously leaking gas, and made Monsieur Bayard an offer of £12,500 for the balloon, half his asking price. In the end du Clos and the Defence Committee had to add another £5,500 from their own pockets and this was accepted. The War Office subsequently decided that the cost of replacing the envelope could not be justified and the airship was scrapped.

The Lebaudy airship flew over Sussex on its way to Farnborough on 26 October of the same year, and was over Brighton at ten past two in the afternoon. A captive balloon had been hoisted at Black Rock to act as a guide to the airship, and five minutes later the airship hovered over St Georges Road, Kemp Town, and it was there a worker from the nearby Kemp Town Brewery found a message wrapped in a red, white and blue ribbon. This asked the finder to hand the message to the nearest telegraph office for despatch. The note was in fact from the *Morning Post* reporter Walter Allen, and gave details of the flight. It was taken along to Morgans Library, the sub-post office next to the brewery, and sent off without delay. The patients out on the balconies of the nearby Sussex County Hospital had an excellent view of the airship, as did the diners at the Hollingbury Golf Course as it resumed its journey.

The success of the flight was somewhat marred when the airship, 337ft long with a diameter of 39ft, descended at Farnborough. The ground crew walked it to the new hangar, which had been specially built for it. Despite the utmost care, the balloon snagged the top of the hangar, and the envelope was holed, with a subsequent escape of gas. It turned out that the balloon makers had given the wrong dimensions of their balloon to the contractor who built the shed. Later repaired, the airship was taken out for a test flight, but there were handling problems due to faulty rigging. When it was eventually released, it shot up in the air and slid across the main road with the ground party in hot pursuit, making straight for a nearby house. The officer's wife in the upstairs bedroom saw the enormous gasbag coming nearer and nearer before it engulfed the house. Fortunately, someone got to the airship and turned off the petrol before the gas started to seep out. Once again, the War Office decided the airship was too badly damaged to be worth repairing.

Lieutenant Dunne completed his prototype swept-wing, tailless aircraft in 1907 and it was transported to Blair Atholl in Scotland for secret trials, which continued into the following year. By the end of 1908 Cody had designed and built his Army Aeroplane No. 1 and taken it into the air for a brief flight. Dunne and his followers, however, remained convinced that his design would in the end, prove superior. It was after this that a sub-committee of the Committee of Imperial Defence suggested that expenditure incurred on these aviation experiments (some £2,500) was too great for the results achieved. So, both Dunne and Cody received their marching orders, but as the former had gained some influential backers, he continued the work under the title of the Blair Atholl Syndicate. Dunne's own aeronautical experiments seemed to have ceased by about 1914, but he later achieved fame in the field of philosophy. He wrote one book in particular, called *An Experiment with Time*, in 1927, which became something of a cult. Cody, on the other hand, was allowed to erect a shed on Laffan's Plain, to keep his aeroplane with the loan of an engine to enable him to continue his experiments.

In February 1911 it was decided to form an Air Battalion, to be divided into two companies, one concerned with kites and balloons and located at Farnborough, the second being concerned with aircraft being located at Larkhill. The aeroplane section had twelve officers, two-thirds of which were Royal Engineers with four officers from line regiments, who were really regarded as interlopers. One of these was Basil Barrington-Kennett from the Grenadier Guards. Basil had been born in Brighton on 19 November 1889 and was the eldest of the four sons of Lieutenant Colonel Brackley Herbert Barrington-Kennett, late King's Bodyguard of the Grenadier Guards. His uncle had died after a balloon ascent with Hedges Butler in 1903, as has been recounted earlier.

Basil had been on a number of balloon flights and became keenly interested in flying. In 1910 he joined the New Forest Flying School in Beaulieu, Hampshire, as a pupil. He passed his RAeC brevet tests at Hendon on 31 December 1910, gaining certificate No. 43.

On Sunday, 3 September 1911 Basil set off to fly home in a Bristol Boxkite, leaving Larkhill, Salisbury Plain, at about 5.30am. Thick mist and crosswinds forced him down at Hambledon near Portsmouth, some 20 odd miles from his destination. The weather finally cleared at about 5.30pm and he resumed his flight, coming down some forty minutes later on an old football pitch at Tillington near Petworth. As the whole village and others had assembled to see him, Basil took the aircraft up for a fifteen-minute exhibition flight, after offering a small Boy Scout a flight that was vetoed by his anxious parents. After this, he had some tea and attended an evening service with his parents and two of his brothers, Victor and Aubrey. Next day he took off at 6am and flew on to Farnborough.

He was considered one of the most promising pilots in the RFC and on 14 February 1912 flew in a Gnome-powered Nieuport monoplane with Corporal F. Ridd in an attempt on the Mortimer Singer prize for a non-stop flight by an Army pilot covering the greatest distance. This he won with a flight of just under 250 miles at an average speed of 55mph in four hours thirty-two minutes.

It was two months after this that the Government decided to accept some further recommendations to form the Royal Flying Corps with an Army and Navy Wing and a centralised flying school. While the plan was theoretically feasible given goodwill, it turned out the Army and Navy were not congenial bedfellows. To be fair, they faced totally different operating conditions and requirements and the Naval Wing split away to become the Royal Naval Air Service in July 1914. The new Commanding Officer of the Military Wing was Major F.H. Sykes, friend of Rudyard Kipling and a regular visitor to Kipling's house Batemans near Burwash. The first adjutant of the RFC was Basil Barrington-Kennett, who for some time had nurtured an ambition to merge the discipline of the Guards with the technical knowhow of the Royal Engineers. Now he was in charge of discipline and personnel, he was able to put this dream into practice, persuading some NCOs in the Guards to join the new corps. This did not go down too well with the Engineers, but Basil, although a disciplinarian, was a popular figure to both officers and men. He always knew everybody's name and exchanged a cheery word with them on his rounds.

It was decided at one stage that a number of NCOs should be taught to fly and given the title of '2nd Class Pilots', and it was here a problem arose with one particular Guard sergeant who was not only ham-fisted but also bone-headed. His instructor spent hours in trying to get him ready to go solo, and tried to explain what was required but the NCO merely drew himself up and shouted 'Sir', which the instructor did not feel advanced the situation. In the end he was sent up and managed more by luck than judgement to bring the aircraft down in one piece.

Early risers near Lindfield Common, near Haywards Heath, on 20 April 1912 saw an Army lorry with a detachment of Royal Engineers, from the then Balloon Battalion at Farnborough arrive and set out a large canvas cross in the middle of the Common. The news was soon abroad that an airship was visiting the village, and in no time at all, a crowd began to gather. The day was fine and bright, and the airship 'Gamma', which started off at 6.15am made the journey via Guildford, Cranleigh, Horsham, Cuckfield and Haywards Heath before hovering over the Common. There was little wind, and the ground party had no difficulty at all in handling the balloon's descent. The 'Gamma' was nearly 170ft long and powered by two 40hp Iris engines, which had swivelling propellers to improve handling near the ground. The airship was piloted by Captain Broke-Smith, the Adjutant and Chief Balloon Instructor at Farnborough. Also on board was Captain Maitland, two officers under instruction with an NCO and two mechanics.

While the crew were provided with refreshments by the villagers, Captain Broke-Smith paid a visit to Lindfield House, where his father-in-law Admiral Twiss resided, which, as one reporter said, explained the choice of landing site. Although the crowds were allowed fairly close to the airship, they were forbidden to smoke. Their stay was quite short and by 9.30am the crew re-entered the airship car and, after casting off, ascended on their return journey to Farnborough, which they reached in two hours. Four days later the airship made a voyage to London and back, circling St Paul's Cathedral, in eight hours.

During the rest of the year, Army balloons came over Sussex on a number of occasions in free-ballooning training flights. One descended at a sewage farm, near Ferring Grange and another on the Felpham Golf Links, narrowly missing a dip in a nearby river. In

September 1913 the airship 'Eta' passed over Sussex and the pilot Lieutenant Wilson dropped a message to a relative at Crawley at 8.30am. The airship then passed over Preston Park before making four circuits of Brighton and returning to Farnborough via Worthing, Littlehampton and Chichester. On 1 January 1914 all Army airships were handed over to the Royal Navy, and in March some naval trainees landed in a rough coppice at Heathfield and it took thirty men to lift the balloon and rigging into an adjoining field before the envelope could be repacked and taken to Heathfield Station to be sent back to Farnborough by goods train.

Chapter 5

The First Aviation Pioneers in Sussex

Three men made their contribution to the advancement of aviation in the county during the years 1901–11. Two of these, Jose Weiss and Harold Hume Piffard, known as Hal to his intimates, were by then well-known and successful artists. The third, Alec Ogilvie, was to go on to play a significant part in the development of British aviation.

Jose Weiss was born in Paris in 1859, his interest in flight arising when he was a boy and watching the eagles soar over the mountains of the Tyrol. Although he studied science and engineering, he had already shown a natural talent for painting. On leaving university he started in the wine trade, but later moved over to the wool business. This involved him in regular visits to England and he stayed in lodgings at Southsea, near Portsmouth.

On journeying to London by train, he was greatly struck by the beauty of the Sussex countryside, and determined to paint some local landscapes (by then he had already had a painting of a French landscape exhibited at the Royal Academy). Taking a few days' holiday, he obtained lodgings at the village post office near Amberley Railway Station and painted a local scene in oils. He received many compliments on the finished canvas and on taking it to the Goupil Gallery in London's Bond Street he sold it for £12.

It was then he realised that it might be possible for him to make a living from painting, but it was not until the 1880s that he gave up his job and rented Meadow Cottage in Amberley. As it turned out, his confidence in his artistic ability was fully justified. In his lifetime he was said to have painted over 2,500 canvases. At the time there was a buoyant market for English and French landscapes in America, Canada and South Africa in particular. Well-to-do immigrants bought them to remind them of their mother country and to add a touch of culture to their houses. Weiss seemed, unlike many artists, to have been a very astute businessman and made a comfortable income from his prolific output. On one occasion he sued a gallery owner for selling his pictures at inflated prices but lost the lawsuit. He was said to be able, when in a good mood, to rough out two or three canvases on site in a day and complete them in his studio in another two or three days.

In 1894, with more of his paintings on exhibition at the Royal Academy and his income assured, he married, and two children and three years later, moved to Houghton House. Weiss had, for some time, taken a great interest in the progress of flight and the death of Otto Lilienthal, the great German glider pioneer, in a flying accident, spurred him to work systematically on the building and testing of gliders based on the natural shape of birds such as the albatross. As time went on these gliding experiments took up more and more of his time, and were only interrupted when he went out into the countryside to sketch and paint to provide more funds for living expenses and his aerial research. His gliders were now getting quite large, some with wingspans of 6ft or more, and were fitted with lead weights of several pounds each. The basic framework of the glider body was bamboo glued with tyre cement, which was then secured with tarred twine. As one visitor said there was always a seafaring aroma pervading his workshop and the surrounding area.

From 1902 onwards Weiss began to launch these large models from both Amberley and Houghton Hill, using a ramp. Those that flew across the fields and over the chalk cliff often went into the river and were recovered some 2 miles away by the local lads, who would be rewarded with a copper or two for their trouble. In the succeeding years, Weiss made regular visits to London to visit the galleries and to attend meetings of the Aeronautical Society of Great Britain, where he regularly gave lectures on his gliding experiments and theories. Weiss was always happiest when pottering in his Amberley workshop in his knickerbocker suit and loathed wearing formal attire. He was also a person who was congenitally incapable of getting to an appointment on time. Each of his visits to the metropolis required the whole family to be mobilised, to bully and badger him into his best clothes, and have his cycle ready for his ride to Amberley Station, which was three-quarters of a mile away. One of his elder children would precede him by bicycle and, standing on the station footbridge, wave and shout to encourage him to hurry. If, as was normal, the train was already in the station, his son or daughter would at the same time be pleading with the stationmaster or guard to hold the train until their father would arrive. It seems that all of this effort was rarely wasted, since Weiss almost always managed to catch the train, to the universal relief of his family, the railway staff, and his fellow passengers, who became quite inured to the performance and, as Englishmen and women, treasuring a true eccentric. On one occasion Weiss took his son Bernard to London with him as a treat and, after leaving an art gallery, went on to lunch. It was only when he was eating his dessert that it struck him he had started out with one of his children. Retracing his steps, he found Bernard curled up and asleep on one of the gallery's sofas.

As related earlier, the work by Lieutenant Dunne on his swept-wing aircraft was proceeding under conditions of secrecy and it caused Colonel Capper some alarm when a press report of the Weiss gliders showed they were of similar design to the Dunne models. He therefore motored down to Amberley with Lieutenant Dunne and was relieved to find that the Weiss gliders did not have the wing curvature of the Dunne designs. They were also not displeased when all the flights of the Weiss models crashed in spiral dives all that afternoon. A similar situation arose when Major Baden-Powell and some Army officers also visited Weiss for a demonstration of some of his models. With the wind coming from the north, the models all veered round and crashed into the hill. Although these failures depressed Weiss, they also made him more determined to prove his theories.

In February 1908 Weiss was introduced to Frederick Handley Page, then a young electrical engineer who wanted to break into the nascent aircraft industry. Despite their differences in age and outlook, the two men seemed to hit it off from the start and visited each other's homes during the year. Weiss was more than happy to expound his theories on the need for inherent stability in aircraft and the viability of large aircraft. Handley Page listened with flattering interest, which was by no means his normal style. As Handley Page later became the head of a large aircraft company, producing many large aircraft, it would seem the ideas promulgated by Weiss fell on fertile ground. Towards the end of 1908, Noel Pemberton Billing, later to be the founder of Supermarine Aircraft Company, became interested in an empty hydraulic crane factory at Fambridge in Essex. It had ample accommodation and workshops covering 1,600 acres of reclaimed marshland, and he visualised forming an 'Aircraft Colony' for small aircraft manufacturers. Meantime, Handley Page had been commissioned to build a Quadraplane for a would-be aviator and inventor and visited Fambridge to see if it would be suitable for flying trials. It has been suggested that he met Weiss there with two companions, Alexander Keith and a would-be painter Gerald Leake, and offered Weiss a chance to exhibit his new powered glider on a stand he was taking for the Aero and Motor Boat Exhibition at Olympia in March 1909. In fact, it seems unlikely that Weiss and his companions moved to Fambridge before the Exhibition was over. At Olympia they were joined by a wealthy aviator, Malcolm Seton-Karr. He had bought a Howard-Wright biplane, which had been designed by W.O. Manning, and on which he hoped to learn to fly. No doubt the agreement to jointly share the Exhibition stand was agreed at an earlier meeting. As a quid pro quo, Weiss allowed Handley Page to use his patented wing on any aircraft he might design without royalty payments.

When the show at Olympia opened, the new Weiss powered aircraft and one of his scale model gliders were on prominent display on the Handley Page stand, with the man himself wearing a new and shiny top hat to add some distinction to the proceedings. A notice on the stand offered replicas of the Weiss powered machine at £500 each accompanied by a flight guarantee. No buyers were forthcoming, which was perhaps just as well as the machine was never capable of a sustained flight.

It was also at this exhibition that Eric Gordon England made his appearance. Born in Concordia, Argentina, in 1891, his parents had come back to England where he was educated, and they now had a rented house called Oakwood in Haywards Heath. By this time, he was an apprentice at the Northern Railway Works at Doncaster, but he too was bitten with the bug of flying. He had extracted promises from his parents that if he could get a paid job in aviation, he could give up his apprenticeship. He therefore visited all the stands, explaining his 'agreement' with his parents, and asking if they might like to employ him. Although he was received kindly, only one person, Pemberton Billing, showed wholehearted approval for his enterprise and initiative. He offered him the job of manager at the Fambridge site (he was then just eighteen) at a princely salary of 25 shillings a week, subject to Pemberton Billing meeting his father. This meeting took place in a pub near Fambridge, where Gordon England's father and Pemberton Billing got along famously. On the other hand, Gordon England's grandmother was aghast to hear of the proposal and assembled three elderly pillars of the Establishment to lecture him and his parents on the myth that aviation had any future whatsoever. His parents refused to retract their promise, and Gordon England was obdurate. He was banished from his grandmother's house for some eighteen months until she relented and allowed him back in the family circle. Within five years he was earning over £2,000 per year as a test pilot.

When he first arrived at Fambridge, Gordon England soon found his duties were somewhat nebulous, but in no time he was using his skill and knowledge to assist Weiss and his helpers, who had little or no expertise on aero engines. Gustavus Green, who lived at Bexhill, had originally started up a cycle business, but had turned to producing internal combustion engines for cars and later aeroplanes. A 35hp water cooled in-line Green aero engine was tried on the Weiss glider but despite Gordon England's efforts he could only get it to run intermittently. Green had no more luck, so it was eventually returned to him. Weiss had decided to adopt the Wright brothers' method of launching his new powered aircraft using a derrick and a pulley with a large weight. Recalling this period, Gordon England said it never seemed possible to get a successful sequence of events. If the weight on the pulley worked correctly and propelled the aircraft, the engine failed to start at the crucial moment. On the other hand, if the engine worked properly, the winch did not function. Eventually the Anzani engine's crankshaft broke and the engine had to be dismantled and returned to the manufacturer for repair.

By now Pemberton Billing was finding that he needed more tenants if Fambridge was to continue, and he warned Gordon England that he might shortly have to terminate his job. Gordon England mentioned this to Weiss and he was offered the job of helping on glider construction and acting as test pilot for future flights, Weiss being too old and too heavy and rotund for the task. Weiss decided that while they awaited the return of their engine, they would go back to Amberley and resume gliding trials with the 'Olive', all of the Weiss aeroplanes being named after his children.

On 27 June Gordon England made a flight from Amberley Mount. The glider got into a thermal and achieved an unofficial British record, which was later described by Gordon England as follows:

> The Olive was launched down a precipitous north face. I suddenly found myself high above Weiss' head and in fact in soaring flight. I was able to keep the machine head to the wind and proceeded to glide out of the valley and out of the up-current; after what seemed a long time, the Olive came gently to rest on its keel in a ploughed field at the bottom of the hill. There I remained seated until a breathless Jose Weiss arrived and announced his stop watch had clocked 58 seconds flat and the machine had soared high above the starting point.

Although Eric Gordon England and Gerald Leake made other successful flights of up to half a mile, they never bettered that sustained glide. By the autumn of 1909 Weiss had left Fambridge, as had Seton-Karr, who had moved to Camber, near Rye in Sussex, and Pemberton Billing had to give up the site. Having put the engine back in the 'Olive' and fitted another to his 'Elsie', Weiss, Gordon England and helpers moved down to Littlehampton for more flying trials from the open beaches. The Duke of Norfolk allowed Weiss the use of a fort-like building on the foreshore for storage of equipment. The trials in April 1910 were unsuccessful. On the first flight the aircraft nosed over on take-off and Gordon England was dragged face down along the sands, so Weiss decided to transfer the aircraft to Brooklands, where he had a hangar near the sewage farm, an ever-present danger to the tyro flyer of the day. From the middle of 1910 onwards both Gordon England and Leake attempted to fly both aircraft with only minimal success. Finally, after a particularly successful painting foray, Weiss bought a brand new 40hp ENV engine and this was installed in the 'Sylvia', which Gordon England also now fitted with a conventional fixed fin, rudder and tail. Preliminary taxying trials and short hops convinced Gordon England that the aircraft would now fly. He therefore took off, made a number of circuits and then climbed over the Brooklands Paddock and made a wide turn over the sewage farm.

Suddenly two struts gave way, and although Gordon England managed to keep the aircraft the right way up, it suddenly dived into the slimiest part of the sewage farm. He emerged covered with green slime and with the help of the sewage workers, who had ample practice in rescuing would-be flyers, got the aircraft to the bank. Weiss rushed across, but once he was sure Gordon England was all right seemed quite unperturbed, saying that strengthening of the struts would solve the problem once the aircraft had dried out. Although Gordon England continued his flights, he found his sojourn at Brooklands was introducing him into a much wider circle of aviation enthusiasts, such as Oscar Morison, Jimmy Valentine and, particularly, Graham Gilmour. The latter had recently secured himself a job with the British and Colonial Aeroplane Company (later called the Bristol Aeroplane Company). Gilmour made it plain to Gordon England that he was wasting his talents with Weiss aircraft, and arranged for him to have an interview at Bristol, where he was offered a job as an instructor/ test pilot/designer. Gordon England, therefore, said goodbye to Weiss with some regret and later said that he was an aviation pioneer who did not get the recognition that he deserved. Weiss and Alexander Keith then turned their attention to designing a flapping wing glider called the 'aviette', which had two pedals to operate the mechanism that beat the wings through an arc of 3ft. The machine was tested in free flight and launched successfully, but little else seems to be known about it.

Alec Ogilvie, the second Sussex pioneer, was educated at Rugby and Cambridge and constructed many flying models before graduating to full-size gliders. On one never-to-be-forgotten occasion he was towing a quadraplane glider behind his car when the tow rope snapped. The glider, with his brother in the cockpit, suddenly shot up some 40ft into the air and his brother was ejected out of the cockpit and fell through the four sets of wings before emerging bruised and somewhat shaken from the wreckage. During 1908 Ogilvie formed a partnership with a T.P. Seawright, a keen motorist who was also interested in aviation, and they gave themselves the title of the Aviation Manufacturing Company, with the intention of designing their own aircraft. They seemed to have built one at Finchley, but it never succeeded in getting off the ground. At the end of the year, Ogilvie made a grand tour of leading aircraft manufacturers in France, and on 16 December made a detour to Le Mans, hoping to see Wilbur Wright flying his biplane. He later wrote in his diary:

> W. Wright made two wonderful flights this afternoon, all kinds of evolutions, turning, skimming, close to the ground, gliding without an engine from 200ft. A true and complete flying machine. No chance of speaking to Wright.

Later he did manage to see the great man, and they had a long talk and later formed a warm friendship. Ogilvie, like many others, found Wilbur an impressive character, absolutely honest and sincere with great intellectual powers. At the end of the month, Ogilvie placed an order for a Wright biplane, six of which were built under licence by the Short Brothers, at a cost of £1,000 each. Sometime earlier in 1909, Ogilvie and Seawright took a lease out on some land on the foreshore at Camber near Rye, and erected a shed some 50ft × 60ft with 10ft-high doors. With the delay in delivery of the Wright biplane, Ogilvie had a glider built based on the Wright glider except that it was fitted with an upright seat for the pilot. He made a number of good glides over Camber, the maximum distance he covered being 300 yards. The Wright aircraft, called the 'Baby', was delivered on 7 November and Ogilvie flew in it the same day. On the following Tuesday, he flew 2 miles at 40mph, the next day 8 miles, and then two days later covered 10 miles, but then a piston blew out, igniting the petrol in the cylinder. Although Ogilvie switched off the engine, a sheet of flame shot up before the biplane dropped 150ft, ploughing into the foreshore sand damaging the propellers and the airframe.

On 24 May Ogilvie took his Aero Club brevet certificate at Camber under the eyes of the official examiners from the Aero Club, passing without difficulty and gaining Certificate No. 7. In June he was visited by members of the Hastings and St Leonards Aero Club Association, and he demonstrated the controls of the Short-Wright machine, the Wright type glider and also the various wind gauges fitted to the ground to ensure conditions were suitable for flying. The members of the Club were also shown the Howard Wright biplane, which Seton-Karr had moved from Fambridge and which was now housed in an adjoining hangar, the designer W.O. Manning often visiting the site.

During the summer months Ogilvie participated in a number of flying meetings, and was at Bournemouth when C.S. Rolls was killed flying his French Wright biplane, the first British pilot to be killed in a flying accident. Ogilvie also accompanied the popular flyer Claude Grahame-White and James Radley to America to contest the Gordon Bennet Cup at Belmont Park near New York. Grahame-White won the contest of twenty laps in his racing Blériot monoplane. On returning to England, Ogilvie decided to participate in both the British Michelin Cup for the longest distance flown by a British pilot and aircraft, and the Baron de Forest £4,000 prize for a British long-distance flight to the Continent. On Wednesday, 28 December Ogilvie took off from the East Cliff Rye in a Wright biplane and landed some four hours later, having lapped a distance of 147½ miles. This beat an attempt earlier by S.F. Cody, who covered 115 miles. Two days later, Ogilvie started out at ten o'clock in the morning for his attempt on the de Forest prize, before a large crowd of locals and well-wishers. Attired in a leather jacket, fur boots and a cork life preserver, Ogilvie rose into the air and then banked but the onlookers could see the aircraft was rocking and they all rushed to the sandbank to get a better view, and saw the aircraft diving towards the sands, which it struck with a loud crash, damaging the lower wing and tearing the fabric. By the time they reached the aircraft Ogilvie had dismounted and told a friend: 'When I turned, the machine stood quite still and then fell.' The machine was put on to a trolley and taken back to the hangar for repairs, and Ogilvie was soon helping to dismantle the wings. A number of machines had already been lost in the de Forest contest. Grahame-White crashed while making a low turn and was badly cut by the flying wires of his Bristol Boxkite, while Cecil Grace disappeared attempting a Channel crossing and was never found.

The next morning, Ogilvie found that there was a heavy fog over the Channel and decided to abandon the de Forest contest but attempt to improve his Michelin Cup flight. After lapping 55 miles, he had to land, saying that the new wing that had been fitted was making the machine unbalanced, and in compensating for this with the controls he was finding the strain too great to continue. He made another attempt after lunch but this time had engine trouble and the aircraft had to be returned to the hangar. Here Ogilvie received a telegram telling him that T.O.M. Sopwith had clocked 150 miles for the Michelin prize, but had been finally pipped at the post by S.F. Cody, who had flown 185 miles. Sopwith had, however, won the de Forest prize with a 177-mile flight to the Continent.

In April 1911 Ogilvie was picked as a member of the Technical Reserve Advisory Committee set up by the War Office to advise them on technical matters on aviation. By now his lease at Camber had expired and he was persuaded by his Royal Aero Club friends (the King granting the Royal prefix in 1910) to move to their new flying ground at Eastchurch, Kent, where Short Brothers was also setting up a factory. Ogilvie left Camber at 8.45am on 23 May, landing at Ashford, Kent, to refuel, and arrived at the Isle of Sheppey at 10.45am covering the 90 miles in an hour and a half. One result of his sojourn in Camber was his air speed indicator for aircraft, which he patented in November 1913 and which was subsequently adopted on all service aircraft.

The third and last of this trio of pioneers was Harold Hume Piffard. Born in India in 1867, where his father was the Clerk to the Calcutta Courts, he was sent to Lancing College at the age of ten. Here he soon established a reputation for his artistic and histrionic abilities and as an inveterate practical joker. At the age of twelve, success in some school theatricals made him decide to abandon his studies and go on the London stage. In mid-winter and after the Sunday roll call, with three shillings and sixpence (17½p) in his pocket, he walked to the metropolis, reaching there on the Tuesday. His applications at the stage doors of theatres and music halls for artistic employment met with no success and he had to sleep on the Embankment for several nights before he reluctantly returned to Lancing. His dream of a stage career unfulfilled, he then had to face the displeasure of the headmaster.

One of his most famous exploits perpetuated in the annals of the college took place on Sunday afternoons, when he would meet the local train. As it came into view approaching the railway bridge at Beeding near Steyning, he would execute a war dance on the rails (there were no electric trains then!) and when the engine came up on the bridge he performed his coup de grace, daredevil dive, into the river below through a hole in the track. As he wore little or nothing, the effect was said to be more than satisfactory on the more staid passengers.

In 1883 Piffard left Lancing and re-joined his parents in India, being employed in a Darjeeling tea plantation, the eventual intention being to set up on his own. The death of his father led him to return to England and start art studies, for which he had a decided talent. Admitted as a student at the Royal Academy, he completed his studies, then moved on to Paris to join the Julian's Academy of Art, living in the Latin Quarter. Meanwhile, his continuing interest in the stage led him to continue to practise tap-dancing, juggling acrobatics and also master a number of musical instruments. He used to entertain his fellow students between breaks when the life models were given rest periods. On one vacation Piffard undertook a walking tour of Spain, starting from Gibraltar and crossing the Pyrenees into France. He covered a total distance of 1,120 miles on foot and often used to give variety turns in the courtyards of inns in exchange for meals and his lodgings.

On his return to the Academy, a fellow French artist suggested he might turn his entertaining talents to his financial advantage and introduced him to the manager of the Montmartre Vaudeville theatre, the Divan Japonais. He was given a nine-month contract and other engagements followed at the Eden and the Gaiety Montparnasse. At the last named he met two Americans, Reed and Jillson, who had previously appeared at the Folies Bergère. They decided to form a trio under the name of the Pinuads. They returned to England and toured music halls in London and the provinces.

During, this time Piffard continued his studies and in 1895 he painted a large 5ft × 4ft canvas entitled the 'Last of the Garrison', which depicted an incident in the Franco-Prussian War. It was accepted and hung in the Royal Academy and he decided to concentrate on his painting. A gifted artist, he flourished as a military painter for some years. His martial subjects were all cast in the heroic mould, and one reproduced in the *Illustrated London News* showed the execution of the Duc D'Enghier before an open grave facing the firing squad with his faithful dog by his side. Piffard later derived his main income from the thriving magazine market, drawing for *Pearsons*, the *Windsor* and the *Illustrated Bits*, among many others.

It is not known when Piffard first started to take an interest in aviation, but he made many flying models and gained a number of prizes for his efforts. It may be that he took up ballooning sometime after 1904, although since he did not join the Aero Club until 1909, it seems unlikely that he used their balloons, or even the services of their professional aeronauts. We know that Piffard designed and built his first aircraft with some kindred spirits at North Ealing in 1909, where he erected a hangar-cum-workshop. The aircraft was a pusher biplane with wings of equal length and both front and rear elevators, similar to the Farman, powered by a 40hp ENV engine fitted with a propeller of 7ft diameter. Originally Piffard had designed the engine to slide on its mounting to enable the centre of gravity to be adjusted, but fortunately W.O. Manning persuaded him to abandon this idea as highly dangerous.

Like Weiss, Piffard spent a substantial part of his income on aircraft experiments and since, also like Weiss, he had little mechanical aptitude, had to employ a mechanic to care for the engine. At this time Piffard also had a trainee art student who was supposedly studying painting under his tuition. She was Barbara Blanck, who found art definitely took second place to flying in the mind of her tutor. Although she was the only woman among a group of males who helped Piffard, she seems to have made no complaint, eventually marrying W.O. Manning.

Piffard tested his first home-built aircraft in late 1909, and in December actually rose a few feet in the air in a hop of a hundred yards or so. Ever the optimist, he pictured himself flying over

London, but these dreams were shattered when, in a violent storm shortly afterwards, both the hangar and his aircraft were wrecked. Fortunately, by then, he seemed to have come into contact with a solicitor, George Arthur Wingfield, who was seeking a suitable site for an airfield, which he saw as a profitable investment. At that time, he had narrowed the potential sites to two, one of which was Shoreham. No doubt Piffard's recollections of his schooldays and the flat site in front of Lancing College helped Wingfield finally to select this candidate. He took an initial six months option on the land at New Salts Farm in 1909, and also obtained permission to erect a large shed for Piffard and his acolytes to build a new aircraft and eventually test it, to ensure the site was really suitable for an airfield. Piffard and his crew would motor down from Chingford in his Darracq car, which was of doubtful reliability, but the aeroplane was not ready until about April, so Wingfield had to extend his option. The shed was 40ft square and sited in one corner of the field near the railway line between Worthing and Brighton. It was soon apparent that Piffard's recollection of the site was somewhat flawed, as the area was badly drained and often waterlogged, being next to the River Adur. To get sufficient room for take-off, some of the numerous ditches for drainage had to be covered over. One fairly clear run was found that only had one ditch, and this was boarded over and a flag put up at each end so that it could be identified from the air when landing.

When finally completed, the 'new' aircraft was ready by May. It differed little from the type built at Ealing. It had its first test flight that month, and rose from the ground at the first attempt, although there was some difficulty with the back wheel until this was replaced by a skid. By now Piffard was making a number of long hops, or flights, as he insisted on calling them. The landlord of the nearby inn, the Sussex Pad, had in a fit of generosity promised Piffard a case of champagne when he could fly over and collect it. Piffard's initial flights and those for some time were 'straights', that is he flew in a straight line and landed, turning the aircraft round manually and then flew back to his starting point. Nevertheless, he was gaining confidence, but alas, on one flight while returning to the shed, the aircraft was struck by a gust of wind when at about 30ft. When Piffard regained consciousness, the doctor was stitching up a cut in his leg. He also had a large bump on his head and a good shaking, but he soon recovered. The machine, on the other hand, was almost a write-off, only the engine, wings and tail tips surviving in one piece.

As Piffard always displayed a red flag when he was likely to attempt to fly, he had gathered a large following of local supporters, who had taken him to their hearts as a source of continuing entertainment in a spot that had very little other excitement. Wingfield did make an attempt to extract money from this audience, but since they could see perfectly well on the boundary, he eventually gave it up as a bad job. The supporters did, however, set to with a will to help repair the shattered aircraft, which was known locally as the 'Humming Bird'. By late June, the rebuilt aircraft was again ready for testing. Unfavourable weather meant that it was not until July that further flights were possible, to satisfy Piffard that the lateral balance was correct. He had planned a flight over Brighton, but this was again delayed after his next landing when he collided with his shed, carrying away the skid, the front elevator and part of the right wing. After all this was repaired, a cylinder in the engine fractured and had to be replaced. By now it was late August. Piffard made another test flight but had only just got into the air when the aircraft started to shudder and shake, so he hastily returned to terra firma. There he discovered that one of the bracing wires on the wing had snapped and snagged a propeller blade, breaking it off. The broken piece was found although the repair caused a certain amount of consternation since it meant splicing a new blade on what was left, but this was done. Three bolts secured the new blade, and these and the joint were covered with material from an old pair of dungarees and doped. The same thing was done on the good blade to balance it up. Amazingly this seemed to work, although those in the know kept out of the plane of the propeller when the engine was started up!

In August 1910 the Vincent family were on holiday in Shoreham, and Stanley Vincent, the youngest, his brother and father spent a great deal of time watching Piffard and helping him when required. To the young boy, Piffard was a bit of a disappointment; he was not of the material of which daredevil aviators should be made. He was a short, tubby man, over forty and a bundle of nerves. A chain smoker, his consumption of cigarettes increased rapidly when he decided to take to the air. He was also short-sighted, and in consequence he was never quite sure when he had to cut the engine to come into land near the shed. He had two vacation students, who had joined him to act as fitter and rigger and have some fun. One of these solved the problem of when to cut the engine by procuring a whistle and giving a sharp blast when Piffard was in the right position to switch off the engine and land. One day, when the 'Humming Bird' came back over the field, the whistle was mislaid and panic set in, with the helpers running about whistling but not achieving the pitch that would be heard above the noise of the engine. In the confusion, Piffard made a late landing, but luckily hit a bell tent that took the strain without any really adverse effect on either him or the machine.

One of the problems encountered with the engine was having no revolution counter, so it was difficult to tune the engine correctly. One day the engine was running exceptionally well and Vincent's father, who was a Doctor of Music, said that was a 'G' on the musical scale, so he bought a 'G' tuning fork. From then onwards, according to Stanley Vincent, the engine was run up and everyone would hum in the same key, the engine was cut and the tuning fork was twanged. If it did not match, the engine would be retuned, as near the correct key as possible.

On 11 September, the weather improved and Piffard went up on another test, the propeller proving satisfactory without any noticeable loss of thrust and an attempt on the champagne stakes was considered. But again, a cylinder in the engine failed and Piffard had to await a replacement. When it arrived and was fitted, Piffard took his courage in both hands and essayed a turn to reach and land next to the 'Sussex Pad' and claim his prize. This took forty seconds but he found it was impossible to get a clear run to fly back owing to the ditches, and it then took Piffard and all his helpers an hour and a half to get the 'Humming Bird' and the crate of champagne back, using planks and gates to struggle across ditches.

By now Piffard was becoming extremely confident, and performing 'straights' and quite tight turns with panache, receiving some compliments on his flying from the local press. As a result, he had a visit from a movie cameraman anxious to get one of his flights on celluloid. Piffard agreed, and showed the cameraman where his take-off would start and suggested other suitable shots. The cameraman demurred, and pointed out that there was a ditch 150 yards in his path, but Piffard dismissed this airily, claiming he would be at least 50ft in the air by the time he reached that point. When all was ready, Piffard took his place in his machine and then realised a following wind had sprung up, so he not only failed to rise as promised but went straight into the ditch. Piffard was not hurt, but his aircraft was badly damaged, as was his reputation. Although Piffard explained at great length to the cameraman why the accident ought not to have happened, he did not seem to be paying much attention, being as it turned out more than satisfied as to the outcome. It was many months before Piffard could attend a cinema showing without seeing his crash on the screen.

Once more the aircraft was trundled to the hangar, but it was not long before it was repaired, enabling Piffard to practise full turns, which he had now mastered. On one occasion, however, this led him off his usual course, and on landing on his right wing he caught a wire fence at a speed of 25mph, the machine swinging round and catching another fence, damaging the skid, right wing and tail. It was early October before Piffard ventured out again, and by now the weather had changed for the worse, and the lease on the field was about to expire, so he decided to make a final flight. On 4 October, with a gusting wind, he took off and the 'Humming Bird' shot up in the air some 40ft. Piffard struggled with the controls and managed to right it, but then was struck by another gust. Again, he got the machine level, but another even stronger gust struck the aircraft and this time it crashed, striking the ground with the tip of the right wing and cartwheeling, to the horror of those watching. Fortunately, Piffard emerged more or less unscathed, but the aeroplane was a complete write-off, apart from the engine. Piffard comforted himself with the thought that the machine had been so spliced and repaired over the year that it was of very little use for experimental work and that he would build another machine, his third in the same number of years.

So Piffard, Barbara and his acolytes returned to London, satisfied that their pioneering efforts had resulted in the first flights over Shoreham. Piffard spent the winter producing magazine illustrations to finance the new 'Humming Bird Mk II', which cost another

£600 (less the engine). When this sum had been accumulated, the studio was turned back into an aircraft factory, echoing to the sounds of sawing and hammering. This time Piffard determined to modify his design to a hydroplane, or seaplane as it was later renamed by Winston Churchill. These machines were on trial with the Navy and it may be that Piffard was influenced by the commercial prospects. On the other hand, he may have thought, like others, that there were fewer problems in flying from water since there was no need to find and rent a flat space free of trees or other obstructions. By June 1911 the new seaplane was housed in a dismantled state in an old lifeboat shed near the present Good Shepherd Church on Shoreham beach. The following month it had been assembled, said according to one report, with collapsible air bags for floats, which was supposed to be a new idea! In trials in August, the machine capsized, throwing everyone in the water, but it was soon righted, even if everyone got rather wet in the process. It seems the more conventional-type floats were then fitted, and brief items subsequently in the local press refer to trips of considerable distance by water including a trip to Hove but there are no firm reports of it actually flying. It is possible the type of float used would not 'unstick' from the water or that the machine was underpowered for take-off from the sea.

The machine, like the first one, was eventually destroyed on Shoreham beach during a storm at the end of 1911, but as Barbara Blanck said many years later, they had some wonderful parties on the beach at Shoreham, which were some compensation for all that unfulfilled effort. So Piffard faded from the scene, as did Weiss. In an article Piffard wrote for one aviation magazine, he suggested aeroplanes belonged to the female gender: capricious, fascinating, expensive and generally speaking an infinite source of pleasure and pain. He can, however, claim to be the first flyer from Shoreham airfield, which still survives as the only operational airport from the first six airfields originally set up in this country.

Chapter 6

Sussex Airfields and the First Flight to Brighton

The arrival of the aeroplane coincided with the new era of popular pictorial journalism for the common man and woman. It did not take the press long to realise that flying had all the newsworthy ingredients necessary to sell newspapers: drama, personalities and, on occasion, sudden death, so that flyers and their machines became headline news. Lord Northcliffe and his paper the *Daily Mail*, started a campaign entitled 'Wake up England' to warn the public of their lack of defence against aerial attack. He also pursued his conviction (not entirely from disinterested motives) that aviation had a shining future and offered substantial monetary prizes for flights, which undoubtedly led to technical advances, while increasing his readership.

Magnus Volk, the inventor of the Volks Electric Railway that ran along the foreshore of Brighton beach, was keenly interested in flying. In December 1908 Magnus cycled with his son Herman to Issy-les-Moulineaux in the hope of seeing the Englishman, Moore-Brabazon fly his new Voisin aircraft, but unfortunately the aviator only managed to make a few short 'hops'. Three months later he again cycled with another son to Pau near the Spanish frontier, to see Wilbur Wright fly his biplane in a number of demonstration flights. In a later visit to France, to the first international flying meeting at Reims in 1909, he watched Glenn Curtiss win the Gordon Bennett Cup in the Golden Flyer, little realising that Curtiss would take him up on a flight from Brighton some four years later. By now aviation meetings were becoming increasingly popular and well-known aviators of the time, mostly French, could charge thousands of pounds to appear and give exhibition flights. In September that year it was proposed to hold

74

a flying meeting north of Devil's Dyke, and a number of aviation experts, including S.F. Cody, were approached but nothing came of it. At the end of the month a report appeared in the *Sussex Daily News* giving details of Government proposals to set up an aviation school on the Sussex Downs between Brighton and Lewes. The next day there was a brief item saying the Government had selected a place near Trevone Head in Cornwall for their 'aerial experiments'. Whether either of these items had any factual basis is not known.

In October, Eastbourne Council decided to set up a committee to report on making the town an 'Aviation Centre', as the Duke of Devonshire, a large landowner in the area had 600 acres that might be available for aviation, with other sites on the marshes that could be used as landing places.

A few days after this, the *Sussex Daily News* informed the public that it was the intention of G.A. Wingfield, the chairman of the Aviators Finance Company Limited, to secure the site at Shoreham at New Salts Farm for an aerodrome. Its many advantages were extolled: it abutted the River Adur with access to Shoreham Harbour, while the south boundary had rail services between Brighton, Worthing and London, with the Old Shoreham Road to the north. H.H. Piffard was quoted as saying that the site was the best he had seen in the country. This was, of course, some eight months before he actually managed to get the 'Humming Bird' to fly over the waterlogged ground. Ten days later a meeting was held at the Hove Town Hall with the Mayors of Brighton, Hove and Worthing present. The audience was first addressed by W. Pettett, secretary of the Company, then the managing director G.A. Wingfield, and their architect, R.J. Lovell. Pettett, a Hove garage proprietor, was also the inventor of the Pettett petrol pourer; a device that was screwed on to a 2-gallon can to admit air as the petrol was poured out. He told the meeting that the land at New Salts Farm was being acquired by the Company with the firm intention of setting up an aerodrome, and that they were already in discussion with the railway company regarding the building of a new station on their southern boundary, to give access to the south coast and London. When completed, the aerodrome would have a 10-mile flying circuit over the flat surrounding countryside and they intended to hold an International Flying meeting when it was opened.

There would be stands to hold 20,000 people and a flying club, while land not needed for flying would be turned into a golf course. It was agreed that the proposals would be considered by the three councils.

In June 1910 Wingfield obtained a further option to purchase the freehold of the river bank and foreshore of the River Adur next to the proposed airfield. There was also a meeting in the month of the Air League at the Hotel Metropole, Brighton. Its president, Sir Theodore Angier, a local wealthy shipowner, told the meeting he had been asked to associate himself with Aviators Finance Company so that a flying ground could be built in Sussex and he had agreed. This was the subject of general approbation among the members present. Subsequent speakers stressed the need for Britain to be in the forefront of aviation, and the proceedings closed with a patriotic recitation from Rudyard Kipling. Sir Theodore was, in fact, a good friend of the Wingfield family, whose wife often visited Lady Angier. Wingfield's son Lawrence, however, found the noble knight rather a nuisance. He was a physical fitness enthusiast and known as the Pocket Hercules, and would insist on seizing Lawrence and throwing him into the air, which was regarded as very unseemly by a boy of twelve years old. In March 1911 there was a rumour that the Army and Navy Association, another patriotic organization, was considering establishing an aviation ground at Park Barn, Cuckfield, close to the golf course. Needless to say, this was soon squashed as being likely to affect property values in the area.

Meanwhile, Worthing Council were considering an offer made by the company Aircraft Courses Limited to arrange for an aviation meeting to be held in the town, but their General Purposes Committee turned it down. Hove got a little further when the company approached them and actually selected a site. Then they discovered that under the terms by which they had originally purchased the land it could not be used for the purpose of aviation and the whole thing fell through.

It was on Wednesday, 15 February 1911 that the first aeroplane flew over Brighton, arriving from Brooklands in little over an hour. The pilot was Oscar Colin Morison, of Scots descent, aged twenty-seven years and he had studied electrical engineering. He had first worked in England before going over to the United States and Canada. Returning to England in March 1910, he went to the Blériot school at Pau, in France, to enrol as a pupil. After some tuition, he went on safari to East Africa. He returned to Pau in October to complete his flying lessons. Although he had not passed his brevet tests, he decided he would fly home from France, but his first attempt in a Blériot failed when he got lost in fog and had to come down at a French military airfield. He made a second attempt from Issy-les-Moulineaux airfield. This time his machine got caught in a gust of wind on take-off and plunged into the ground from 30ft. The aeroplane was wrecked, but Morison made the first of a number of miraculous escapes without injury.

Ordering a new Blériot, with a 50hp engine, he moved on to Brooklands aerodrome. He soon earned himself a reputation as a dashing and fearless pilot, even amid flyers such as Graham Gilmour, James Valentine and Eric Gordon England. Morison and Valentine took their Royal Aero Club brevets in January 1911, numbers 46 and 47 respectively, and became firm friends. Morison made a number of cross-country flights in the area, and raised the Brooklands height record to 6,000ft. On the morning of 15 February, he flew to Cobham, while Gilmour took off in his Blériot for a test flight, intending, it seems, to fly to Brighton. Engine trouble forced him to return, and he found the fault could not be rectified that day. On Morison's return, Gilmour suggested he might make a flight to Brighton, and Morison rang the resort's Royal Albion Hotel and booked a room. This was the hotel run by Harry Preston, the hotelier, who afterwards encouraged flyers to stay there. Morison's flight was uneventful, except that as he came over the shore, he realised he was at Worthing as it had only one pier, while Brighton had two, so he turned eastwards. At the same time that Morison left Brooklands, two cars followed him, one driven by Gilmour with two of Morison's mechanics, and the other by a party of their friends. Since most airfields were off the beaten track, a car was almost essential, although the aviator motorist found himself regarded as a dangerous maniac when driving but a brave airman when they were in the air. Morison had already had several brushes with the Surrey constabulary for speeding, while Gilmour positively delighted in being as obstreperous as possible to the police on all occasions. PC Pickard was later to give evidence at Byfleet Court that at 4.15pm Gilmour was driving towards Cobham at an excessive speed. Coming round the corner on the wrong side of the road, he missed a horse and cart by inches and then had to swing to the offside to avoid two school girls who abandoned their bicycles and leapt for safety, Gilmour's car leaving two deep ruts in the road. Under examination, the constable said Gilmour already had four summons for speeding that week. Gilmour professed to recollect nothing of the incident, saying he would have remembered if he had to avoid anyone. The Byfleet bench was unconvinced and fined him £10 with costs. Three days later he was fined a similar amount at Woking Court for misdemeanours during his return car journey from Brighton on Thursday, 16 February.

Morison had been told that it would be possible to land near the Brighton Aquarium, but as news of his flight had become known, the crowds had appeared. Worried by a possible shortage of fuel, he decided to land on the foreshore as the tide was partly out. He selected a patch of sand near the Volks Electric Railway Station near Paston Place, but as he came into land, he realised that he was landing on shingle, not sand. In consequence, the aircraft stuck in the stones, breaking the propeller and damaging the landing gear. Morison emerged to be greeted by a large crowd of spectators and be welcomed to Brighton by its chief constable. As his friends arrived and started to dismantle his aircraft, Morison was escorted to a car and driven off to the Royal Albion Hotel a short distance away. The aircraft was later removed to the Prudential Garage in King Street, reassembled as far as possible, and an entrance fee of one shilling (5p) charged to the public.

Morison's flight created a great deal of interest in the town, and it was decided to hold a commemorative dinner in his honour at the Royal York Hotel on 20 February with the Deputy Mayor, Alderman Geere, in the chair. Giving the toast 'Our Guest', Geere said that although it had been their pleasure to welcome visitors to Brighton under various means of locomotion, this was the first occasion on which a visitor had dropped in by aeroplane. Events were crowding in on them so fast, they were apt to regard great discoveries as commonplace, yet in their lifetime they had seen phonograph, cinematograph, the telephone and wireless telegraphy, and today the aeroplane. Mr Morison had lunch at Brooklands and, seeing the nice day, called for his aeroplane and an hour later arrived in Brighton. 'It was astonishing – it was epoch making.' He then presented Morison with a gold cigarette case, suitably inscribed on the behalf of the members of the Sussex Yacht Club, as a memento of the occasion. Morison rose to his feet amid much applause, and modestly said that it had been his ambition for some time to visit Brighton and he naturally felt proud of having achieved that distinction.

It was some two weeks before Morison's Blériot monoplane was repaired and the weather suitable for flying, but on 7 March the machine was taken into the yard of the Prudential Garage and secured with ropes so Morison could test run the engine. An hour later his aircraft was on the Hove Lawns, where every vantage point in the area for spectators was full to overflowing. Another hour elapsed and Morison appeared, by which time the crowds, now estimated to number about 10,000, were becoming impatient. He finally took off in fine style, and was soon out to sea before turning westward on his way to Shoreham, while his mechanics packed up their gear and followed him by car. Morison landed at Shoreham about fifteen minutes later and told a waiting reporter that he intended to make the new aerodrome his headquarters for the present, although he would be returning to Brooklands eventually. It seems Messrs Pettett and Wingfield had persuaded Morison to stay over at Shoreham, probably offering a free hangar for his Blériot and incidental expenses to provide some additional publicity for their new venture. It also seems that Gilmour had persuaded the British and Colonial Aeroplane Company to loan Morison a Bristol Boxkite to be housed on the airfield so he could take up passengers. Again, the purpose seemed to have been to gain favourable publicity for that Company.

Morison had not been at Shoreham long before he received an invitation to Sunday lunch from the headmaster, the Reverend Bowlby of Lancing College. Gusty winds prevented a visit until the afternoon but at four o'clock Morison took off, climbed to 1,000ft and circled the chapel before coming in to land on the college cricket pitch. Here the ground was so smooth that Morison overran and struck some rising ground known as Grubber Bank, slightly damaging the Blériot's elevator. Morison was soon surrounded by an admiring throng of pupils, who plied him with questions on his aircraft and flying in general and clamoured for his autograph. He was detached with some difficulty from his admirers, and taken to tea with the headmaster and later shown around the college and the grounds. Morison decided to leave the Blériot overnight and get his mechanics to repair the tail next morning. After thanking the headmaster and his staff for their hospitality, he was photographed beside his machine and left by car for the Royal Albion Hotel. In the next few weeks Morison encountered some problems with his Gnome engine, but by mid-April, after getting some spare parts from France, the engine was running smoothly. It seems with hindsight that he was waiting on the arrival of the Boxkite before selling his Blériot, but fate was to intervene. On 15 April Morison flew to Eastbourne, covering the 31 miles in less than an hour.

After looking for a suitable landing ground, he finally decided to land in the town's Devonshire Park. By eleven o'clock it was quite crowded, and he came down on the grass some 50ft from a pathway next to the Music Gardens. Morison then saw some telephone wires, and in trying to avoid them, his machine struck an electric light standard with such force it was broken off at the base. The aeroplane's tail had caught in the branches of a tree and the front of the machine smashed into some chairs, with Morison still in the cockpit, leaving the aircraft in a perpendicular position. His first words on being assisted from the aircraft were 'Where am I?' Interviewed by a reporter, he said both of the wings were broken, as were the elevators and propeller. He estimated that the machine would cost £200 to repair, which was unfortunate since he had planned to sell it the following week. The wreckage was later taken from the park and returned to Shoreham for rebuilding.

It was another fortnight before the Boxkite arrived at Shoreham Station, and it was loaded on to two horse-drawn trollies and a van to be taken to the aerodrome, where assembly started straight away. A local reporter appears to have been carried away by the sight of the new aircraft, describing it as 'like an enormous bird … a beautiful sight, so graceful, symmetrical and examined in detail so replete with wonderful workmanship'. Bad weather delayed Morison's first test flight, and the machine was not ready to take part in the first

Brooklands to Brighton Air Race, much to Morison's disappointment. After the race, two of the contestants, Gilmour and Pixton, decided to stay over at Shoreham. Advertisements for passenger flights started to appear in the local press, the minimum charge for a flight with Morison being £5. Mrs Buller, the wife of the chairman of the Shoreham and Lancing Land Company was Morison's first passenger; indeed, a large proportion of his passengers turned out to be female.

Eric Gordon England, now employed by the British and Colonial Aeroplane Company, was also at Shoreham and invited both Pixton and Gilmour to spend the weekend at his parent's home at Haywards Heath. Gilmour, who was also visiting a relative at Portsmouth, declined, but Pixton accepted, and flew there on Sunday. His arrival caused great interest, as few aeroplanes had been seen in the area and crowds gathered to see his Avro biplane. Gordon England was having trouble with his Boxkite and was unable to get home, so Pixton left early on Monday morning to return to Brooklands. In the meantime, Morison was still taking passengers up at Shoreham, so Gordon England suggested they might go up to Oakwood that Monday evening. They left Shoreham at 6.45pm in Morison's machine and flew via Brighton, arriving over Haywards Heath twenty-five minutes later. The locals, who now appeared to be developing a taste for flying, saw the machine lose height and land 2 miles south of the town. As a result, there was a rush of motorists, motor cyclists and pedal cyclists along the Burgess Hill to Haywards Heath road, plus many walkers hurrying in the same direction. It turned out Morison had run out of petrol, and he and Gordon England were invited in for a cup of tea by a local farmer while some cans of petrol were procured. When the aeroplane was refueled, they resumed their journey. Morison, noting that the field at Oakwood was a little small, landed in the adjacent field, where they were soon found by the pursuing crowds. It was here that an 'unpleasant incident' occurred, as the press described it. It seems the field was part of the Holy Cross Home, and someone appeared and demanded a fee of £5 if they intended to leave the aircraft overnight. Gordon England's father protested vigorously at this imposition, but Morison simply took off again and landed in Oakwood's field. The disagreement was smoothed over the next day, the Reverend Mother sending a message expressing her regret at what had happened and offering the use of her field if the aviators needed it for their departure, a somewhat ambiguous remark in the circumstances. On the Tuesday evening Morison and Gordon England set off on their return journey but had reached only 200ft when the engine cut out completely. As the Boxkite without power had the gliding angle of a brick, the machine fell on to a large clump of trees some 30ft high, with its tail hanging towards the ground. It was impossible for either of the occupants to get out until some ladders were obtained for their rescue. On reaching the ground, Gordon England rang Shoreham and arranged for Morison's mechanics to come over the following day and dismantle the aircraft in situ.

By now the souvenir hunters were starting to gather, and the police had to stop people crossing nearby gardens to pick up pieces from the crashed machine. The furore from Morison's visit did not die down for some time. There was a long and acrimonious correspondence with the solicitors acting for the owners of Oakwood, who protested that admission charges had been levied, and complained that the spectators had trampled down fences and hedges. These complaints were dismissed out of hand by Gordon England's father, who told reporters that it was his intention to introduce even more aviation into the area!

The accident put back the proposed air race from Shoreham to Black Rock in East Brighton, where Charles Green had ascended in 1821, and Magnus Volk was offering a prize of £25 to the winner. Finally, another replacement Boxkite was flown down to Shoreham and the race was fixed for 13 May, which fortunately turned out to be a fine day with a cloudless blue sky and sunshine. In the event the only two competitors were Gilmour and Morison, and their aircraft were on display at Shoreham aerodrome before the race, when the Kent Brass Band rendered various musical selections to an appreciative audience of spectators. At 4.45pm everything was ready. Gilmour took off first and started to climb, while Morison kept quite low. The crowds had gathered on the Brighton and Hove seafront, the two piers, and the cliffs at Black Rock, and were alerted by a maroon when the flyers took off. There were shouts of 'There they are' as the machines were seen approaching the piers. Morison was still very low and now just in the lead as he passed the finishing post at Black Rock in exactly fifteen minutes, followed closely by Gilmour. Then Gilmour circled and made a sweeping turn to land on the tennis courts at Roedean Girls School, Morison followed. Once again, he overran on the smooth surface and hit a fence and damaged his skid. An account of the race was given by Miss A.L.G. Eady in the *Roedean College Magazine* of the time:

The Aeroplanes at Roedean

When we first heard that two aeroplanes were coming to Roedean there was wild excitement. It was Saturday afternoon, and we were playing cricket, but the game did not progress very rapidly, as every two or three minutes someone would cry out, 'Look quickly! I am sure it is one of them! Do you see, just over there?', at the same time pointing to a poor harmless seagull flying away over the sea, or a dark speck of cloud in the distance.

Immediately the game was forgotten, and we looked eagerly at the spot indicated, only to give vent to disappointed 'Oh's' as we found out the mistake. But this could not go on forever.

At last quite late, after tea, we heard a gun fired. It was the signal that the aeroplanes had started from Shoreham. At once we flew to the terrace, those of us lucky enough to have cameras grabbing them up in our wild haste, hoping to take some photographs. For some time, there was nothing to be seen. Then came a murmur of excitement. Two black specks appeared! Could these be the aeroplanes? No, they were not getting any bigger! What a disappointment! But that front one surely that seemed to be coming nearer. Was it? Yes! Yes! and so was the other! They really were the aeroplanes! At this point nearly everyone went half mad with excitement. Slowly at first, then quicker and quicker they came until 'Bang' another gun fired showed they had passed Black Rock, which was the goal of the race (for the two were having a race). Nearer, yet nearer they came. Surely that was a man we could see in the front one? Then, we held our breath, the foremost aeroplane swept over our heads and circled round the school. The second soon followed.

Helter skelter we ran to see them both appear again and, what was this? The second aeroplane had turned again. Was it going to fly round the school a second time? No, it was settling on the Flat Pitch skimming the ground like a bird, and pulling up just in time not to collide with the fence. This was splendid! To fly round the school was what we had expected but to settle on the Flat Pitch! This was beyond our wildest dreams. The first aeroplane had now seen the action of the second and not wishing to be outdone came flying back as fast as it could, but a little too fast, in fact, for when alighting, not being able to stop in time, it went crash into the fence breaking the latter and also the back part of the aeroplane.

The second aeroplane did not wait long, flying off after a quarter of an hour, but the first one had to stop to be mended. In the meantime, we all formed up in patrols, and marched down to the Flat to see the broken flying machine, and took many photographs of it and Mr Morison, who was driving it. All the evening until about seven o'clock we waited to see the aeroplane start off again, and then came the message saying it could not go all that night, but would wait until two o'clock on Sunday afternoon, so all of us might see it. At two, however, it was so misty that it could not go up, so again we had to curb our impatience. At last we heard all was ready, and that the mist had gone, it was going to start. Immediately we dashed out in time to see the bird-like machine skim across the Flat Pitch and mount higher and higher into the air. The aeroplane turned and circled round us adding to the excitement, then away it flew to Brighton, getting smaller and smaller in the distance, until it disappeared altogether from our sight, leaving us gazing with eager eyes at the spot where, a moment before we had seen it.

Morison's son Richard (Air Vice Marshal Retired) said that the landing at Roedean Girls School caused much ribald merriment among his father's friends, and he had had to suffer much leg pulling for months.

On the following Monday another heavy mist prevented any flying in the morning, so it was late afternoon before Morison, Gilmour and Gordon England motored over to Shoreham to make some flights. Although they all flew Boxkites, the spectators soon learned to identify them by their headgear. Morison wore a crash helmet that he replaced with a rather battered trilby on landing. Gordon England, on the other hand, wore the more conventional cloth cap, which he reversed when flying in the true intrepid aviator style. Gilmour seemed to scorn such headgear and affected a somewhat baggy woollen Tam-o-Shanter. The aerodrome was almost deserted on their arrival, and they started to open the hangar doors to get their machines out when Police Inspector Marsh of the Shoreham police arrived. Taking Gilmour aside, he informed him that he was under arrest on a warrant for manslaughter. It later emerged that this related to an accident when a small boy was struck by Gilmour's car and killed. The three friends went with the inspector to Shoreham Police Station, where Gilmour was held pending the granting of bail. Rumours soon circulated about his arrest, but details of the accident were soon common knowledge. It seems Gilmour was driving to the Bristol Company's airfield at Amesbury and overtook a tip cart. The boy in question, hanging on the back, suddenly jumped down in the path of Gilmour's car, making it impossible for him to pull up in time, the boy dying of his injuries despite medical attention. The coroner's jury exonerated Gilmour at the subsequent inquest, so the arrest gained him much public support. When the case was heard later at Warminster Assizes, the jury only took ten minutes to find him not guilty of the manslaughter charge.

Next day Morison continued with his passenger flights, and probably achieved the distinction of being the first pilot to take a Boy Scout aloft. The Scout concerned was Lance Corporal Digby Cleaver of the 1st Shoreham Troop, whose parents were living, during the summer, at Lazylands on Shoreham Beach. A constant visitor to the aerodrome, Digby was regarded as their mascot by the flyers and mechanics.

At the end of the month, Morison went to Paris to collect a Morane Borel racing monoplane, which he had bought to enter in the Circuit of Europe Race, due to start from Paris, and in which Jimmie Valentine was flying a Deperdussin monoplane. Unfortunately, the Morane was not ready until shortly before the race, and the organisers refused to allow Morison to make a test flight before the start. The subsequent overfilling of his petrol tank also meant he lost his place in the take-off sequence and engine trouble forced him to make a forced landing in the Champ de Manoeuvres, damaging his machine so he had no alternative but to withdraw. When his machine was repaired, he again demonstrated his flying skill by crossing from Paris to Shoreham in just over twelve hours. Setting off from Paris on 8 July at 4.40am, he met dense fog and had to land at Calais. After a rest and some refreshments, he resumed his flight and crossed the Channel. Arriving at Dover, he turned westwards for Eastbourne, which he reached at 3.30pm and landed to be refuelled at the bus depot, the manager and staff quickly topping up his tank, so he got to Shoreham at 4.45pm.

This was really Morison's swansong in Sussex. On the following weekend he returned to Brooklands. A week later he probably had his most spectacular crash. Coming back from Hendon, he landed at Brooklands at 70mph with a 30mph tailwind. As the Morane's port wheel touched the ground, it buckled and a stay in the undercarriage snapped. Thereupon the aircraft cartwheeled and finally landed upside down with a horrifying crash. People ran to the aircraft from all directions, but Morison, to everybody's astonishment, crawled out unhurt. An aviation magazine of the time made very critical remarks about aviators who still had to learn to always land into the wind. On Tuesday, 13 August at 4.10am Morison took off in his Blériot from Sandgate Plain in Kent to fly via Shoreham to Ventnor on the Isle of Wight. There he intended to meet Valentine and England for some exhibition flights over the island.

Two miles out at sea the engine failed again, and he had to land in the water. The boat that went to his rescue found him sitting on the wing with water up to his knees, quite unperturbed and smoking a cigarette. The aircraft was towed ashore, overhauled in the railway station yard and then sent on to Huntingdon. It had been bought by W. Rhodes-Moorhouse, who was to be the first member of the

Royal Flying Corps to gain the Victoria Cross in the First World War, posthumously.

Apart from a visit to the Steyning Magistrates in September, when he was summoned for not producing his licence for endorsement for speeding, Morison's last visit to Shoreham aerodrome seems to have been on 11 December with James Radley and Graham Gilmour. There were probably two main reasons for his giving up flying, apart from running out of aircraft. Firstly, it was now becoming a very expensive hobby, but secondly, he had become engaged to Digby Cleaver's sister, Margaret. She, perhaps, thought his luck in escaping serious injury might be running out. The happy couple were married at St Peter's Church, Brighton on 26 November 1912, and their best man was James Valentine.

Chapter 7

1911

The first air race in Sussex took place on 6 May from Brooklands to Brighton, after three postponements owing to bad weather. The contestants were Gustav Hamel (Blériot), Lieutenant Snowden Smith (Farman), Graham Gilmour (Bristol Boxkite) and Howard Pixton (Avro biplane).

Gustav Hamel, twenty-two years old, was of German-Danish extraction, his father being a distinguished medical practitioner and physician to Edward VII. Although his parents wanted Gustav to study medicine, he became interested in motor racing and flying. His first flight was in a balloon with Frank Hedges Butler, from London to Peterborough. He, like Morison learned to fly at Pau, and Blériot thought him one of his best pupils. He got his French brevet in February 1911.

Before the actual race, Hamel had a dummy run on 12 April, flying from Brooklands to Hove, a journey of an hour. He had earlier telephoned Richard Preston, brother of Harry of the Royal Albion Hotel, informing him of his intentions, who arranged for the police to remove the railings from the Hove Lawns to give a clear landing run. After lunch at the hotel, Hamel took off at four o'clock for the return journey, but ran out of castor oil, the lubricant used in his Gnome engine. Forced down at Littleworth near Partridge Green, he immediately telegraphed Dick Preston for a fresh supply, which arrived an hour and a half later. Resuming his flight, he found the engine was not giving full power and had to land again. This time he came down near West Grinstead station, gliding down into the meadow north of the Cowfold Road. A train had just arrived at the station, and he was soon surrounded by some hundred travellers who deserted the train regardless of their destination, to see him and his aeroplane. He again wired, this time for his mechanics to come and repair his engine, and meanwhile was offered hospitality by a local resident. His machine was towed tail-first to a nearby barn. With the engine and the wings outside covered with a sheet, a watch was kept on the machine all night.

On the day of the actual race, a large white cross was placed in the centre of the Shoreham aerodrome as a marker for the aviators. A company of Boy Scouts, from Worthing, had positioned themselves at the end of the Norfolk Bridge with their field telephones to provide communication between the aerodrome and the Bridge Hotel in Shoreham High Street and thence to Brighton. Up to three o'clock in the afternoon cyclists and motorists were still arriving from all directions, and crowds made their way on foot from the railway station to the aerodrome or all adjoining high points around the airfield. The first competitor to be seen was Hamel, his Blériot monoplane being quickly identified by Pettett, now manager of the aerodrome. After circling, he went on to Brighton, to be followed by Lieutenant Snowden Smith, who skirted Shoreham before setting a course for Brighton. The third machine, piloted by Graham Gilmour, then appeared over Lancing College, and turned for Brighton. Then Hamel's machine reappeared and swept in for a landing on the airfield, the crowds surrounding him and giving him three cheers for his win. Although second to land, Lieutenant Snowden Smith was disqualified because the stewards were not satisfied he had kept to the agreed course, so Gilmour was given second. Pixton, it was learned later, lost his way and landed on the Plumpton Racecourse to find out where he was. Once again, his arrival caused a stir, one rubicund yokel saying with a broad grin to his friend Bill: 'No need to go to Brighton to see 'em, we seed them grand here!' Pixton, who was by now feeling distinctly peckish, made his way to a nearby hostelry for a hearty lunch and did not reach Shoreham until 6.30pm. He had to ask some of the crowd to restrain his machine while he was running up the engine and a beefy peasant broke one of the fuselage spars, necessitating a temporary repair with a broom handle.

The newly titled Brighton and Shoreham Aerodrome Ltd was officially opened on 20 June 1911, after a luncheon for the mayors and mayoresses of Brighton, Hove and Worthing and many local worthies. In the speeches during the course of the luncheon all spoke of the rapid advance of flying, and the company was assured it would receive their maximum support for their enterprise in setting up in Shoreham, the first Sussex airfield. The managing director and company chairman George Arthur Wingfield replied, saying he had visited many of the aerodromes in this country and none had the ample flying space of nearly 1,000 acres free of trees or other obstacles. It was their intention to build a magnificent club house with a swimming pool and many other sporting facilities to attract members and tourists to the area. He finished by thanking the company secretary and the manager of the aerodrome, W. Pettett, and his staff for the magnificent work they had done in getting the airfield ready. Next week the airfield would be the venue for the competitors taking part in the Circuit of Europe Air Race, and the following month the Circuit of Britain would take place under the sponsorship of the *Daily Mail*. The visitors were then given a tour of the aerodrome and shown the all-British Valkyrie monoplane, a tail-first or canard aircraft with a 35hp Green engine, which was housed in one of the ten hangars that had been built on site. The gusting of the wind prevented any flying that day.

Horatio Barber had set up his own company, the Aviation Syndicate, in 1909, to promote his designs. The Valkyrie was reasonably successful, and the firm then moved from Salisbury Plain to Hendon, where Barber also set up his own flying school. His agreement with Wingfield's company was that he would get a payment of £50 for the week of his stay, plus 50 per cent of the gross and net takings on the best day. He in turn had to pay 15 per cent of any prize money he might win outside the aerodrome during that period. Unhappily for the company, a strong westerly wind prevailed throughout the week and in consequence Barber made no exhibition flights all week. Barber had earlier agreed to fly a consignment of Osram electric light bulbs for the General Electric Light Company as a publicity stunt during the Electric Congress that had been held at Brighton a week or two earlier. There was a diminution of the wind on the evening of 4 July, and a searchlight was placed in the Marine Park Hove to assist his landing and subsequent return to Shoreham. Even then he had to land at 70mph with a 20mph tailwind, but got down safely and the bulbs were unloaded and put on a Page and Miles truck. This has always been claimed as the first time cargo was transported by air in Britain. Barber soon made his return flight to Shoreham and the next day flew back to Hendon, accompanied by a young female pupil from his flying school.

The Circuit of Europe, which was jointly sponsored by the *Standard* newspaper and the Paris *Le Journal*, was the first international event to take place over Sussex.

The title was a bit of a misnomer, as only four countries were covered: France, Belgium, Holland and Britain. The prizes were awarded for individual stages so that more of the competitors could share in total prizes of £18,000. The stages were: Paris–Liege, Liege–Spa–Liege, Liege–Utrecht, Utrecht–Brussels, Brussels–Roubaix, Roubaix–Calais, Calais–Dover, Dover–Shoreham–London. The return was much shorter: London–Shoreham–Dover, Dover–Calais and finally Calais–Paris. The race started from the French airfield at Vincennes on 18 June, and nearly half a million French people were said to have camped outside to see the dawn take off of forty-three participants. The three hot favourites were Lieutenant Conneau of the French Navy, who always flew under the civilian pseudonym of 'Beaumont'; Jules Vedrines, who at one time had been a mechanic for Robert Loraine, the British actor/flyer; and Roland Garros. As stated earlier, the only British participants were Morison, who crashed early on, and his friend, James Valentine.

Bad weather dogged the competitors, and three pilots were killed on the first day, so by the time the race had reached Calais for the Channel crossing only a dozen pilots remained. Valentine, flying his Deperdussin monoplane, had to make a forced landing at the first stage and failed to complete the stage in the three days allowed but he re-joined the race at Calais. The flyers reached Dover from Calais at 4am, and, led by Vedrines, protested that they should make an earlier start than the original 7am take-off to Shoreham to avoid the threatening weather that was building up over the Channel. So it was that the first aircraft took off early and arrived at Shoreham from 7am onwards, when only a few spectators were on the aerodrome. Fortunately, the three mayors and their wives were there and welcomed the aviators. Vedrines was first, followed by Gibert, Vidart, 'Beaumont', Kimmerling, Garros, Valentine and Tabuteau. The French competitors were astounded at the poor turnout of spectators compared with the response they had received in their own country. Vedrines won £200 for being first at Shoreham, while Gibert took the prize for the fastest Channel crossing. Three of the competitors who crossed the Channel fell by the wayside on their way to Shoreham. Barra, flying a Maurice Farman, had to land in a field at Holban's Farm near Tottingworth Park, Heathfield. A reporter hurrying to the spot was told by a local: 'One of 'ems down in the valley over yonder!' By the time he got there the farm was crowded with motorcycles, cars, bicycles and ponies and traps. Monsieur Barra, rather nattily dressed in a grey suit, white sweater and cloth cap, was surrounded by a large circle of spectators and was sitting in the middle chatting away to everybody in excellent English. He told a reporter he had been losing power from his engine and found his aircraft scarcely had enough power to climb over the Downs. He had sent for his mechanics, who were to go to Brighton for a more powerful propeller, and hoped to continue his flight that afternoon. As time passed, the farm began to assume the appearance of a country fair, with local school children getting a half day holiday to see the aeroplane. Some of the farm labourers present then started to cut down some 30 yards of hedge to give Barra more room for his take-off, which he finally achieved at five o'clock to cries of 'Bon Voyage' from his assembled admirers.

His team mate Renaux, in a similar machine, was also in trouble. With his passenger, a Monsieur Sencques, he force landed in a field near Park Farm, Bodiam, in the Rother Valley. Again, a large crowd gathered and provided food for the aviators to have a picnic while they waited for the mechanics to arrive. This time the trouble was diagnosed as a fault in the petrol feed, and the flyers left for Shoreham by midday. The third unfortunate was Train, in a monoplane designed and built by himself. Some three months earlier, during the Paris to Madrid Air Race, he had to come down suddenly on the airfield, scattering spectators. Finally, he had run down the French War Minister and killed him, also seriously injuring the French Premier Monsieur Monis. A forced landing at the beginning of this race had been overcome because the bad weather had given him time to repair his machine. This time he had to land on a hill at Heighten, near Newhaven, and the aircraft then ran backwards down the slope, hitting a fence and damaging the rudder and one wing. As the rudder could not be repaired locally, he had to withdraw from the race.

Next day a straggler appeared over the Channel, a Monsieur Duval who, at seven o'clock that evening, had lost his way. A Mr Wildish of Crowhurst insisted to a local reporter that the Frenchman came down very low and hailed him, asking the way to Brighton and that he, Mr Wildish, pointed in the direction of Bexhill, waving his hand to indicate that he must turn right from then onwards. As Duval came down at West Cliff near Lewes and did not speak English, having difficulty in understanding the directions given to him, Mr Wildish's gestures do not appear to have had much effect. Eventually Duval took off again and landed at Convent Field near Lewes. He finally abandoned his entry the next day after consultation with helpers, to universal relief.

On the return flight from Hendon to Shoreham, Vedrines was again first, and was seen arriving over the chimneys of the Beeding Cement Works, gaining another £200 for the feat. He was hotly pursued by Garros and 'Beaumont', the latter having by now gained the overall lead. Nevertheless, Vedrines' mechanics rushed out to meet him and quickly refilled his tank with petrol, so after two minutes he was off again. The rest of the field arrived before the appointed time, so again there were not many paying spectators to see them. Valentine had to drop out after reaching Hendon, and in the final result 'Beaumont' was first, winning £6,500. Garros came second, winning £2,200, Vidart third with £2,100, and Vedrines ended up forth, getting £2,000. The remaining prize money, some £6,000, was divided among five other contestants.

A fortnight later the Circuit of Britain began, and although the distance covered was much the same as the Circuit of Europe, the rules were stricter. Contestants could not replace their machines, and five points on the engine and fuselage were sealed, and at least two had to be intact at the end of the race. Thus, the race depended more on reliability as much as the skill of the pilot. The overall route was Hendon via Harrogate and Newcastle to Edinburgh (343 miles), Edinburgh to Bristol via Glasgow, Carlisle and Manchester (383 miles),

Bristol to Brighton via Exeter and Salisbury (224 miles) and finally the last lap from Shoreham to Brooklands (40 miles). This time ten of the seventeen pilots were British, including Valentine, Hamel, S.F. Cody (now a British citizen) and Bennie Hucks. The ones who fell out were Oscar Morison, who suffered temporary damage to his eye when he was running up his engine; Eric Gordon England, whose engine was faulty; and Graham Gilmour, who had been suspended by the Royal Aero Club for low flying over the Henley Regatta and other misdemeanours. The opposition included that redoubtable pair 'Beaumont' and Vedrines, two other compatriots and pilots from the USA, Austria and Switzerland. There was another enormous crowd to see the start from Brooklands, with cars double parked round the track for 2 miles. It was an exceptionally hot day, which led to an hour's delay in the start. There was similarly a large crowd, said to be equal to that for the Circuit of Europe for the second lap from Hendon, many thousands spending their night round campfires in the neighbouring fields. Only three competitors completed the journey to Edinburgh on 24 July: Vedrines, 'Beaumont' and Valentine. The last named became lost in a rainstorm on the next leg, and on landing broke his propeller and rudder. In the end only 'Beaumont' and Vedrines were left in contention, the former being one hour and fifteen minutes in the lead when they reached Bristol on the return leg. They both agreed that they should complete the Bristol to Shoreham leg in one day, Wednesday. So, for the third time their arrival at Shoreham was somewhat earlier than anticipated, and many local people went home for breakfast and returned to find Vedrines had arrived first, again having glided down to make a perfect landing in the middle of the airfield. He was escorted to the official stand by a welcoming crowd, most of whom appeared to be French nationals. One newspaper said Vedrines was soaked through with rain and worn out with lack of sleep and excitement resulting from the closeness of the race. In a state bordering on collapse, he was extricated with difficulty from the hero-worshipping crowd and taken to a camp bed set up in one of the hangars, where he fell into a fitful sleep, continually starting up thinking he heard the roar of 'Beaumont's' engine. When 'Beaumont' did arrive, Vedrines realised that he had little chance of beating his rival, the handicapping system meaning that Vedrines could not take off again until 2.41pm, while 'Beaumont' could leave at 1.28pm. 'Beaumont' settled down for a rest, leaving promptly when his time came. Vedrines, meanwhile, gave up all attempts to sleep and prowled around the hangars until he could take off again, when a strong south-westerly wind sped him up the Adur Valley and over Lancing College. The *Brighton Herald* struck a somewhat discordant note amid the congratulations of other papers by pointing out the 'vandalism' of the Aerodrome Company in destroying the charms of the district by erecting lofty corrugated hoardings that seemed to have little or no justification, as the great bulk of spectators who came to see the race remained outside the aerodrome.

Valentine persisted as a competitor to the very end, reaching Shoreham at seven o'clock in the evening of 4 August and thus winning the Brighton Hotel's Association Cup for the first Englishman (and the only one) to reach Shoreham. Valentine actually arrived before the telegram he sent to the race officials at Shoreham but Captain Danvers, representing the Royal Aero Club, checked all his seals and found them untouched. Valentine left at 9.30am the next day as there was a rumour that S.F. Cody was also on his way to Shoreham on his last lap. Valentine had to land at End Place, Horsham, when he noticed that some of his flying wires had loosened, and he motored to Brooklands to get some spares. He returned in the afternoon to replace them, arriving back at Brooklands in the evening.

In fact, Cody did not reach Shoreham until Saturday, 7 August at six o'clock in the morning, and was highly amused to hear of Valentine's haste to reach Brooklands in case he pipped him to the post. Cody told the few people who greeted him on arrival that as he had the wind against him all the way from Salisbury the journey had taken two and a half hours. Checks of the seals showed they were all unbroken, and after a hearty breakfast in the Club Secretary's office, Cody took off again at 8.25am and arrived at Brooklands an hour later.

All in all, the two races, despite national and local press coverage, did not result in the Aerodrome Company getting the spectators through the turnstiles they had anticipated. There seems to have been two main reasons for this. As the competitors were able to vary their arrival and departure times to suit weather conditions, many people found the aeroplanes had already left when they arrived at the turnstiles, and, as the *Brighton Herald* had pointed out, most of the spectators got an equally good view of the events from the surrounding heights.

On 31 July Barber appeared again at Shoreham with a passenger. This was Miss Trehawke Davies, a woman of independent means who suffered from ill health but still seemed to crave excitement. She wrote one article in which she said it was her ambition to participate in a South American revolution. Her hope may have been that flying might enable her to arrive in a country while the revolution was still in full swing. She had travelled widely, was keen on motor racing, and had been injured in a number of motor accidents. It appears she took up flying (as a passenger) after going to Hendon to watch the return leg of the Circuit of Europe. Grahame-White, the airfield owner, agreed to take her up, and she later began to hanker to become the first woman to fly from London to Paris.

By now she had made a number of flights with Horatio Barber, and on 6 August she booked a return flight between Hendon and Shoreham with him. Barber took off with her at 5.55am and battled against a strong headwind. Arriving over Lancing College, he realised that his petrol was almost exhausted and he alighted in a 4-acre field near Steyning to wait for the wind to blow itself out. Later he took off with only 3ft to spare in a gap in the trees and within five minutes landed at Shoreham. Next morning the wind had increased to about 35mph, but they managed to reach Horsham. Judging discretion to be the better part of valour, although his passenger seemed to be thoroughly enjoying the unruly weather, Barber landed on the town's golf course, calculating his speed from Shoreham to be in the region of 95mph. The wind started to increase to gale force, and Miss Davies and Barber were put up at Warnham Court for the night. They made a really early start next morning and reached Hendon at 6.10am. Miss Davies did not seem at all put out by the experience, and wanted Barber to arrange to fly her on a Continental tour from London to Paris and back. Barber, it seemed, showed a lack of enthusiasm for this scheme, so she sought other pilots.

It is possible that the poor financial return from the two air races led the Aerodrome Company to initiate another venture. This was to be an air race between Shoreham and Dieppe, with English pilots flying to France and the French to England. This was later extended to pilots crossing the Channel and returning to base. A committee was set up, presided over by the Mayor of Hove. The first date selected was 12 August, but this was found to be too early and the event was deferred to 2 September. The total prizes were £1,000, of which £600 would go to the winner. A meeting was arranged with the Mayor of Dieppe and the Dieppe Fetes Committee, but unfortunately, when the Mayor of Hove and G.A. Wingfield arrived at Newhaven to meet the SS *Dieppe*, the French mayor was not aboard, having stayed behind to welcome Vedrines, who had flown back from Hendon to Dieppe that day.

However, two French representatives were taken by car to Shoreham and shown round. They were most impressed with the aerodrome. Vincennes, from which the Circuit of Europe started, was only half its size, they said, while Reims, which had almost the same area, had few of the admirable qualities of Shoreham aerodrome. It was at this point that the French visitors were seen as more than an adequate substitute for the Mayor of Dieppe. In the evening a dinner was held in their honour at the Princes Hotel in Brighton, and a toast drunk to the 'Channel Race'. The French visitors once again praised their hosts, saying that the Dieppe people were deeply interested in the proposed race. Wingfield replied, saying he was delighted that the two mayors had taken up the proposed race with such enthusiasm, which boded well for its success.

On 17 August, however, the scheme was submitted to a Royal Aero Club meeting, where it was decided that it would not sanction the contest on the grounds of danger for the contestants in having to fly some 80 miles over water, both there and back, to participate. This led to a very aggrieved letter from Sir Theodore Angier, protesting vigorously against the view that it would be too dangerous. He pointed out the French had agreed to provide torpedo boats to patrol the Channel, and Sir Theodore also hinted that the fact that the majority of the committee members were balloonists who were nervous of crossing the Channel could have influenced their decision. This seemed to have cut little ice, and Wingfield and his company abandoned the project, no doubt considering that to upset the Royal Aero Club would not be in their own interests in the long run since they controlled aviation generally and sanctioned all aerial meetings.

The eventual setting up of the second aerodrome in Sussex, at Eastbourne, came about after a meeting between F.B. Fowler and W.E. McArdle. The latter was a pioneer motorist and resident of Bournemouth who sold his garage business to take up flying. He gained his wings in France at the Blériot School at Issy-les-Moulineaux on 19 April 1910 and then set up his own flying school, near Beaulieu, in partnership with J. Armstrong Drexel, a wealthy American, calling it the New Forest Aviation School. Drexel passed his RAeC brevet there (No. 14) on 21 January 1911. The school was one of a number that were mushrooming over the south of England, a proportion of which, according to *Flight* magazine, had somewhat dubious reputations. The two flyers held a number of flying displays at the airfield and three pilots gained their brevets, but by early 1911 the partners appear to have decided to give up the venture.

Frederick Bernard Fowler was born in Eastbourne in 1883, the son of a farm bailiff at Tilton near Selmeston. Leaving Eastbourne School in 1901, Fowler was apprenticed to Vickers Sons and Maxim at Erith, Kent, and eventually graduated to work on the Thornycroft car. In 1905 he left and joined the Climax Motor Company, became a foreman, and drove their cars in reliability trials in Scotland and Ireland. He lost his job when the company gave up making cars, and returned to live with his parents in Eastbourne.

Fowler's interest in aviation appears to have been kindled by Blériot's crossing of the Channel, and a meeting with McArdle culminated in Fowler agreeing to buy five Blériot aircraft from the New Forest Aviation School. Fowler could not then fly, and had nowhere to house the machines, but during the next month he went to Beaulieu and virtually taught himself to fly. In the meantime, he found a 50-acre site of water meadow with drainage ditches (shades of Shoreham!) below the gasworks and St Anthony's Hill, and rented this along with a further plot for erecting two hangars. Hearing of a corrugated iron church belonging to the local council, he offered £70 for it, which was accepted. It turned out to be an ideal workshop for making and repairing aircraft.

Another would-be aviator of the time at Eastbourne was Victor Yates, who had earlier built an aircraft on Blériot lines with tubes and fittings from the bicycle shop where he worked. The engine was a 35hp Anzani and the aeroplane was put together in a makeshift shed in a field at Wilmington. It is not known whether it actually flew, but he was offered a post as an instructor at the new Fowler Flying School, due to start on 1 December 1911, and he accepted.

Another person of some importance in aviation was F.W. Lanchester, who was born in Lewisham in 1868 and came to Hove when his family moved there two years later. His father was an architect who designed and supervised the construction of a number of houses in the town. At the age of fifteen, Lanchester went to the Hartley Institute in Southampton and later moved on to the Royal College of Science. Although he left without any formal qualifications, after a stint at the Patent Office he got employment at the Forward Gas Engine Company in 1899, and was made Works Manager after four years. Sir Harry Ricardo, the famous Shoreham engineer, said that Lanchester was a rare combination of a great scientist, engineer, mathematician, inventor and true artist in mechanical design. He became a major force in the field of car design and construction, and in his spare time became greatly interested in flight and the problems involved. In 1907 and 1908 he published two volumes of *Aerial Flight*, which received very favourable reviews in technical journals.

Norman Thompson, a Cambridge graduate, had decided in 1908 that his future lay in the field of aviation, and made contact with Lanchester. He also succeeded in getting the financial support of an old family friend, Dr Douglas White, who agreed to fund an experimental aircraft without expecting any financial return. Lanchester was initially sceptical, telling the two that they would lose their money, but Thompson would not give up, saying they were not looking for profit, but wanted to produce a machine that would help Britain to take its place in the world of aviation. Both Thompson and Lanchester first went to the Reims Flying Meeting in France, and Lanchester examined and analysed the various forms of aircraft there, many of which were just capable of getting into the air but not of making sustained flights. On their return, Lanchester started work, arranging for the Daimler Motor Company to build the body work and engine mounting for his proposed aircraft. He specified a weight, including a pilot, of 800lb and a speed of 90mph with inherent stability. The actual design was very much ahead of its time, a pusher biplane with all metal wings and a streamlined nacelle built of steel sheets with a four-wheel pneumatic undercarriage.

Sheds for the new White and Thompson Company were erected at Middleton, near Bognor, where there was a foreshore of good firm sand some miles in length for flying trials. Since the Government made it plain that they were interested only in two-seater aircraft for pilot and observer, the design was modified by lengthening the fuselage, despite strong protests from Lanchester.

By the time it had come for the completed prototype to be tested, the beach had changed owing to an earlier spell of stormy weather. This had brought to the surface chalk boulders and seaweed, and pools of water covered the whole area. The first trial with Thompson as pilot almost resulted in lift off when the aircraft was at its maximum speed, but two wheels suddenly buckled and the aircraft flipped over. Thompson was unhurt, and it was found the structure had suffered little damage from the impact. After repairs, more trials were carried out and a new propeller and larger wheels were tried but it was felt that there was insufficient wing area and engine thrust to get the machine in the air. Although it did start to rise on one occasion, the undercarriage collapsed for the second time and the machine overturned.

Lanchester later maintained that, if the original design had been built, success would have been more likely, and that an experimental design should not be subjected to commercial pressures. Thus, he parted from the company, although he remained friendly with Thompson and White.

At Shoreham there seems to have been a hiatus after the excitement of the two air races, but as the year neared its end the Aerodrome Company persuaded the Chanter Flying School, which had been at Hendon, to move to Shoreham. By the middle of November their two Blériot aircraft were in use for instructing pupils. Chanter had also designed a small Nieuport-type monoplane, which he flew very successfully in December. Another new arrival at the aerodrome was Lieutenant J.C. Porte, late Royal Navy, who had been invalided out of the service after contracting tuberculosis, no doubt during his time as a submarine officer. He had learned to fly at Reims and had made a number of glider flights from Portsdown Hill near Portsmouth with a fellow officer in 1909. Porte had now joined the Deperdussin Company, which intended to set up a factory in England to demonstrate its aircraft to prospective buyers.

Two other prototype aircraft had also come to Shoreham for trials – the Metzgar and Leno pusher monoplane, which resembled Horatio Barber's Valkyrie, was brought down by road in early July, and two months later had completed ground trials. It later made a few 'hops', but never seemed to have flown any distance. Another arrival was the Collyer-England biplane. The latter gentleman was B.H. England (no relation to Eric Gordon England), a Sussex man from Slindon near Arundel who had been educated at Steyning Grammar School. In 1910 he went to the Brighton Technical College, and then tried his luck at Brooklands. A partnership with Collyer resulted in the construction of their biplane, and though trouble with the engine and the search for a suitable propeller caused problems initially, the machine did eventually get into the air.

Chapter 8

1912

Although Fredrick Fowler had arranged to bring four of the Blériots from Beaulieu by road to St Anthony's, Eastbourne, he decided to fly the 50hp Gnome-engined Blériot over himself. On 8 January he took off from Beaulieu. Conditions were very misty, and when he reached the Solent, he ran into a thick bank of fog that blotted out all of the landscape except Calshot Castle. Fowler told a reporter from the *Eastbourne Gazette* what happened next:

> My machine was being tossed about like a cork, and it took me all of my time to keep her on a level keel. I still, however, did not like to give up, and keeping on I soon found myself over Southampton Water. Here matters became worse, I could scarcely see one hundred yards ahead and as I did not want to become completely lost, I decided to turn. From this point my serious trouble began; as soon as I commenced to turn the machine started to drop, and although I tried every means to keep up, she absolutely refused to rise. Gradually the water got nearer until the final crash came and the next thing I knew was that I was under the machine struggling hard to get to the surface. Luckily my clothes had not caught in anything, so I did not have much difficulty about it, but the sensation was not pleasant. The rest of the tale is soon told. The Coastguards at Calshot Point had seen me and were soon on the scene. Within a quarter of an hour the machine was high and dry on the beach a total wreck, owing to my having fitted an air bag it floated.

the mud. By four o'clock in the morning the fire was under control. The damage was assessed by Mr Hamilton Ross, the manager of the Chanter Flying School, which had lost all its aircraft, and Messrs Wingfield and Pettett also appeared to survey the damage. The cause of the fire was never really established. The total damage was assessed at £1,000 to replace the hangars, which was covered by fire insurance, but it seems unlikely that the Chanter machines were covered, since the school disappeared from the scene shortly afterwards. Emile Gassler moved over to Eastbourne to register with the Fowler Flying School shortly afterwards.

On 24 April the Brighton Shoreham Aerodrome Company Ltd made a claim for the sum of £65, which it alleged was due under a contract made with Horatio Barber, and also made an alternative claim for £50 for withholding information of a flight for the General Electric Company. It seems that G.A. Wingfield, the Managing Director and a solicitor, felt he should have received a proportion of the payment in respect of Barber's earlier transport of the Osram bulbs to Hove. During the course of the case, Pettett emphasised that Barber had agreed the company would take 15 per cent of any prize money he won on any outside flights. When on 4 July Barber flew with the light bulbs from Shoreham to Hove, he received a £100 fee from the G.E.C., but the plaintiffs had not, they claimed, received the share to which they were entitled. In the witness box, Pettett said he was aware that the flight to Hove had been arranged for 3 July, but it did in fact take place on the following day. He agreed there was no concealment of the flight by Barber, but said if they had advertised the trip, they could have got more spectators to the ground. When Wingfield gave evidence, he said he was determined to sue Barber when he found the arrangements with the G.E.C. existed during the period of the company's contract with him.

When Barber was cross-examined, he said he agreed the terms for the first week's contract but argued that when the week was up, he told Pettett he would have to leave unless further money was forthcoming; now the week had expired. He had made the short flight to Hove with the bulbs on 4 July, returning to Brooklands on the following day. The judge asked Barber how it was that the contestants in the European Circuit Race were able to fly on 3 July and he was not, Barber said that all the participants were 'regular daredevils' with no money and flying for prizes up to £18,000, which was ample inducement for them to risk their necks.

As far as the flight for the G.E.C. was concerned, he contended that the posters advertising the flight were all over the aerodrome, and that Pettett had been told about it two days earlier. Barber also pointed out he could have made the flight from Hendon if the weather had allowed him to leave Shoreham earlier. This was confirmed by the manager of G.E.C., who explained that the original flight had been planned to coincide with an earlier Electrical Congress at Brighton but when bad weather prevented this, it was immaterial to the company when or from where the flight was made. In his summing up the judge said that Barber was entitled to stay at Shoreham until the weather improved, and while he did not suggest that the Brighton Shoreham Aerodrome Company had given evidence wrongly, it was quite possible with the lengthy discussions that had taken place some misunderstanding had arisen. He therefore gave judgement against the company, with costs, but saw no reason for awarding damages to Barber. Three weeks later the company reappeared in court regarding building work, probably in respect of the aerodrome fire. The builder had been paid only half the sum due to him, and the company contended that he had not completed the work according to specification.

At Eastbourne great excitement was caused by the sinking of the P & O liner *Oceana* off the town, some 4 miles west of Beachy Head at 4pm on Saturday, 16 March. The *Oceana* collided with the German barque *Pisaque*, which struck the liner on the port side abreast of her foremast. Lights and rockets from the *Oceana* were seen by the coastguards at Beachy Head, Eastbourne and Newhaven. At a later enquiry a court found the collision was the fault of the chief officer of the *Oceana*, who had attempted to cross in front of the German vessel, with the ensuing loss of seventeen lives occurring when one of its lifeboats was swamped and the people thrown into the water. Another lifeboat in serious difficulty was fortunately brought ashore safely by the Eastbourne lifeboat. The *Oceana* finally sunk at 10am the following morning, leaving her foremast above the water. Her cargo was estimated to be worth about £1 million, of which three-quarters was silver bullion, much of which was later recovered.

This sunken vessel was the subject of an experiment to determine whether such a ship could be detected from the air, as she lay in 70ft of water. The *Sphere* and *Tatler* magazines commissioned the pioneer aviator and balloonist Frank McClean to photograph the wreck, and he left Eastchurch on 17 June in his 70hp Short tractor biplane, flying via Tunbridge Wells. When he landed at Eastbourne after flying the 60 miles, Hugh Spottiswood, the owner of the magazines, had already arrived in the town and was making arrangements for a photographer to accompany McClean. Unsuitable weather delayed the flight but the aircraft was fitted with floats in the meanwhile. Four days later the aircraft took off at 10am from St Anthony's airfield despite some gusty squalls, and a number of photographs were taken. These later appeared in the *Sphere*, and clearly showed the outline of the sunken vessel under the water. With increasing build-up of submarines in the German Navy, the value of this experiment was not lost on the naval authorities, who now realised that aircraft could perform an important role in any future conflict. In fact, of course, the conditions were unusual, considering the size of the vessel and its proximity to the shore. Nevertheless, it was found in later trials that a submarine periscope could be detected from an aircraft in good weather.

On his return from Eastbourne to Eastchurch, McClean became involved in a legal imbroglio. An action for damages was brought against him by a farmer, Thomas Partridge, who claimed that low flying over his farm at Cowbeach, had frightened a 'valuable mare'. The farmer claimed £30 for the mare's depreciation plus veterinary fees, a total of £45. The legal implications for aviation were deemed very important by the RAeC, which obtained counsel's opinion. Since, however, McClean was about to set off on an astronomical expedition to the Pacific, he settled the matter out of court for £25, an undoubted large pecuniary loss to the legal profession generally.

It was in July that the citizens of Brighton had a foretaste of the use of seaplanes, when one appeared off the beach between the two piers. Two Short tractor biplanes had set off to fly from Sheerness to Portsmouth, a distance of some 100 miles. The intention was that the machines should undertake exercises with the Fleet, and this was one of a number of long-distance flights that naval aircraft were undertaking. One of the two seaplanes was piloted by Lieutenant

Spencer Grey, who was forced to alight off Newhaven with engine trouble, but its crew managed to repair the fault after they landed on the water. The second Short, which came down between the two Brighton piers, had a similar problem. The holidaymakers on the piers saw a torpedo boat and two attendant motor boats alongside the seaplane. The audience on the West Pier who had previously been listening to the band melted away to watch what was happening. They soon saw that the boats had moved away to allow the seaplane, which was piloted by Commander Samson, to take off in a shower of spray and then set course for Portsmouth, with the vessels setting course in the same direction.

Lord Northcliffe's crusade to make Britain strong in the air was continuing with his 'Wake up England' campaign, in which aeroplanes visited the main centres of population to give demonstrations and passenger flights to the public. At coastal resorts seaplanes were used, and visits were made to Brighton, Eastbourne, Hastings and Bexhill in Sussex. This first Flying Week, as it was called, started on 23 July at about 12.30pm when Claude Grahame-White arrived over Brighton after leaving Hendon at 11am. Grahame-White was undoubtedly the golden boy of British aviation at this time, as he flew with panache. Virtually fearless, he had a large measure of luck in his early flying career. He had recently moved his flying school from France to Hendon, which he selected as the ideal site for an airfield in the London area.

His new aircraft was the latest Maurice Farman, which could be used with either wheels or floats, the latter taking about ninety minutes to fit. The Farman's fuselage was mainly constructed of steel tubing, and the aircraft had a wingspan of 57ft. Its 70hp Gnome engine gave it an exceptional take-off and it had a very flat glide. Adjourning to the Royal Albion Hotel, Grahame-White had lunch with his wife, the former actress Pauline Chase.

One of the attractions dangled before the public was that Louis Paulhan, Grahame-White's erstwhile rival, who beat him in the 1910 race from London to Manchester, would also be flying, from Paston Place in East Brighton, with J.L. Travers another pilot in reserve. The Paulhan-Curtiss seaplane had been brought to Brighton by rail and was being assembled at the Volk's Electric Railway Station in Paston

Place. The railway brought the public to see the aircraft in its hangar, a building that was specially designed by Herman Volk, who was now taking an increasing interest in aviation, having become friendly with Eric Gordon England.

Hamilton Ross, the former manager of the Chanter Flying School, had bought the Barber Viking when Barber gave up aircraft manufacturing and had it fitted with floats. A hangar had also been set up on the beach next to the West Pier, and Hamilton Ross was offering passenger flights to the public, without a great deal of success.

The local press were most interested in Grahame-White and on Wednesday morning he made his first passenger flight around the two piers. In the afternoon a much-heralded race took place between Grahame-White in his Maurice Farman and Harry Preston's new fast motor cruiser *My Lady Molly*. One paper compared it with matching the Shoreham Tramway against the crack railway train the Southern Belle. The course was from the Volk's Station at Paston Place to Hove and back. The cruiser was given a twelve-minute start, while the aircraft had to complete the course twice. As usual Grahame-White gave a very good display, alighting on the water halfway through and then climbing again to make a swoop, which meant he passed the motor cruiser some fifteen seconds before it could reach the final marker. His victory was marked by the presentation of a silver cup by Sir John Blaker.

Later Grahame-White made an evening flight with his Maurice Farman bedecked with coloured light bulbs. This seemed to bring out a poetic streak in the *Brighton Herald* reporter, despite his earlier cynicism about the afternoon's race:

> Black night shrouded the sea, a brooding, heavy darkness made blacker still by the contrast with the brilliant shore. The Palace Pier was a blaze of myriad lights. Suddenly there was a flaming portent. The dark night opened an eye of fire; then closed it into the darkness. Again, the light shone in the darkness. It took shape, as of two parallel lines, joined to a broader, vaguer glow below. Here was the waterplane illuminated with electric lights and reflected in the water beneath. The two lines below the

glow took motion, they glided together in the far away darkness ... But it was sailing over the Palace Pier, and in the great glow of light that poured upwards upon it, its shape became visible, a dim ghost of the waterplane we had seen in the daytime flying in the sunshine. As it bore landwards growing amazingly in size, people on the Aquarium Terrace could hear the music from the Municipal Orchestra swell out in a great Wagnerian crescendo as the bird of light sped away in the distance and slowly settled like a dying swan on the water, the music fading in the thrill of the muted violins!

The following day, one of the mechanics who had been assembling the Paulhan-Curtiss seaplane was called urgently to his home at Dijon. As he had missed the train connection for the Newhaven steamer, Grahame-White flew him to Newhaven in time to make the connection and also brought back a passenger on the return journey. Paulhan arrived at the weekend, but the weather now turned very windy, and although both pilots flew in the morning, flying had to be abandoned that afternoon and the next day. Indeed, the wind was so fierce on Sunday that the tent and tarpaulins used to protect the seaplanes were blown down and the aircraft had to be shackled with baulks of timber to prevent them moving. Plans for the visit to Worthing had to be cancelled, and the proposed visit to Eastbourne for four days could not start until Friday. At 5.30am the few inhabitants of Eastbourne awoke and, near the beach, saw Grahame-White land on the shore, followed by Travers. Grahame-White's first passenger was the famous novelist, H.G. Wells, the flight lasting for ten minutes. Wells said afterwards that he had enjoyed the flight, and found the aircraft 'as steady as a motor car running on asphalt'. Later he confessed that he found his study a very dull place after all the excitement of the flight.

In the afternoon Grahame-White was said to have a slight indisposition, but it is more likely that getting up at the crack of dawn was not to his taste, and he had retired for a nap. Travers flew in the afternoon, circling St Leonards, but it seems that the Eastbourne public were rather reluctant to part with five guineas for a flight until one, a local garage proprietor named Mr Lovely, appeared with his small son, Arthur. Arthur, dressed rather inappropriately in a sailor suit, was said by his father to want to be the youngest aviator in Europe. Arthur, according to his father, thoroughly enjoyed the flight, although he had to be restrained for his own safety when waving wildly to his mother, and we are told he burst into tears when they landed and wanted to go up again.

The following day Travers took up an enterprising Army officer from the Surrey Yeomanry who was encamped at Polegate. He wanted to make a reconnaissance of a camp of the Surrey Infantry Brigade at Whitbread Hollow, east of Beachy Head. He told reporters on his return that he had located the outposts round the camp and would be reporting to his commanding officer accordingly.

At twelve noon, next day, Grahame-White appeared and set off for Cowes, but stopped at Bognor. Unfortunately, the choppy conditions offshore prevented him from taking up any passengers, but the locals said his later take-off for Cowes was some compensation for the missed flights. A further planned visit to Eastbourne in August was again marred by bad weather, and the two flyers – Travers and Noel – damaged their machines on the journey to the town, which precluded them from flying anyway. One disgruntled local commented ironically on the slogan 'Wake up England' painted on the side of their aircraft, saying that while he did not want the flyers to risk their lives, if no flying was possible, they could at least display notices accordingly.

At Shoreham, two new flyers appeared at the aerodrome. One was a Frenchman, Salmet, known to his friends as Samlet, who flew in from Folkestone in his 70hp Gnome Blériot. He was, it appears, both young and keen, speaking fluent English. Welcomed to the aerodrome by the manager Pettett, he refused a cup of tea and insisted his aircraft be refuelled so that he could give an exhibition of low flying for the waiting spectators. This he did, and was cheered heartily on landing, when he seems to have had a burst of patriotic fervour, and after calling three cheers for the King and the Entente Cordiale, was again cheered by the onlookers.

A few days later, Robert Slack flew into the aerodrome, being described in a local report as the 'aviator Slack' as opposed presumably to the earlier type of gentlemen who were now finding flying an expensive hobby. A letter to *Flight* magazine on aviation insurance bewailed that a person of position and means who took up flying would find it not only risky and expensive but also extremely inconvenient, in that practising flying had to be undertaken in the early hours when the air was most likely to be calm. Slack, a student aviator, was being sponsored by the International Correspondence School to advertise their courses by travelling round England and giving exhibition flights. During the next week he flew to Lancing, Worthing and Brighton, where he landed on the racecourse.

Another visitor to Sussex was Corbett Wilson, who flew the Channel from Calais early in September but was forced down at Herstmonceux with engine trouble. He then got as far as Eastbourne and managed to press on to Hamsey Place near Lewes, then went to Ashurst, near Steyning, when he was forced down by a broken engine valve. Finally, at 6.10pm on Saturday the engine failed again, and he had to land at Sharpenhurst Hill opposite the boy's college of Christs Hospital. An extract from the Hospital magazine *The Blue* takes it from there:

The First Aeroplane to Visit Christ's Hospital

The small number of residents who kept holiday at Christ's Hospital during September, were startled about 6pm on 7 September by seeing a monoplane buzzing over the Cricket Pavilion, with its nose pointed earthwards, as though to plunge headlong into Eastman's Copse. They were relieved to see it disappear over the wood, and to learn very soon that it had descended safely. A rush was made for Sharpenhurst Hill, people seeming to spring from nowhere, and in a few minutes no less than fifty were crowding round the machine, stretched out like a huge dragonfly on the slope of the hill, just below the Bar. The aeronaut was Mr Corbett Wilson, an old Etonian, on his way from Paris and Dover to Farnborough. We learnt that he had been compelled to descend at Ashurst through his engine misfiring, and that it had again failed him when in sight of Christ's Hospital. A motor car was despatched along the Worthing road to cut off his mechanics. Fortunately, they were waylaid and turned up after dark at the Headmaster's House, where Mr Wilson was entertained for the nights of Saturday and Sunday. The monoplane was housed for the night against the east side of the Barn, and the watchers were told off to guard it. The mechanics worked all Sunday and until midday Monday, putting the engine to rights, the crowds of sightseers being kept off with some difficulty with ropes. At last all was pronounced ready and Mr Wilson decided to start at five o'clock. After a game of croquet and some tea, he walked up the hill with the Headmaster and his family. Quite a crowd was still there, eager to see the ascent. The monoplane was wheeled close to the second golf green, its nose pointing towards Shelley Wood. Mr Wilson climbed in to his frail looking seat; the two mechanics helped by Maynard and Tappenden, hung on the sides to keep the bird from flying, while the engine was set going for a final test. There were sounds of mis-firing again, but these soon ceased; Mr Wilson held up his hand, the men let go, and the monoplane glided swiftly along the grass, turning slightly to the left; as it reached the sloping ground the nose was cleverly tilted, and up went the bird-like thing, its huge wings gleaming in the sun, some 200 feet above our heads in the direction of Shelley Wood, where it slowly turned, and went buzzing away for Pitch Hill. Mr Wilson had previously been shown the right line was Handscombe Hill, and we all thought he had missed his direction. When he had gone about a quarter of a mile, to our astonishment the aeroplane came slowly round, heading back from the place whence it had started. Slowly back it came descending lower and lower until it was not a 100 feet up, just over the second green. All thought he was going to land again; but no, for a second poised above the heads of the crowd, when the engine appeared to be going at full speed, the machine made a magnificent sweep westwards, rising upwards as it turned, and going straight over the reservoir at a tremendous speed against the wind, it was soon a speck in the distance and finally lost in the gathering mists over Hanscombe Hill. A telegram arrived next morning announcing Mr Wilson's safe landing at Farnborough about 5.40pm.

Meanwhile, the Eastbourne Flying School was beginning to attract more pupils. Up to then Emile Gassler had been fortunate in having almost continuous tuition. However, his presence was to some extent providential in that Fowler was building up his workshop as part of the Eastbourne Aviation Company and now had the capacity to produce aircraft on a one-off basis. Since Gassler wanted to design aircraft, the stage was set for their co-operation in this new venture. A number of pupils coming to Fowler were servicemen who wanted to volunteer for the RFC Military or Naval Wings. They had a strong motivation to succeed since they could reclaim their fees from the authorities if they were successful. Two of the naval types were R.J. Bone and T.A. Rainey, of whom we shall hear more later. By September, the school had ten pupils, and Fowler found he needed another two-seater. He decided to buy a Bristol Boxkite, the British version of the Maurice Farman, and also engaged the services of J.J. Hammond as an instructor. The first New Zealander to learn to fly at the Bristol school, Hammond had married a Seaford girl after coming to England on holiday in 1908. He then joined the company as a pilot and went back to Australia to give exhibition flights in a Boxkite. Here he had a slight difference with the company and left its employ. He had previously had an adventurous life as a sheep worker in Australia, a prospector for gold in the Klondike, a trapper in Alaska, and like Cody, a cowboy in a Wild West show. Now a very experienced aviator, he had never had an accident and got on well with the service pupils, who took over control when he took potshots at passing game birds. On 9 September, Yates finally took his brevet and passed, taking up instructing, while Gassler passed his tests a month later. He also assisted in instructing when required. One of their new pupils was Cyril Foggin. Flying solo in an Anzani-engined Blériot at a height of 60ft over St Anthony's Hill, he was caught by a gust of wind. The aircraft twisted round, dived earthwards, and turned over on impact. When Foggin staggered out he was dazed and shocked, but uninjured since he was wearing one of the new crash helmets for aviators.

In October, the Avro Company, based at Brooklands, received an offer to house its depot and flying school at Shoreham at a competitive rate. This meant its aircraft could be tested there, as could the seaplanes it was now starting to build. The chief instructor of its flying school was then H.R. Sims, and the new manager of the aerodrome was Mr H. Gonne, who had taken over from Pettett. Shoreham now boasted a club house, a pavilion, tennis courts and a croquet lawn. There was also a golf course adjacent. One contributor to *Flight* magazine extolled the virtues of Shoreham by the seaside, five minutes' walk from the bungalow town on the beach. He asked could anything be more ideal than to live in a maisonette and spend the summer learning to fly?

Chapter 9

1913

The year opened with the Brighton Shoreham Aero Club Dinner at the Royal York Hotel, attended by G.A. Wingfield, Sir Theodore Angier and W. Pettett and wives, with the brothers Harry and Richard Preston of hotelier fame, plus Roger Wallace KC of the Royal Aero Club.

Wingfield said that although the Shoreham Aero Club was growing, more members were always needed. In the past twelve months a dozen first-class aviators had visited the aerodrome, while Messrs Avro had been assisted to open a flying school on site and pupils had been procured. He rather spoiled this happy picture by making reference to some Aero Club members, who, as he put it, 'seemed to expect for their two guineas more than could be obtained for a hundred pounds'. The Mayor of Hove made a patriotic speech on the need for increased air defence, and closed by saying that Shoreham aerodrome should be subsidised from national funds, which was heartily applauded by all present, the dinner closing with a toast to the chairman and mutual approbation.

Wingfield was subsequently successful in coming to an agreement with the War Office, after much negotiation, whereby it would have the use of one hangar at Shoreham with landing rights at the airfield. A fee of 4 shillings a day was levied for each aeroplane using the hangar, but despite a fair number of occupants the agreement did not produce the income expected and it lapsed after one year. Meanwhile, Fowler, who had some spare time, decided to expand his passenger flights and took up a local reporter for a flight on a bright January morning. The journalist described his feeling of exhilaration and the total confidence he had, both in the pilot and the machine. After the flight, Fowler gave the reporter a tour of Eastbourne Aviation Company and airfield and told him that Hammond would be leaving shortly. In a later interview with the press, Hammond told them he would be flying to Paris to pick up and fly back a new type of water plane and give exhibition flights and take up passengers at Eastbourne. This would be his last venture in this country before he and his wife returned to New Zealand to resume ranching. Nothing seems to have come of this scheme, and it is believed Hammond subsequently joined the RFC. Fowler was now presented with the opportunity of expanding his company. Frank Hucks, brother of Bennie the well-known aviator, approached Fowler with proposals to combine his Waterplane Company with the EAC. The Hucks company was formed early in 1912 with the financial assistance of Charles William von Roemer, an electrical engineer at Herstmonceux. The company had two 70hp Gnome-engined Maurice Farman seaplanes, which were used to tour seaside resorts for passenger flights. When the Waterplane Company was absorbed into the EAC, Fowler became managing director and Frank Hucks took over as secretary, the company capital being increased to £5,000.

In April the inhabitants of Brighton fortunate to be on the seafront were treated to an exciting exhibition of low flying by Gustav Hamel, who was again piloting Miss Trehawke Davies in her two-seat Blériot. At one point the wingtip was said to have touched the water, and the wheels skimmed the waves. The aircraft landed at Shoreham and the two stayed overnight before resuming their flight to Dover. Here Miss Davies disembarked and her place was taken by a journalist, who accompanied Hamel on a trip to Cologne. This trip was undertaken it seems so the paper could point out that if such a flight was possible by aeroplane, it could also be undertaken by a Zeppelin.

In May the familiar and cheery face of Eric Gordon England reappeared at Shoreham aerodrome. After two years with Bristol, he was both a highly skilled pilot and designer. A chance meeting with James Radley in November 1912 had led him to agree to their joint production of a new type of water plane. No formal partnership agreement was entered into; indeed, the financing was done by Radley, with Gordon England contributing his expertise in design

THE DAWN OF AVIATION

as a paid employee. The water plane was built at Huntingdon near Cambridge, where Radley had a financial interest in the aerodrome. It had two very unusual features: as there was no known engine of sufficient power, three Gnome 50hp engines were in effect harnessed together with chain drives to a single propeller shaft. The second novelty was that the pilot and two passengers were seated in one float and the other held three passengers. It was perhaps best described as a hybrid between a seaplane and a flying boat. The river at Huntingdon airfield – the Ouse – was not deep enough for flying trials, so the seaplane was sent to Shoreham. Its first take off from the River Adur was made on 1 May but bad weather prevented its removal to the Volk's station at Brighton. Eventually it was towed the 6 miles by motor boat.

On 26 May the Radley-England Waterplane came out of the Paston Place hangar for a press preview and for photographs. A reporter from the *Daily Mail* did not appear for a promised flight, so it was offered to George Aitchinson, a local reporter from the *Brighton Herald*. Aitchinson, who had never flown before, was understandably nervous, and his confidence was not restored when Herman Volk, the son of Magnus, arrayed him in a thickly padded coat, which he was told had to be buttoned up the neck or else the water would get in and he could end up floating face down in the sea. Before he knew what was happening, he was given a piggyback through the surf by Robins, Gordon England's mechanic, who slipped so they both fell into the water, much to the delight of the assembled crowd. Aitchinson got to his feet and climbed into the float to escape any more humorous badinage.

As soon as he was in, Gordon England in the other float gave the thumbs up signal, and with a tremendous roar the engines started up and the seaplane hurtled over the water with spray everywhere. The machine was soon 50ft up, and Gordon England climbed further before putting it through its paces, much to the discomfort of the reporter, who was not strapped in and was clinging grimly to the side of the float. But Aitchinson began to enjoy the sensation as they flew over the chalk cliffs and sea with the hills of the Downs in the background. Then, looking over, he saw Gordon England gesturing towards the engine to show he was going into a dive. As they came near the surface, the reporter was flung forward and spray some 12ft high sprung up behind them as they planed down and touched the water. But as they slowed down Aitchinson realised the aircraft was tilting backwards as Gordon England's float was holed and taking in water. It was found later the float was damaged when it struck some floating debris. Gordon England was, however, quite unperturbed and, swinging himself on the stays of the aircraft, came over to the float Aitchinson was in, suggesting they should get on the prow to balance the machine. Soon boats appeared and Robins managed to fix a line to the engine supports to tow the sinking machine back to the beach.

It was by then almost a total wreck, although the engines were salvaged. It was subsequently rebuilt to participate in the *Daily Mail* prize for £5,000 for a circuit of the coast of Britain in seventy-two hours. New floats were built by the Sussex Yacht Agency and the engine had to be replaced with one of British manufacture, a 100hp Sunbeam, to comply with the rules. The resultant machine was unsuccessful; the floats, despite their superior constructional finish, would not 'unstick' from the water and the engine was a continual source of trouble, never running properly at full power. In the end the water plane was sold to Noel Pemberton Billing, who, ever the optimist, said he would use it for a daily service between Southampton and Cowes. Needless to say, this never materialised.

The new Avro 503 seaplane was first flown from the River Adur at Shoreham on 28 May, with Fred Raynham piloting and with Jack Alcock as a passenger. It became airborne after 180ft and cleared the adjacent railway bridge by 100ft. The following day it was flown down to the Volk's hangar at Paston Place and alighted on the open sea to be manhandled up to the beach. It proved a very successful aircraft; one machine even being purchased by the German Government.

An approach was made by Cedric Lee and George Tilghman Richards to Radley and England, who sought their expertise to build a radical new circular wing or annular aircraft, which was duly dubbed the 'Flying Doughnut' by the less scientifically minded of the Shoreham population as it had a hole in the middle. The original patent had been taken out by Isaac Henry Storey, who lived in Westmorland, but the first person actually to construct such an aircraft was George Kitchen. He took out a further patent in 1912, and kept the machine in a hangar at Middleton Sands near Heysham. It was bought by Lee, who was later joined by Richards.

In May 1913 the two Pashley brothers, Eric and Cecil, moved permanently to Shoreham from Brooklands, where they had learned to fly. They had taken up gliding in 1908, and in July 1911 Cecil got his brevet (No. 106), while Eric was successful two months later (No. 139). Within a few days of their arrival they were up in their Maurice Farman-type aircraft, which had been built by Hewlett and Blondeau, giving passenger flights in the area. At most places they landed on the foreshore when the tide was out and took up passengers for a ten-minute flight, which proved a reasonably profitable venture in the holiday season.

Another two brothers, Roderic and Geoffrey Hill, spent their summer holiday at a farmhouse near Lewes building a biplane glider. Roderic was then nineteen years old, his brother being one year younger. Roderic, an amateur artist, financed the project from some drawings he had sold to the *Sphere* magazine. The brothers tossed a coin to decide who would make the first flight from Firle Beacon. Geoffrey won, and made the first short hop. The brothers returned the following year to make further successful glides.

It was about this time that Fowler's two naval pupils arrived, both of whom proved very adept. T.A. Rainey was in the pilot's seat after only a couple of days' flying and went solo the same day. However, in coming in to land he was too high, but succeeded, much to Fowler's surprise, in losing height, and making a reasonable landing. Fowler then sent him up again, pointing out how he had to lose height on landing. This time, to Fowler's horror, Rainey tried to lose height by switching off his engine but then succeeded in making a tremendous right-hand turn, missing a public house by inches, to fly straight towards the gasworks before making yet another right-hand turn to miss a gasholder by about 2ft, finally landing and breaking a tailskid and two struts. Fowler was so relieved his pupil was still alive that he muted his strictures on his landing. Rainey passed his brevet a month later, but stayed on to get more practice.

Reginald Albert Bone was one of a new breed of submariners who turned to flying. When his ship was in dock at Sheerness, he came to Eastbourne to take flying lessons. He later recounted how early on he

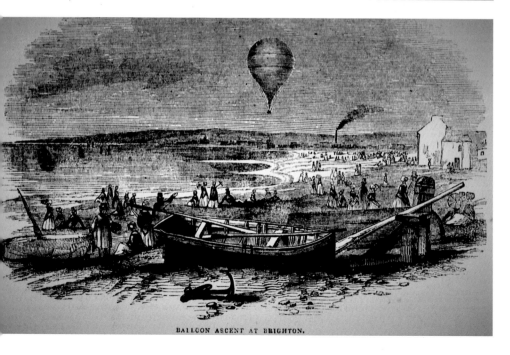

Right: Zambecarri's first public balloon experiment at Moorfields, England, 1783.

Below: Charles Green and his balloon ascent at Brighton, Sussex, 1821.

THE AIR BALLOON.

Which was Launched in the Artillery ground Nov.ʳ 25. 1783.

Publish'd Dec.ʳ 5 1783 by I. Marshall & Co. N.º 4 Aldermary Chur.ʰ Yard Bow Lane London.

BALLOON ASCENT AT BRIGHTON.

Left: Lt. George Gale, pictured in 1851.

Below: Harold Piffard, the first man to fly a heavier than air power machine over Sussex.

Harold Piffard, in the Hummingbird at Shoreham with Lancing College in the background.

Piffard hydroplane on Shoreham beach before it capsized.

Above: Piffard crashes attempting to get to Sussex Pad.

Right: Advert from 'Flight' magazine showing the exploits of Mr Alec Ogilvie in September 1912.

MR. A. OGILVIE FLYING HIS LONG DISTANCE FLIGHT 14½ MILES 28-12-1910.

Alec Ogilvie over Camber Sands in Sussex nr Rye.

The Weiss glider (Olive) flown by Gordon England at Amberley Mount in 1909.

A small amount of mail was unofficially carried much to the displeasure of the post master general.

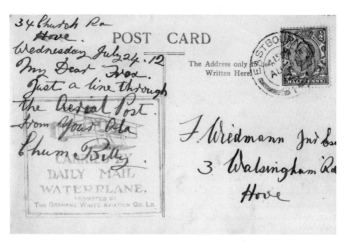

Arrival, almost certainly of Travers, at Eastbourne during the tour.

Claude Graeme White flew to Newhaven Harbour with Paulham's mechanic to catch the ferry to Dieppe, 26 July 1912.

Travers and Noel at Eastbourne – note the 'Wake up England' slogan on the fuselage.

A card signed by Bleriot pilot Robert Slack – he flew in almost impossible weather conditions and his plane seemed to be travelling backwards in strong winds after leaving Shoreham.

FLIGHT

The I.C.S. Tour in Southern Counties.

IN spite of the rough weather, Mr. R. S. Slack, on the I.C.S. Gnome-Blériot, last week put in a good deal of work in the neighbourhood of Brighton. On Monday, Sept. 2nd, he flew from Shoreham, along the sea front, round the Brighton piers, and around Kemp Town to the Brighton racecourse, where the machine was inspected by members of the Corporation and others. He went back over Preston, to the Dyke, Southwick, and over the front to Shoreham, and did some exhibition flights in the evening. On Wednesday, Worthing and Goring were visited, the machine then going along the Brighton front to Rottingdean, and back *via* Portslade. Although the weather was very rough on Thursday, Mr. Slack ascended, trying to fly to Worthing to keep engagement, but had to give up after ascending to 700 ft. and remaining aloft 18 mins. The anemometer was registering 50 m.p.h. gusts. He kept his promise on Saturday, and flew to Worthing, descending near Broadwater Green. Later, he went over to Goring, and returned by Worthing front to Shoreham. Several exhibition flights at Shoreham on Sunday.

A write up by 'Flight' of the I.C.S tour.

was in one of Fowler's Anzani-engined Blériots, which was used to roll along the ground to let the pupil get the feel of taxying an aircraft. Normally incapable of flight, the machine got caught in a strong gust of wind and actually took off. Bone had no real idea of what to do, but managed to make a half turn and bring it down safely. Feeling rather pleased with himself, he was taken aback when his instructor told him off under the impression that he had done it deliberately. Despite the gaps between his lessons due to being away at sea, Bone got his brevet in August and then applied to transfer to the RNAS. The authorities were reluctant to lose a trained submariner, but Bone was very persistent. At a final interview he produced a photograph of the *Oceana* sunk off Eastbourne but still visible from the air, to convince his interviewers of the importance of flying to the Navy. They finally capitulated and he got his transfer.

At the end of June, the first fatal flying accident occurred at Shoreham aerodrome when Richard Norman Wight, who had learned to fly at Brooklands with the Vickers school, was killed. He passed his brevet in April (No. 462) and, like the Pashleys, had only recently arrived at Shoreham. The following account of the accident was published in the *Sussex County Mail* on 5 July 1913:

Terrible Disaster as Shoreham Aviator Burnt to Death
(A full and authenticated account by our special correspondent)

Sunday evening last will live long in the memories of Shoreham and Bungalow Town generally, but more especially will the awful happening upon that day live in the minds of the witnesses.

It was a beautiful summer's evening and people were gazing skywards, attracted by the humming of a biplane near the Brighton-Shoreham Aerodrome, when, in a second, their interest was turned to apprehension. The aeroplane had dived suddenly to earth. A rush was made towards the spot which proved to be the garden attached to New Salts Farm, Shoreham, and upon arrival there a fearful sight presented itself. A biplane badly broken and crumbled, with its engine partially buried in the ground and the engine and fuselage a mass of roaring flames and horror! In the midst of it all, the unfortunate pilot making fruitless efforts to get free. None but those who have seen a petrol fire can appreciate the significance of the spectacle nor the great personal risk which a rescue demanded, but we are proud to say there were men present who had no thought but their fellow creature's need, were willingly, at a moment's notice, to face serious danger in a horrible form. The first man on the scene was William Bowyer, who in company with William Burrage, was stabling a horse at the farm nearby. Hearing a crash Bowyer exclaimed: 'Bill there's a motor car run into the gate,' but on going out they saw an aeroplane in the farm garden, enveloped in flames. Hurrying to the spot, they were followed by Messrs Wallace, (Doyle) Wimble, an ex-Senior Fire Brigade man of Shoreham, Jack Patching and Byrne (of Kittiwake Bungalow). Mrs Tucker also arrived from her home nearby, and was of the greatest service, assisted by Mr John Thompson who also rendered valuable help. On their arrival Bowyer and Burrage found the aviator standing upright in the fuselage, trying to extricate himself, and calling out 'For God's sake pull me out of this' as he did so. After making a fruitless effort to do so Bowyer replied 'I will as soon as I can get help, sir.' Bowyer, Doyle, Wimble, and Burrage then took hold of the hands and shoulders of the aviator, who was leaning over the outside top of the fuselage. Whilst the three were trying to pull him out, however, Bowyer suddenly exclaimed 'God's sake Doyle, his legs are tangled up with the wires'.

This was only too true, poor Wight's right ankle was firmly held by wires. Glancing desperately round, the would-be rescuers espied an old scarecrow overcoat lying on the ground, and this, with the greatest presence of mind, they bound round the unfortunate man's head and shoulders, and then dashed around the outer side of the fuselage and seized the entangling wires, which they tried to cut with a knife, but failed to do so, whereupon Patching, who is a very powerful man, endeavoured to tear the wires from their fastenings by main strength, but was not successful. Poor Wight moaned in agony meanwhile. Had it been possible to rescue the unfortunate man by pluck and self-sacrifice Bowyer and his helpers would have done so, but it was not to be.

There now arrived on the scene, Mr James William Goodbarne, the manager of Messrs Fletchers butchers, Shoreham Branch, whose conduct can only be described as gallant in the extreme. Although the unfortunate aviator was still surrounded by petrol flames of the most terrifying description, Goodbarne rushed forward, and making a quick dive into the middle of them, threw his arms round the struggling man and tried to drag him away, but found to his dismay that the aviator's foot was still entangled. After an effort to wrench him free, Goodbarne was compelled to retreat owing to the fierceness of the flames, but only for an instant, for when horse cloths had been brought out from the farm to try and quench the flames, he seized one, and rushing into the flames wrapped it around poor Wight to protect him from the flames. The conduct of Mr A.E. Geere, manager of the Avro Flying School at the Drome, who with great presence of mind brought down wire nippers with him in case of emergency, is worthy of the highest praise. He dashed repeatedly into the heart of the flames in his endeavours to free the unfortunate man, and placed still more horse cloths over him, as the victim's desperate struggles shook them off.

Mr Ernest Cheeseman of Brunswick Road, Shoreham, was also extremely useful and succeeded in severing the wires which held the deceased in his terrifying position. Mr Philip Paine, who was at the aerodrome at the time, rendered valuable assistance, when on seeing the disaster he at once secured a fire extinguisher and in company with Messrs Jolly and Smith drove to the spot at high speed in his B.D.P. cycle car. It was owing to the efficient wielding of the extinguisher by Mr Jolly that the rescuers were enabled to reach and cut the wires which held the victim. We understand that the extinguisher was a No 3 Simplex, manufactured by Nather and Platt Ltd, whose Head Offices are at Queen Anne's Chambers, Westminster. Immediately the extinguisher touched the flames they went out, and had it been available earlier, no doubt the young aviator's life would have been saved. After this Mr Paine drove off for the doctor. Such assistance as could be rendered to the fearfully injured was rendered by Mrs Whiting, a trained nurse from 'Watergille' Shoreham Beach, who dressed the burns with some oil which she had been most fortunately able to secure from the farm. Valuable assistance was also rendered by Mr J.W. Smith who holds the St. John and Red Cross Certificates and whose efficiency in time of need has been mentioned before in our columns. Police Inspector White dealt with the accident very smartly, when he arrived, PCs Rose and Greenfield also assisting under his orders. The injured man was conveyed to the Sussex County Hospital, Brighton, in a motor car which was driven at a terrific speed, traffic being warned by a whistle blown continuously during the journey. Great credit is due to the gentleman who so promptly placed his car and service at the disposal of the authorities for the whole evening.

Wight was admitted to the hospital at 7.30pm and expired at 10.45pm the same evening. The aviator's last words were spoken to Mr Jolly (one of Eric Gordon England's engineers), who accompanied the injured man to hospital, 'after bidding him goodbye, he asked Mr Jolly to say goodbye to all the boys for him ...'

The coroner, summing up at the inquest, said the young pilot had been imprudent in doing more than was justified, Geere having said

Wight had been told he could take the machine up but that he was also to restrict himself to straight flights and then come down. However, a subsequent Royal Aero Club Accident Committee Report stated that the propeller fitted to the Avro biplane was unsuitable, while the engine revolutions were 100 below normal. While agreeing that the pilot had committed an error of judgement in attempting an extended flight, they pointed out that this was the fourth recent accident where a pilot had flown a machine with insufficient power for a safe flying speed, and those responsible should take measures to prevent pilots' lives being put at risk. It seems Simms, the previous chief instructor at Shoreham who had resigned in March 1913, had pointed out the unsafe condition of some of the older Avros to the company and suggested they should be scrapped.

Despite the gloom the accident cast over the aerodrome, flying continued as usual and Geere was in the air with bandaged hands and a new pupil in a few days. On Sunday the Pashley brothers' parents visited Shoreham and saw their sons giving exhibition and passenger flights. Eric had just completed one flight when one of the Avro Flying School pupils ran him down on a motorcycle and broke his leg. Eric was taken back to his lodgings and a doctor was called, but it was nearly four months before he was lifted into an aircraft to make another flight. Cecil, in the meanwhile, extended his passenger flights inland to Lewes and other towns, and by the end of the year he estimated the brothers had flown over 10,000 miles.

Late in July, a Breguet biplane was brought over to Shoreham by the firm's test pilot, Henri Bregi, with Mrs Buller, who first flew with Oscar Morison as a passenger in 1911. Mrs Buller had taken her brevet at Douai in May 1912 and now had her own aircraft. Asked by a reporter if she found it difficult to control an aeroplane, she laughed, saying, 'Not a bit, I am at home in the air just as I am driving a car.'

On Thursday, 31 July Grahame-White arrived again at Paston Place with his 80hp Morane Saulnier seaplane, having flown from Sheerness in two hours including a twenty minutes descent at Newhaven. This was his second 'Wake up England' visit to Brighton for the *Daily Mail*, and this time his companion was Salmet, the Frenchman. Salmet did not arrive until the next day, landing his 80hp Blériot at Preston Park where a hangar had been erected.

Later Salmet took off and circled the Preston Valley before flying over Brighton, returning thirty minutes later to make a good landing. Both aviators made a number of flights in the following days before Grahame-White flew off again to Cowes on 4 August to continue his tour. Salmet was not so fortunate. Leaving next day, he had to make a forced landing at Ore near Hastings, from where it seems he had to continue his journey to Folkestone by taxi. In a later flight in Dorset, Salmet took up Hatton Turner, who was with Coxwell when his balloon landed at Goodwood in 1863. When the sun got into his eyes on landing, they both ended up in a hedge. Turner, who was by now seventy-five years old, took it well, and presented him with a copy of his book on ballooning.

At midday on Friday, 17 June, a Maurice Farman flown by Lieutenants Granville and Small left Larkhill for a flight to Shoreham. Encountering fog en route, they lost their way and onlookers at Portslade and Hangleton saw their machine descend and apparently strike Hangleton Church. A crowd hurried to the scene, fearing the worst, but found the aircraft had succeeded in avoiding the church, striking a wall to the east of it. Neither of the airmen were injured. Lieutenant Granville explained that he had to descend owing to engine failure, and in avoiding the church and pond had struck the wall. The aircraft was badly damaged and was put on a lorry and taken to Shoreham.

On 7 August Britain was stunned by the news that the popular S.F. Cody and a passenger had been killed testing a new hydroplane he was intending to enter in the *Daily Mail* race. His funeral cortege to Aldershot was followed by many hundreds of local people, proof of high affection and respect he had gained in this country. During the summer, Fowler came to an arrangement with the *Eastbourne Gazette* and the *Illustrated Visitors List* to give some of their readers free flights. Readers had to complete a coupon from the papers, and six were picked out of a hat daily. The lucky ones then collected their tickets and made arrangements with Fowler for a suitable time and date for their flight. The scheme was a great success, and in the opening weeks 90 per cent of the would-be flyers were women. The continuing publicity of reports of winners' flights in the papers encouraged others to pay for flights, and Fowler seems to have spent more time on taking up passengers than instructing. There is an account of one young woman who had a ticket to fly in the evening. Finding Fowler was not flying from the beach in the morning, she telephoned him at the aerodrome and was told the machine would start flights at three o'clock that afternoon. Six women had to go up before this determined flyer, who had to wait and forego both her tea and dinner. It was 7.10pm when she had her turn, and as she put on her bathing cap Fowler commented that it was the most sensible headgear any of his female passengers had worn. She described the flight as perfectly lovely and well worth the wait, and was very taken by Fowler's kindness in providing for a motor car to meet her when they landed. The sponsored flights finished early in October, which was just as well, because on 11 October Fowler married Miss Josephine Oakey, the daughter of the sandpaper magnate, Herbert Oakey. Fowler's mechanics formed a guard of honour outside the church.

On 23 August, Brighton was squally with misty rain when a Sopwith Bat Boat landed on the water close to the sheltered side of the Palace Pier. The flying boat's sea anchor was lowered and another rope stretched from the boat to the pier so that it could turn to the wind. The Sopwith machine was the first flying boat purchased by the Admiralty, and was powered by a 90hp Austro-Daimler engine. Originally delivered to Calshot, the flight to Brighton was one of a series of proving flights. The pilot, Lieutenant Spencer Grey, was accompanied by Rear Admiral Mark Kerr. Arrangements were made with Captain Shirtcliffe, the Pier Master, that Lieutenant Grey would return at about five o'clock to check the weather. If it had improved, he would resume his flight to Calshot. In fact, the strength of the wind continued to increase throughout the day, and the pier master and his staff became increasingly anxious about the safety of the flying boat, as freshening winds were causing waves to break over the hull. As Grey did not arrive at the time arranged, they finally located him at the Hotel Metropole at eight o'clock that evening. After some discussion, it was agreed that Grey would come to the pier at five o'clock the next morning and, if the conditions improved, continue his journey. Otherwise the flying boat would have to be brought ashore to be beached and housed in the seaplane hangar at the West Pier.

By next morning the weather worsened, with the waves now some 4 or 5ft high and breaking over the flying boat's bows and cockpit. As the sky became lighter, some of the pier staff took a boat out to the machine and found that the cockpit was rapidly filling with water. Attempts to bale it out soon showed that the sea was gaining on them, and the aircraft was becoming waterlogged. By eleven o'clock the tail was under water, and the aircraft was assuming a perpendicular position. It was then that Lieutenant Grey finally realised that the machine would have to beached, and called for aid from the coastguards, also getting confirmation that the aircraft could be stored in the nearby hangar. Ropes were fastened to the machine and after much difficulty due to strong winds and tides it was eventually dragged up over the shingle. Breakers were still buffeting the flying boat, and as the machine was pulled up the shelving beach the elevator and tail snapped off. This in turn loosened the control wires and the wings collapsed, and had to be sawn off. By now only the engine and hull were in one piece, while the rescue attracted so many spectators, they impeded the salvage attempts. The hull and engine were later used in a rebuilt flying boat some twelve months later.

The Waterplane Race, a flight round the British coast sponsored by the *Daily Mail*, had to be completed by 30 August in seventy-two hours and was due to start from Southampton Water. As S.F. Cody had been killed and the Radley-England Waterplane entry had to be withdrawn, Harry Hawker had a clear field, but by the time he reached Yarmouth in his Sopwith seaplane he was so ill from sunstroke and the engine fumes he had to give up. On his recovery he tried again and got as far as Dublin before crashing when his wingtip struck the water. Hawker escaped injury but his passenger broke an arm.

At the end of the month, Volk's Station at Paston Place was again the place to go due to a further visit from Lieutenant Conneau (Beaumont), who was bringing over a French flying boat, his manager Monsieur Schreck, two other aviators and two mechanics. Herman Volk had invited him over, since the visit would boost the use of the Volk's railway. The flying boat was brought over by boat to Newhaven and assembled on the beach with the help of spectators, who also took it down and lowered it into the water. Alighting at the Paston Place Station, the lieutenant received a rousing welcome from the assembled crowd of some 2,000 people, the Frenchmen present shouting 'Vive la France!' To enable him to get through the crowd the police had to form a cordon and carry him shoulder-high into the shelter of the seaplane hangar. At noon the following day the Frenchman took up a number of passengers. Those in the afternoon included the hotelier Harry Preston and Magnus Volk, this being his first flight. Both of these flights were filmed by the cinematograph operator from the Palladium cinema at Brighton, and aroused much interest when shown later in local cinemas. A lunch was given in Beaumont's honour at the Royal Albion Hotel later that afternoon. On Tuesday Beaumont had to leave for Newhaven, as his Government permit to fly had expired. Beaumont took Herman Volk on the flight back to Newhaven, taxying up the landing stage to beach the machine and dismantle it for the return on the cross-Channel steamer. Herman – interviewed on his return to Brighton – said he was very impressed with the new flying boat. It was intended to build them at the Donnet-Lévêque factory in France, where they would be produced in quantity by the Franco-British Aviation Company, of which Beaumont was the managing director.

In October, another flying boat made an appearance at Paston Place. This was the Curtiss Model F, which Glenn Curtiss had brought over. The machine had been ordered by Captain E.C. Bass, an American who had acquired the agency rights to sell the machine in Britain. This flying boat had already proved very popular with wealthy sportsmen in the USA, and Bass apparently thought the aircraft could be marketed over here. At this point a number of inter-connecting strands came together as a result of the visit and flying demonstrations. The British Deperdussin Company, in which Lieutenant Porte had invested most of his savings, had failed, and he had taken the post of test pilot to White and Thompson at Middleton. Porte was already firmly convinced that the flying boat had a great potential for submarine hunting, so he was particularly interested in the Curtiss machine with its possibilities for development. Captain Bass had arranged for White and Thompson to undertake maintenance of his machine, and the company later purchased the British rights to manufacture the Curtiss machines in this country.

The new flying boat created a great deal of interest, and spectators queued to look at the machine in the hangar. A number of distinguished visitors from abroad also found their way to Paston Place, including representatives from the German Navy. The first test flight after the assembly of the machine was undertaken by J.D. Cooper, an Englishman who had learned to fly at the Curtiss Flying School and now had considerable experience with flying boats. Gordon England and Lieutenant Porte were both invited to go to Paston Place to see the machine and were given test flights. Porte had a long conversation with Glenn Curtiss, and they both seemed equally impressed with each other. Curtiss did not stay long in Brighton before going on to his European sales tour. In mid-October Captain Bass held a small party at Paston Place to christen his new flying boat the Pioneer, the well-known comedy actress Daisy Irving wielding the champagne bottle. A month later the flying boat was flown to Middleton for White and Thompson to modify the Curtiss controls, and remained there because the Paston Place hangar closed for the winter.

Bass also moved from Brighton to Bognor and became involved with White and Thompson, becoming a stockholder in the company. Early in 1914 he narrowly escaped a month's prison sentence for attacking the driver of a grocery cart who, he alleged, had obstructed his motor car. However, on appeal the sentence was reduced to a fine, after an apology by Bass and a promise to pay compensation to his victim for the assault.

The second Hendon to Brighton Air Race took place on 8 November. This was a handicap race with a trophy and £100 for the winner and a second prize of £50, donated by the Sussex Yacht and Motor Club. Nine competitors took part; six were English, including Gustav Hamel, the previous year's winner, and Raynham and Slack; there were two Frenchmen, Messieurs Verrier and Marty; while W.L. Brock of the USA completed the line-up. Hamel, like two other participants, flew in a Morane-Saulnier monoplane. The start was delayed by bad weather, but the aircraft finally got away by 12.30pm. The field was soon reduced to five, and in the meanwhile the crowds were building up at Shoreham. Wingfield and Pettett were also standing by to welcome the flyers on behalf of the Aerodrome Company. Arrangements had been made for the participants to have a formal lunch at the Royal York Hotel, but this had to be cancelled owing to the delayed start. The airmen, therefore, had to snatch a hurried meal at Shoreham before completing their final leg to Hendon, where Verrier won the trophy and Hamel had to be satisfied with second place and the £50.

At 6am on the morning of 23 November, after nearly seven months' work, the Lee-Richards annular monoplane was rolled out of the hangar at Shoreham for its initial test flight. Its construction had been undertaken in strict secrecy, and it was even suggested that armed guards had been employed to keep away intruders. It was a cold morning, but Gordon England was well muffled against the weather and started taxying trials. He had received strict instructions from the partners not to take the aircraft up in the air. Within a few minutes, however, Gordon England found that the aircraft handled well on the ground, the controls proving most effective. On increasing engine power and reaching 30mph he found to his surprise that the machine was becoming airborne, and without hesitation decided to give the aircraft her head. Increasing the power, he climbed to about 300ft and levelled off at 400ft, circling over Lancing College and the surrounding area before turning west and flying over Worthing.

After half an hour he returned to the airfield and, turning over the railway embankment, started to descend. Suddenly and without any warning, the engine cut out. Spectators on the field said the aircraft stalled at about 100ft before turning turtle and crashing, striking some telegraph wires alongside the railway track and flinging Gordon England out of the cockpit. Though shocked, and with one black eye and a cut over the other, he escaped serious injury. At the time he had not realised that he had torn some tissue in one knee, and this took some time to heal and needed an operation. Trains on the Brighton to Worthing line were delayed for some time until the wreckage could be cleared from the track. An investigation suggested that the accident had been caused by faulty weight distribution, so that when the engine stopped the aircraft became tail heavy and then uncontrollable. A mystery that was never cleared up was that the petrol tank had been fully filled on the previous night, but the undamaged tank, when examined, was found to be completely empty. Work was started immediately on another modified machine, using the salvaged engine and the propeller.

Also, in November James Radley decided to close down his workshop at Shoreham, although Gordon England was still owed money for salary and payments he had made for materials. All of England's efforts to get payment from Radley proved fruitless. Fortunately, Cedric Lee made arrangements to take over so the work on his aircraft could continue, and Gordon England was retained as works manager and test pilot.

Chapter 10

1914: Peace and War

In January 1914 the Royal Aero Club announced that they would select three competitors to represent Britain in the forthcoming Gordon Bennett Air Race, to be held in Paris in September.

Cedric Lee decided to build two more annular monoplanes in the hope that they might be chosen for this prestigious event. The second aircraft was ready three months later, and was almost identical to the crashed prototype except for an additional pair of elevators attached to the top of the fin. Meanwhile, Eric Gordon England's attempts to get James Radley to reimburse him for monies expended on the Radley-England Waterplane were still proving fruitless. Finally, on 30 March, the case came before the King's Bench Division in London. Gordon England's counsel explained that his client had originally been engaged at a salary of £25 a month to supervise the construction of a hydroplane during the previous year. It was the intention to enter the machine for the *Daily Mail* seaplane race around Britain, for which there was a £5,000 prize. During the period April to August 1913 his client had to expend money for wages and material from his own pocket, although he received no recompense. Radley rarely visited the workshop, spending much time abroad. Cross-examined by defence counsel, Gordon England said that Radley had proposed a partnership after the accident to the first hydroplane, but that he had declined the offer. Radley then gave evidence, saying that Gordon England was originally employed at a salary of £4 a week, but their relationship in the Shoreham venture was as partners. He had at no time authorised the plaintiff to pledge his credit while he was abroad. Summing up, the judge said it was a pity the partners had not been more business-like, but that he had to decide the issue on the evidence before him. His decision was that there was no partnership, and he found in favour of the plaintiff that his salary was £25 a month, so there would be a judgement for £145 with costs.

After his experience with the prototype annular monoplane, Gordon England displayed more caution in the flying trials of the second machine. It underwent extensive taxying trials, short hops and landings until he was fully conversant with its handling qualities. In the subsequent cross-country flights, Gordon England reported that the aircraft handled well except for the major problem of maintaining a straight course. The yawing of the machine meant it had to be corrected continually, otherwise it could develop into a flat spin. Although Gordon England spent another twenty-five hours in the air test flying the aircraft, this problem was not resolved, and in later days he described this tendency as 'damned dangerous'. He finally decided to withdraw as test pilot from the trials. Two other pilots were approached, one deciding against the job after one flight, while the other, Gordon Bell, accepted. Taught to fly by Gordon England at Brooklands, three years previously, he was a fearless and some said reckless pilot, and even at that time had flown more types of aircraft than anyone else in the country.

A year earlier, flying a Martin-Handasyde monoplane with an RFC passenger, he indulged in some low flying over an airfield and crashed, killing his passenger. Bell himself sustained severe head injuries and concussion, a silver plate being inserted in his skull and he had to wear a wig. A legacy of the crash was that high-altitude flying caused him great discomfort. The report on the crash by the Royal Aero Club Accident Committee attributed the cause to grave errors of judgement by Bell, and cautioned him on his future conduct, but this stern rebuke seemed to have little effect. His trademarks were a severe stammer and a quirky sense of humour, which was not always appreciated by his more staid fellow beings. After a complaint by the Royal Aero Club Committee on his conduct, Bell picked up a billiard ball and flung it at a framed copy of the club rules, observing with satisfaction that he was the only member to have broken all the rules at once.

Bell was short-sighted and wore glasses, which he frequently lost, and it did not always inspire confidence in the air when his passenger saw him disappearing from view in the cockpit, groping around for his spectacles. Bell did not display much interest when Gordon England attempted to brief him on the handling of the annular monoplane. On his first flight, on 10 April, he damaged the tail skid, and on one Sunday a fortnight later he was at 800ft over the airfield when the aircraft dipped suddenly and spiralled to earth, crashing close to the scene of the original accident. Although Bell was cut about and slightly concussed, he was not seriously hurt, but the machine was badly damaged. A later enquiry revealed that an eyebolt had come out of one of the elevators, jamming them down. Bell was fortunate that as the aircraft came down to 50ft off the ground in its spiral, air pressure on the surfaces freed the bolt. The machine nearly righted itself before it pancaked. Despite these continuing disappointments, Lee and Richards pressed on with the building of the other two aircraft, and additional hangars were erected for their use at Shoreham.

It seems the backers of the annular monoplane were people of influence, one being Archibald Sinclair (later to be Secretary of Air 1939–45). On 9 June the Admiralty yacht *Enchantress* arrived off Shoreham at 4am in the morning. At the first light, the First Lord of the Admiralty, Winston Churchill, disembarked with Sir John French, who was to lead the British Expeditionary Force to France some two months later. They drove to Shoreham aerodrome, where a demonstration flight by Gordon Bell had been arranged, but he again made another heavy landing, with some slight damage. This proved rather fortunate, because Churchill asked to be taken up and it was possible to refuse without causing too much embarrassment. By 8am the party had returned to the yacht and few local people were aware of the distinguished visitors.

At the end of January, Gustav Hamel visited Eastbourne on tour to demonstrate the new aviation craze of looping the loop (or the Apple Turnover as it was nicknamed at Hendon). Earlier in the month Miss Trehawke Davies had risen from her sickbed to be taken up by Hamel and become the first Englishwoman to have looped the loop. As one aviation magazine of the time commented, somewhat disrespectfully: 'No, not keen, meant to be first, that's all.'

Bad weather at the weekend did not prevent Hamel giving a display on Saturday afternoon. One reporter was told by an 'expert' that

Hamel's first loop was marvellous. Instead of diving down he went up against the wind and threw the machine over. On landing Hamel was cheered by the crowds of spectators and surrounded by local schoolboys and girls seeking autographs. Although there was a slight abatement of the wind next day, Hamel decided against venturing out again as he was to give a display before the King and Queen at Windsor on Monday. On the day he performed fourteen loops, landing within a few yards of the Royal personages to receive their congratulations and an invitation to lunch. Hamel had ordered a new Morane monoplane for the forthcoming Hendon to Brooklands aerial Derby, which once again had been sponsored by the *Daily Mail* and was to take place on 24 May. He had earlier, at Winston Churchill's request given a flying display to the RNAS pilots at Eastchurch, and agreed to repeat the performance at Calshot before the race. He left the Morane Works at Villacoublay at 4.30am on Saturday with his new aircraft. Leon Morane, the designer of the plane, saw him off, insisting Hamel wear an inflated bicycle tube as a safety precaution. Hamel reached Lille at 7.30am, he then flew on to Boulogne, rested, had an early lunch and set off across the Channel at midday. He was unaware that, as a result of stormy weather in the London area, the RAeC had already postponed the race. As the afternoon wore on and there was no sign of Hamel or his machine, Winston Churchill ordered an extensive air and sea search. After forty-eight hours the search was abandoned, although rumours abounded, the favourite being that he had been picked up by a trawler. One of his sisters travelled to Pagham Harbour in Sussex after a report he had been seen there. A few weeks later, a body wearing a bicycle tube was found by the crew of a French fishing boat, who kept the contents of the pockets and these were identified by Hamel's mechanics. Despite this, rumours continued to circulate that Hamel had an incurable illness and had become reckless. Later his family had to publicly deny another strong rumour that he had gone to Germany to fly with the new German Air Service.

The onset of the New Year had not brought any increase in new pupils for the flying school at Eastbourne, as the RFC and RNAS now seemed to have enough pilots for their meagre collection of aircraft, and in any case now had their own service school. At this time Fowler had two young pupils who were already proving something of a headache. Brian Hunt, who was twenty-one, was the son of the MP for Ludlow, while John Thorneley, aged seventeen, was the son of a lecturer at Cambridge University. Both had cars bought for them by their doting fathers, and Thorneley's father had also bought shares for his son in the Eastbourne Aviation Company and hired a Maurice Farman for his exclusive use, which was later bought for him.

Hunt had three crashes during his training, the cost of which had to be met by his father. The first was a pancake in a Blériot, and the second when he was taking the first part of his tests for the RAeC brevet. He had successfully completed five figures of eight when an inlet valve in the engine stuck and the engine stopped, the aircraft going into a dive. Then, suddenly the engine restarted and Hunt, perhaps foolishly, tried to bank round the aircraft sheds to land. As he came in over the aerodrome boundary road, the inlet valve stuck again and he had no alternative but to pancake on a new house under construction in his path. He escaped injury but both the house and the aircraft were badly damaged. In February he was making a cross-country flight when he had yet another engine failure over Polegate, the aircraft canting to one side and striking the ground with some force, buckling the fuselage and smashing both top and bottom wings. Again, he emerged unhurt, apart from a severe shaking.

Thorneley, whose flying career to date had been a little less dramatic, had been much fired by the visit of Gustav Hamel and his exhibition of looping the loop earlier in the year. He decided he would emulate the feat in his Maurice Farman and he and Hunt persuaded Emile Gassler, the EAC aircraft designer and their instructor, to strengthen the bracing for the attempt. It seems that Fowler somehow got wind of this scheme and demanded that the attempt would be abandoned. However, as both he and Frank Hucks had to go to London, where the new Gassler biplane was on display on the Eastbourne Aviation Stand at Olympia, the coast was soon clear for the conspirators.

On 23 March Hunt drove over and picked up Thorneley before 7am, taking him to the airfield. After checking his machine, Thorneley took it up for a test flight in a wind of 30mph. Satisfied, he landed and strapped in securely, then took off again with the cries of 'Good Luck' ringing in his ears from his fellow pupils, and a few spectators on the ground. He climbed steadily until he reached 3,500ft and then dived, performing a perfect loop at 2,000ft. He got the machine back on an even keel, and with a sweeping left-hand bank landed to receive the congratulations of Gassler, his fellow pupils and onlookers. He later described his feeling, as he went into the loop as 'like taking a header into the river'. When Fowler heard that his authority had been flouted, he returned hotfoot to upbraid Thorneley. It was, however, pointed out, probably by Gassler, that the exploit had established three records. Thorneley was the youngest aviator to loop, the first to do it in a biplane, and finally his altitude of 3,500ft was a record for the airfield. Since both Fowler and Hucks were in a good mood due to King George V touring their stand and showing great interest in their new aircraft, nothing further was said. In the end Fowler encouraged Thorneley to undertake more exhibition flights elsewhere, and he later toured Germany, giving displays of looping the loop. As Hunt's father subsequently ordered an EAC biplane with a 50hp engine for his son, when the company was not having much success as aircraft manufacturers, all was forgiven and forgotten.

Very little appeared in the local papers about the activities of Frank Hucks following his arrival at Eastbourne early in 1913. He does not seem to have undertaken any regular instruction of pupils. There was, however, a press report that he visited Brighton on 21 April in a Maurice Farman seaplane and landed a quarter of a mile west of the West Pier. As he taxied his seaplane up to the pier, the noise of his engine was almost drowned by the clicking of camera shutters, and on reaching shallow water the machine was drawn up on the beach. In the afternoon he made numerous passenger flights, and this venture into new territory encouraged Fowler to come to an arrangement with the Volk's Electric Railway whereby passengers taking a return ticket to their station at Paston Place went into a draw for a free flight, one in the morning and one in the afternoon. Well-advertised, this gimmick again proved very successful and also attracted other fee-paying passengers to Fowler.

By now the seaplane station at Paston Place was equipped with a turntable and trolley to enable seaplanes to be taken directly down to the water. During the year there was a significant increase in military and naval flights over Sussex by both the RFC and RNAS. There was a fatal crash on 23 February when a new aircraft designed by Geoffrey de Havilland at Farnborough, the F.E.2., crashed at West Wittering near Chichester. The RFC had erected a canvas hangar near the village for gunnery trials, since the new adjutant, Basil Barrington-Kennett, was anxious to simulate the conditions of active service for airmen where possible. The aeroplane was a pusher biplane, the engine being mounted behind the pilot so that a machine gun could be fitted in the front of the pilot's nacelle for offensive purposes. The pilot was a civilian, Ronald Kemp, who was badly injured and his passenger, another civilian E.T. Haynes, an engineer employed at Farnborough, was killed. A doctor in the area rushed to the scene and found Haynes dead with a fractured skull and a broken spine. Kemp had slight concussion and a fractured thigh. At the inquest, eyewitnesses said that the aircraft went out of control at 300ft, going into a sideslip, and a verdict of accidental death was returned by the jury. The coroner said such experimental things were for the good of the country in some form or other and that the nation owned a debt of gratitude to the young men who took their lives in their hands, although, perhaps they had a certain amount of amusement out of it.

On 13 June, Frank Widenham Goodden, who had bought Hamel's Morane-Saulnier, flew to Fairlight, Hastings, to give a flying display and take up passengers at £5 a time. Goodden was born in Pembroke, South Wales, in 1889. His father was a photographer who moved from Tunbridge Wells to Worthing in about 1910, then moving on to the Compton Studios at the Old Town, Eastbourne. Goodden was always interested in flying and first took a job with Spencer and Son, the balloonists, in London. He then became friendly with E.T. Willows, who has been described as the father of British airships. He made a number of flights with Willows, including the first dirigible crossing of the Channel and the first flight between London and Paris.

One of Fowler's former pupils, Lieutenant Rainey RN, landed at Shoreham one day with engine trouble with his Sopwith two-seater. After it was repaired, the weather proved too windy to proceed, so it was a day or so later that he attempted to resume his journey. He was forced to return with further trouble with the engine. After midday he resumed his journey, making off westwards but was again forced down, this time in a field near the Lancing road. His mechanic, who was travelling with him, tinkered with the engine and they took off again, only to get a few feet in the air before the aircraft turned turtle. The mechanic managed to leap clear before impact, but Rainey was severely shaken and was taken to a nearby bungalow to recover. Meanwhile, the Sopwith was dismantled and taken back to Shoreham. It was on 22 June that several B.E.2s of No. 6 Squadron RFC landed at Shoreham on a cross-country flight before returning to Farnborough after midday.

The Naval Review at Spithead in July led to a spate of forced landings by RNAS aircraft along the Sussex coast. On the 10th, for instance, several naval aircraft flying to Calshot passed over Littlehampton early in the morning, one machine force landing on the Clymping side of the river with engine failure. The pilot, Captain Risk, signalled that he needed assistance, but was stranded high and dry on a sandbank until the tide turned. The destroyer *Cynthia* then arrived to help, but by 10am the seaplane was afloat and was taken in tow by the ship. Eleven days later, three Maurice Farman seaplanes passed over the sea off Worthing on their way to Felixstowe, and one developed engine trouble. Flight Commander Rathborne put his aircraft into a glide, but it struck the water with such force it overturned. His telegraphist was struck by debris and Rathborne was stunned momentarily by a crack on the head but both managed to cling to the floats to await rescue. Fortunately, their plight was seen by a Corporation boatman called Bashford, who had already had several rescues to his credit, and he rowed out to them. Hauling the two sodden airmen aboard, he complained later that his head was buzzing due to other seaplanes 'whizzing round his head'. The Coastguard contacted the naval authorities and the wreckage was towed inshore and beached high and dry on the sands opposite Courtlands, at Goring, presenting a sorry spectacle. In the late afternoon, a torpedo boat, a naval tug and a destroyer arrived and anchored a mile off town, signalling to the coastguard station and asking if any help was needed to tow the seaplane to Portsmouth. Owing to the extensive damage to the machine, it was decided to dismantle it and send it back by train to Portsmouth. A party of bluejackets came ashore for the task and the ships left shortly afterwards for Portsmouth. Meanwhile, along the coast at Shoreham, an RNAS Avro Type E biplane piloted by

Flight Lieutenant Littleton (RN) had already been at Shoreham for a week after landing with engine trouble. He had been on his way to the Naval Review, and after two days had attempted to resume his journey. Caught by a gust of wind, he had to land and badly damaged his rudder. This was repaired in the Shoreham workshops, but all efforts to get the engine to run properly failed, and a new one was sent by rail from Eastchurch. After it had been installed, Lieutenant Littleton took the aircraft up again for a test flight in the afternoon. Again caught by a strong gust, he crashed but had the presence of mind to leap clear just before the aircraft struck the ground. Those who saw the crash rushed to the scene and were amazed to find the pilot standing by the wreckage. He was, however, so shocked and dazed he could not give a coherent account of what had happened, and was taken away to rest and recover.

The last incident of the day was yet another forced landing, again by Captain Risk, who had been flying over Shoreham in a 100hp Maurice Farman when his engine cut and he had to come down in the sea. The aircraft was towed up the River Adur to Norfolk Bridge and then beached for repair. So, in one day, one aircraft was a complete write-off, another was damaged but later repaired, and a third temporarily incapacitated.

The month was not yet over when another seaplane suffered engine failure off the Western Lawns at Hove and had to land in the sea. Once again, a Corporation boatman, John King came to the rescue, taking one of the airmen off to row round the aircraft to assess possible damage. A destroyer eventually arrived off the coastguard station after they contacted the Navy. The crew were taken ashore and the seaplane towed on to the beach for repairs to the engine.

The Avro Company appears to have vacated its premises at Shoreham aerodrome sometime towards the end of 1913, perhaps as early as September. It seems probable that G.A. Wingfield asked for an increased rental. The Avro Flying School never seemed to be a commercial success, only three aviators gaining brevets. The first to do so was a German, Herr Rolshoven. It was later suggested that Germans were being sent to Britain to learn to fly so they could identify and photograph military installations. This seems rather implausible, since training aircraft had a limited range and ceiling and rarely ventured far from their airfield. However, it was true that Rolshoven left Shoreham as soon as he got his wings and joined the Germany Air Service on the day war broke out.

Another of the successful pilots was W.H. Elliott, who came from Horsham. During the six months he was learning to fly he became friendly with B.H. England, who had succeeded in coaxing the Collyer-England biplane into the air. They decided that with the move of Avro, they would set up their own flying school, retaining two of the Avro biplanes, which by now were pretty well worn out. A press report when Elliott flew home to Horsham suggests this may have been in September 1913. They soon gathered some pupils and initially Cecil Pashley seems to have helped out as an instructor and discovered his true métier. By about March 1914, it seems Cecil and Eric decided to break away from the Shoreham Flying School and set up their own Pashley School. The Shoreham Flying School was formally registered as a limited company in June 1914 with a capital of £1,000 of £1 shares. The directors were W.H. Elliott, B.H. England, H.H.R. Aikman and G.J. Lusted, the last named having only passed his brevet at the beginning of the month. As far as is known, B.H. England had still not got his Royal Aero Club certificate at this time.

This was also the year that the prime mover behind Shoreham aerodrome, G.A. Wingfield, and fellow directors decided to introduce regular weekend flying meetings at the aerodrome and install a new manager to exploit its commercial possibilities. The scheme was to attract the public and well-known flyers by having aerial races with trophies and money prizes. A new 1½-mile course was laid out with pylons, one being placed in the home stretch so spectators in the stands could see how well the pilots handled their machines as they banked around the pylon. Several new hangars were also to be erected for visiting aircraft, while tea gardens and tennis courts were to be spruced up. A military band was also to be engaged for the entertainment of the crowds while the air races were held.

The first of these events was held on 11 July in beautiful sunny weather, which brought out large crowds by car, rail and foot from the surrounding districts. Among the flyers at Shoreham was J.L. Hall, who gave the inevitable display of looping the loop in his 50hp

Gnome-engined Blériot. Then followed the air races, and in the first two heats the finalists were the brothers Pashley, J.L. Hall and Jack Alcock. The race was won by Eric Pashley, who collected the Shell Trophy and £70 in prize money. On the following Sunday there were again large crowds present, including the chorus girls from the revue at the Brighton Hippodrome. One, a Miss Sylvia Lee, won a free flight and was taken aloft by Eric Pashley. A flying display was also given by a Mr G.M. Dyot in his red monoplane, made to his own design. It took off in 40 yards and he gave, according to a local report, a 'Fantastic display'. As the international situation worsened, another air race was arranged from Shoreham to Tunbridge Wells on Monday, 3 August. A number of well-known aviators arrived at Shoreham by the weekend to participate, including Gordon Bell, S.V. Sippe and Jack Alcock with his Maurice Farman. G.J. Lusted had to make a crash landing after a flight from Hendon, while J.L. Hall arrived at dusk and crashed into a pylon, smashing his propeller and undercarriage. It was then announced that the race had to be cancelled as, with the prospect of war, the Government had issued an order for the cessation of all flights other than those within 3 miles of a recognised airfield. On Tuesday, 4 August the British Empire declared war on Germany and her Allies on the invasion of Belgium.

Major Gerrard, Royal Marines and Captain Longmore RN, subsequently arrived at Shoreham to requisition aircraft and other equipment that might be of use to the armed forces. Jack Alcock's Farman was taken, and it is recounted that he was later seen head in hands sitting on a petrol can at Brooklands, mourning his loss. Emile Gassler, who had been planning to leave the Eastbourne Aviation Company after getting an offer from Vickers, decided to return home. He volunteered for service with the Swiss Air Corps, but was turned down. In 1915 he joined the German aircraft firm Luft Verkehrs Gesellschaft (LVG) as a flying instructor and test pilot, and in 1917 he moved to the Border Aeroplane Repair Works at Potsdam, which worked on Rumpler C biplanes.

For the two weeks before the outbreak of war the small staff at RFC Headquarters were working day and night to organise the movement of RFC squadrons number 2, 3, 4 and 5 to France, with an aircraft park holding reserve aircraft and all necessary spare equipment.

They had to scrape the barrel to do this, but with the British genius for improvisation in an emergency it was accomplished. Thus, the six divisions of the British Expeditionary Force were able to have air support, which was to prove vital in those first few months of war.

The squadrons flew off to France in the middle of August, stopping at Shoreham to refuel. On the next day, Lieutenant L.A. Strange of 5 Squadron, who had to delay his departure to collect a transport driver, started off on his Channel crossing. His Maurice Farman had a Lewis gun mounted in the front, and with his 13st passenger with full kit and rifle, the machine had to struggle to get in the air, let alone reach Shoreham, but he did eventually land there and refuel. On the next lap to Dover, Strange found his driver had smuggled on board a bottle of whisky and was drunk when they touched down at Dover, prior to crossing the Channel. The Dover Military Police put the driver under arrest and in the guardroom to await the continuation of his journey the following day. However, when Strange went to collect him he had disappeared and gone into town. He was finally found and brought back still the worse for drink at about 10.30am. The journey across the Channel took about forty-five minutes, and the overall journey to Amiens, their final destination, two and a half hours. Their landing was greeted by thousands of patriotic French men and women, who were all round the airfield. Unfortunately, at this point, the driver, who it seemed had smuggled another bottle of whisky aboard (and which was of course now empty), rose to his feet with gusto and waved the empty bottle to salute the Entente Cordiale. Strange's Commanding Officer, Major Higgins, known as 'Bum and Eyeglass' to his men, due to a protruding posterior and a monocle, was not at all amused. The driver got fifty-six days' field punishment and Strange tried to avoid contact with his CO as far as possible. Even so, he was luckier than one RFC pilot, who forced landed at Boulogne and was arrested as a spy.

By the end of 1914 the Eastchurch Squadron of the RNAS was at Dunkirk, Commander Samson being its commanding officer. Among the pilots, or band of pirates as Samson affectionately called them, was Lieutenant Bell-Davies, a frequent visitor pre-war to his uncle's house at Rotherfield, and the irrepressible Lieutenant Rainey. Their remit was vague, and included patrolling against enemy aircraft and

Zeppelins and undertaking reconnaissance for the French general at Dunkirk. In September, Bell-Davies was sent to Lille with five aircraft and pilots, including Rainey. On the way Rainey had to force land due to engine trouble in an area where there was fighting between Belgian and German troops. Stepping out of his aircraft on landing, he was confronted by a German Ulhan cavalry man with a lance, and spent the next few minutes dodging round his aircraft to avoid his demise, cursing all the time about leaving his revolver on the seat of his aircraft. At this stage some Belgian troops arrived on bicycles and quickly despatched the Hun. Setting fire to his aircraft to avoid it falling into enemy hands, Rainey rode away on the crossbar of the bicycle of one of his newly found friends.

On another occasion, Rainey returned from a bombing raid and decided to give his comrades below a demonstration of his acrobatic skills. It was when he made a low pass in front of a hangar that they realised one of his bombs was still lodged in the chassis wires of his aircraft. Waving and shouting, they tried to alert him, but Rainey assumed this was applause for his flying skills, and finally landed before taxying up to the hangar, where his fellow pilots had taken refuge. Although the bomb was removed and made safe, Rainey's stock was at a low ebb for some time afterwards.

In September Rainey was sent off with two others to bomb the submarine depot at Bruges. He dropped his bombs on the shed and again suffered engine trouble but managed to coax his aircraft to reach Holland to be interned. It seems the Dutch had a job keeping Rainey in order. He escaped by stowing away in the coal bunker of a ship, emerging in England as black as the Ace of Spades – it is said the Dutch were as pleased about his escape as was Rainey himself.

The war in France, or the Western Front as it became known, cast the RFC in at the deep end, and they had to prove that their fragile machines could operate under active service conditions. Their primary role was one of reconnaissance as the Germans drove through Belgium and swept towards Paris. As the battle progressed, the RFC pilots began to familiarise themselves with the terrain, even if they were operating in retreat. Initially there was some reluctance to accept their reports, but experience showed they were accurate.

Gordon Bell, who was now in the RFC Special Reserve, went over to France with the aircraft park. Their arrival on the quay at Boulogne caused the disembarkation officers much bewilderment as they had never seen such a vast pile of equipment, much of which seemed to be of dubious value in warfare. Bell is said to have distinguished himself in more ways than one in the BEF retreat. His Bristol Scout was hit in the engine by ground fire and he made a forced landing upside down in a tree before he was thrown out on to the ground. There he found he had been wounded in the knee; later investigation suggested he had been shot down by French allies. Shortly afterwards a staff officer galloped up and, looking down on the dishevelled figure of Bell, drawled, 'Have you had an accident?' An infuriated Gordon Bell stammered, 'N-N-No I always l-land like this you d-damned fool.' The staff officer taken aback, was furious and shouted 'What do you mean by speaking to me like that, do you know who I am?!' 'N-No,' shouted Gordon Bell, 'and what's more I d-don't c-c-care and if you t-think you can come round here, p-playing the c-comic policeman, there's my number on my tail and you can d-damn well b-b-bugger off!' As he was sent home with a Blighty wound, nothing more was heard of the incident but the story was cherished by RFC pilots and has been retold many times.

When one RFC reconnaissance flight showed that a large body of German troops was moving towards the British positions at Mons to envelop the British left flank, General French halted the BEF advance and fought a defensive battle on the Mons–Condé Canal. In the following days the movement of the German First Army was kept under constant observation right up to 4 February, when General von Kluck's movement to the south-west exposed the German flank to an Allied counter-attack. Later General French made it plain that the RFC had furnished him with the most complete and accurate information of incalculable value in his conduct of operations. By mid-October the war of movement had died away and both sides dug themselves into trench systems that stretched 475 miles from the Channel to Switzerland.

Chapter 11

1915–16

From 1915 onwards, the trench system involved a war of attrition and siege with terrible casualties. Aircraft on both sides whose initial role was reconnaissance now branched out into aerial photography to plan attacks on trench systems, ammunition dumps and gun positions etc., and aircraft also began to direct the fire of their guns on to enemy batteries. This was particularly important to the British because of the shortage of shells due to production difficulties at home.

So, the demand for more aircraft and crews increased beyond anything originally envisaged and resulted in a decision to concentrate production on the ubiquitous B.E.2c, which led to problems later. Neither was it obvious to the combatants at first that, unlike some machines of war, aircraft had to be developed and updated continuously if they wanted to have and retain mastery of the air. The Achilles heel of the British effort was the supply of aero engines. Both the French and Germans had thriving motor car industries where their expertise could be transferred to producing aero engines in quantity. In the case of Germany, its continuing development of water-cooled, in-line engines for its Zeppelins, which it transferred to its aircraft, gave it a lead throughout much of the war. Engines were so valuable that even when aircraft crashed near the front line, salvage would be attempted. Captain Gordon Bell and four mechanics in October 1915 went to recover an engine from a B.E.2c that had come down only five hundred yards within the French lines. As can be imagined, these salvage parties were not welcomed by the front-line troops since they drew shell and machine gun fire on to their heads.

The increasing activity in the air of aerial photography, gun spotting and bombing led both sides to try and deny their opponents freedom of the skies. Initially the aircraft in use were scarcely capable of carrying machine guns because of the weight penalty, but improved machines meant this became a real possibility. The main problem, however, was that most machines were tractors with a propeller in front, so a system needed to be devised to fire a gun to bypass the propeller. One French aircraft manufacturer became interested in this problem and worked on a system using an interrupter gear to enable the gun to fire after the propeller had passed its arc of fire. Problems arose in trying to get this to work and Raymond Saulnier fitted some deflector blades to the propeller so tests could go ahead, thus ensuring it would not be hit during the trials. Hindsight now seems to suggest his problem lay with the defective ammunition and belts supplied by the French Army for the tests. Anyway, with the outbreak of the war the trials were abandoned. Roland Garros, who had flown in Sussex in the great European Circuit Race, joined the French Air Force at the outbreak of war. He had become increasingly frustrated at the lack of any effective armament for his aircraft, and hearing of the Saulnier trials visited the factory and had the deflector fitted to his Morane. In two weeks in April he shot down several German aircraft, until he was forced down behind German lines. When the Germans realised they had captured the aviator who was causing havoc, they were delighted. There are many different versions of what happened after this, but what is definite is that Anthony Fokker, a young Dutchman who was trying to sell his aircraft to the Germans, produced the first successful interrupter gear and fitted it to his Fokker monoplane. The E.I. Trials convinced the Germans the gear enabled a machine gun to be fired through the propeller and he received orders to supply his monoplanes for delivery with machine guns using this gear.

Initially the Germans did not realise how this new weapon would revolutionise air warfare and put one machine in each squadron to protect their two-seat observation aircraft. Oswald Boelke, who had shown great offensive spirit when piloting a two-seater was, however, given a Fokker E.I and soon realised if used offensively it could decimate Allied aircraft. By the autumn of 1915 he had evolved new tactics for air fighting. Sitting in the sun, he would dive on Allied aircraft and, positioning himself under their tails, the blind spot, rake them with fire. He also saw the advantage of fighters operating in pairs to protect each other. His proposals for new air fighting tactics were accepted by his superiors and he set up a new elite formation, one of the pilots he selected being Max Immelmann, later to become known as the Eagle of Lille, and Manfred von Richthofen, the famous or infamous Red Baron, who awarded himself a silver cup for every Allied aircraft he shot down.

The outbreak of war with the build-up of the RFC resulted in Basil Barrington-Kennett being promoted to captain and eventually major. However, with the small RFC HQ staff, he was under constant pressure day and night. One of his fellow officers remembers someone coming in and waking him in the middle of the night. Basil jumped out of bed, only half awake and said, 'I will do it', as an example of his devotion to duty.

In February 1915 Barrington-Kennett contracted influenza and was forced to go into hospital. He was still unwell when he returned, and was packed off on leave. When he came back, he was told by the medical officer that he must get away from office work into the open air. Offered the command of a squadron, he felt he could not possibly accept this, holding the view that a commanding officer must lead his pilots in the air. He had not flown for some time, so this was not feasible. He, therefore, applied to return to the Guards, and joined the 2nd Battalion at Bethune. It seems he was very happy back with his men, but was killed in an attack on 18 May 1915. Maurice Baring, aide-de-camp to General Trenchard at RFC HQ, who had only known him since the outbreak of war, said the news of his death, an officer he admired more than any other he met, had meant he had the utmost difficulty in coming to terms with his loss even among the general carnage of war.

Corbett Wilson, who had landed at Christ's Hospital on 6 September 1912, had joined the RFC Special Reserve before the outbreak of war in 1914. He served with No. 3 Squadron for eight months, flying a French-built Morane parasol monoplane on artillery observation. On 10 May he set out with his observer and, passing over Fournes in Belgium, was hit by anti-aircraft fire. The machine crashed, killing both occupants.

Another member of the RFC, Second Lieutenant M.W. Greenhow, a native of Eastbourne, who was educated at Lancing College, was serving with No. 8 Squadron, which had been the first to get the B.E.2c in April before they were sent to France. On 25 September, Greenhow was the observer in an aircraft piloted by Lieutenant Washington that set off on a bombing raid to Douai. By now the B.E.2c had been armed with a Lewis gun, which the observer, who sat in the front cockpit between the wings, could fire backwards over the head of the pilot, who occupied the rear cockpit. Although the gun could theoretically be moved to fire through the wings, the slipstream and its weight made it difficult to do this in flight. By now the Germans had put their observers in the rear cockpit of their aircraft to give them a wider field of fire. After crossing the line into enemy territory and coming under anti-aircraft fire, the pilot spotted a train and came down low to drop his 100lb bomb. Then soldiers appeared from some nearby cottages and started to fire at the aircraft with their rifles. Greenhow fired back and they scattered but a machine gun then opened up from behind a gate. The bomb was dropped but missed the train, though it caused some damage from blast. By now ground fire was striking the aircraft engine, and a bullet struck Washington in the thigh, so he turned for home without delay. On the return journey they were intercepted by two Fokker E.Is, who they fought for twenty minutes until Washington was wounded again in both legs, starting to lose a lot of blood. He lost control of the machine, but managed to regain it and make a perfect landing behind German lines. Greenhow lifted Washington out gently, and carried him to safety before setting the aircraft on fire, by which time a German cavalry patrol had arrived. The two German pilots landed nearby, one carrying a first aid kit from which he took bandages and bound up Washington's wounds and supplied the two Englishmen with coffee and cognac before offering them cigarettes. The Germans obtained a horse-drawn ambulance and took Washington off to the nearest military hospital, dropping Greenhow off at a nearby village guardroom on the way. After interrogation, Greenhow ended up in a prisoner-of-war camp at Crefeld. He later found out his pilot had succumbed to his wounds, dying in hospital. It was by no means unusual in that period of the war for German pilots to land after successfully shooting down an English aircraft over their lines and treat their victims' wounds or, if unhurt, take them back to their mess for a meal before they were taken away as prisoners-of-war. It was less common for this to happen with the RFC as Germans rarely ventured over Allied lines.

The first Boy Scout to fly at Shoreham with Oscar Morison, Digby Crunden Cleaver, was educated at Hurstpierpoint College but finished his education in Switzerland. He returned to this country in 1915 and in July joined the RFC, gaining his RAeC brevet in five days; no mean achievement even in those days. On the completion of his training, he was posted to No. 1 Squadron, which was on active service in France.

His CO, Major G.F. Pretyman, took him up on his first flight over the line just before Christmas, flying a French Morane. This machine had a very sloppy control stick, which the pilot had to hold firmly otherwise it would move of its own accord. Major Pretyman turned to say something to Cleaver, who stood up in his cockpit and leaned forward. Inadvertently, Pretyman loosened his grip on the stick and it moved forward and the machine went into a nose dive, flinging Cleaver out to fall into a ploughed field below. Pretyman was horrified and in attempting to land close to the body, overturned the aircraft on the rough ground.

As a result of this fatality, the control stick on this type was fitted with a spring so it was held in a central position. Major Pretyman was seriously affected for some time afterwards about the tragic death of this eighteen-year-old boy, for whom he held himself responsible.

On 27 December, Second Lieutenant C.E. Foggin, who had learned to fly at Eastbourne and was now with No. 1 Squadron, overhauled an enemy Albatros in his Nieuport at Bailleul and fired at him at close range, seeing his bullets strike the enemy aircraft. In turning to renew the attack, a bullet from the Albatros struck his aircraft and splintered, wounding him in the left eye, so he was forced to break off combat and make for home. Some anti-aircraft gunners later reported that the enemy machine had gone down.

The inhabitants of Rotherfield and the surrounding area were delighted when they read of the award of the VC to Squadron Commander Richard Bell Davies in the New Year. Nephew of Dr Clifford Beal of Alan Down, he had made many visits to his uncle in 1913, on one occasion arriving by air to the great excitement of the locals, who had never seen an aeroplane close up before. Bell Davies served at Gallipoli, and with a fellow airman, Flight Commander Smylie, took part in a bombing raid on a railway junction on the Berlin–Constantinople line on which supplies of ammunition were brought to the front. Smylie, who was flying a Maurice Farman numbered H6, was hit by ground fire and forced to land in a dried up water course, with his bombs still aboard. Bell Davies, who had now dropped his bombs, returned to look for his comrade, and he suddenly saw the crashed aircraft explode. To his relief he saw Smylie waving; he had set fire to his machine to prevent it falling into Turkish hands. Bell Davies made a perfect landing, Smylie scrambled aboard his Nieuport and they took off again over the heads of the troops galloping towards the burning wreckage. Bell Davies' report of the incident was brief and in the best naval tradition: 'Returning saw H6 burning in marsh. Picked up pilot.'

Victor Barrington-Kennett, third son of Lieutenant Colonel Barrington-Kennett of Tillington, Petworth was the brother of the late lamented Basil, who had been killed in the trenches early in 1915. Victor had served in the Balloon Corps pre-war, but took his airman's brevet on 5 March 1912 in a Short biplane at Eastchurch. He went to France with No. 1 Squadron in March 1915, and a couple of months later, with his observer Lieutenant F.L. Richardson, had the first squadron combat with an Aviatik. Richardson got in a good burst from his Lewis gun at close range and the enemy aircraft went into a vertical dive, but no claim was allowed as it was not seen to crash. Transferred to No. 4 Squadron in February 1916 as its new commanding officer, Victor was flying a Bristol Scout in the early afternoon of 13 March 1916 when he encountered a German two-seater south of Arras and attacked it. Unluckily, Lieutenants Max Immelmann and von Mulzer then appeared on the scene in their Fokker monoplanes, and Immelmann shot down the Scout, which crashed very near the front line at Serre, killing Victor. On the same afternoon, Immelmann and two comrades were sitting in the spring sunshine when they were told to fly to Douai, where five English aircraft had been spotted. Delayed for fifteen minutes owing to a minor adjustment to his aircraft, Immelmann finally set off alone after learning the British aircraft had been seen heading for Cambrai. There he found four B.E.2cs and, climbing to meet them, fired at one on the end of the formation. Suddenly the B.E.2c heeled over on to its right wing, plunging to the earth and turning over as it went down. It crashed close to the village of Pelves. Both of the occupants who were killed came from Sussex; the pilot, Lieutenant G.D.L. Grune, from Southwick and the observer, Second Lieutenant B.E. Glover, lived in Lewes. He was only nineteen years old. His brother had been killed five weeks earlier when he had been shot down over German lines. Returning to his airfield, Immelmann drove to the site of the crash to find the bodies had been removed and that it was too dark to take photographs of the wrecked aircraft.

The advent of the Fokker monoplane was posing a serious threat to RFC aircraft engaged on reconnaissance, and they had to be escorted on their missions by other aircraft, reducing the number of sorties that could be undertaken. However, the F.E.2b two-seater with a pusher engine was now starting to appear at the front, which gave observers almost unlimited field of fire with their Lewis guns. The DH.2 pusher, like the F.E.2b a de Havilland design, was also in production and was coming into service, the first unit to receive these machines being No. 24 Squadron. Their new CO was Major L.G. Hawker, VC, MC who had already proved himself in combat.

The first day of July 1916 saw the opening of the Battle of the Somme, in which the British Army suffered appalling casualties. The pilots of No. 12 Squadron with the B.E.2cs were sent out on a bombing raid to St Quentin railway station. To enable them to carry a heavier bomb load, they flew without observers and four aircraft were lost. One of these was piloted by Lieutenant Lawrence Wingfield, son of the managing director of Shoreham Aerodrome. Wingfield succeeded in dropping his two 110lb bombs on the station and observed a column of smoke rising to a great height. Turning for home, he encountered a Fokker monoplane, which after fifteen minutes of combat forced him to land on a German parade ground. Surrounded by German troops, he found their officers knew both London and Brighton well, and they questioned him eagerly on whether his fellow countrymen were suffering very much hardship due to the war. Then a small car with three officers of the German Air Force arrived and bore him away to their nearby squadron headquarters in a beautiful French chateau. Given afternoon tea in their mess, he asked what would happen to his aircraft and was told it would probably end up in the Berlin War Museum. His adventures as a prisoner-of-war will be recounted later. The bombing raid, somewhat unusually for the time, proved a great success. One bomb fell on a shed filled with ammunition, causing a big explosion that spread to sixty other trucks also holding explosives. The train allotted to transport the German troops, who had their equipment spread on the platform, was also destroyed, about 180 men being killed or wounded.

This was also the day that the CO of the newly formed No. 32 Squadron, Major W.B. Rees, MC, who had been educated at Eastbourne College and joined the Regular Army in 1905, saw action. Ten German aircraft appeared over Allied lines and were attacked by a BE.12 and Rees in his new DH.2. The joint onslaught caused the whole formation to disintegrate. The first aircraft that Rees fired upon was hit and dived away for home, a second was damaged and only just made it to the German lines. On attacking the third, Rees was wounded in the leg, but kept firing until only 10 yards separated him from the machine and silenced the observer. By now his ammunition was gone, and his wound made it difficult for him to control the aeroplane, so he was forced to turn for home. Until he taxied up to the hangars and asked for some steps to enable him to climb out of his aircraft, it was not realised he was wounded. Sitting on the grass, he asked the MO to get a tender to take him to hospital. He was subsequently awarded the Victoria Cross for his bravery.

An F.E.2b of No. 20 Squadron on an early morning patrol on 26 September was engaged by one of the new Albatros scouts over Ypres. In a very short time, both the pilot, Lieutenant Livingstone, and his gunner/observer, Air Mechanic 1 Fred Dearing, who lived in Shoreham, were wounded, the latter very seriously. Nevertheless, Dearing continued to fire at the enemy scout with his Lewis gun and managed to drive him off. By now the aircraft was badly damaged, but Livingstone struggled to reach the Allied lines and made a safe landing. Dearing was taken out of the aircraft in a coma and rushed to hospital, but died at 1.30pm without regaining consciousness. He was not yet sixteen years old, having joined the RFC as a trainee air mechanic at fifteen and served six months in France. His flight commander wrote to his mother, telling her that the enemy aircraft had been confirmed as shot down, and said:

> He was a mere boy and as game and plucky as any observer I have ever had anything to do with ... a really splendid youngster who feared nothing and was always ready to undertake any work, however dangerous.

In 1915, as a result of a question raised in the House of Commons, it had been agreed that all soldiers under eighteen, many of whom had lied about their age when enlisting, should be sent back to England. It may be that the fear of adverse publicity decided the RFC against making a posthumous award to Dearing, although a report of his death in action, and indeed the letter to his mother from his flight commander, appeared in the local press.

Eric Pashley, who had joined the Vickers Company when the aerodrome at Shoreham had been taken over by the RFC at the beginning of 1915, test flew many of the first two-seat pusher biplanes, the Vickers Gunbus, from its airfield at Joyce Green, Kent. He volunteered for service in the RFC in 1916, and during August visited Hendon, where his brother, Cecil, was instructing at the Grahame-White Flying School. There, according to *Flight*, he gave a flying display on the DH.2 and 'put up some astonishing stunts'. In the following month, he was posted to No. 24 Squadron at Bertangles near Arras, and on 26 October had his first combat with a German fighter in his DH.2, forcing it down. In the next six months he shot down eight aircraft and forced down two others. At this time the British authorities, unlike the German or French, were against publicising individual airmen and their exploits. The unofficial status for an 'ace' was to have shot down five aircraft. Pashley seems to have received no recognition for his efforts, either by promotion or decoration. He was to die, not in combat, but in a flying accident, on active service on 17 March 1917.

Among the local press reports on October 1916 was one relating to the award of the Military Cross to Captain Ernest Leslie Foot, who came from Pulborough. Twenty-one years old, he was described in the report as the 'hero of over ninety aerial flights' and of numerous successful raids, and described as a fearless flyer. In his case the hyperbole was fully justified. Known as 'Feet' to one and all, he was an amusing and erratic character who was continually in scrapes of one sort or another. Tales of his flying exploits and crashes were related with relish and wherever the pilots of the RFC gathered and talked 'shop'. His father, E.G. Foot, was a doctor in Pulborough and the medical officer at Mrs Johnstone's Bignor Park Red Cross Hospital, where his mother was also a voluntary worker. Commissioned in September 1914, Foot transferred to the RFC as an observer in May 1915, returning to the UK before the end of the year to train as a pilot. By March 1916 he was back in France with No. 11 Squadron, which was then flying the first of the pushers, the Vickers Gunbus, with the observer in the front seat. His aptitude for flying soon led to him being given a scout aircraft, although he and his observer had gained three victories in the Gunbus.

By now the Germans were using the Fokker E.I monoplanes in groups, and it was decided the RFC should also form their own fighter squadrons. Thus, Foot and Albert Ball (soon to be Britain's leading ace) were transferred to No. 60 Squadron. This unit had to be withdrawn from the line in August after suffering heavy casualties, and was to be re-equipped with Nieuport Scouts. By mid-September the Germans had reorganised their air force and new German squadrons were appearing, flying the Albatros D.I or D.II.

The unremitting policy of offensive practised by Trenchard already meant that British airmen suffered from the disadvantage of continually operating over enemy lines, so that after combat they had to struggle against prevailing winds to get home. Now they were faced with new aircraft of a superior performance armed with two forward-firing machine guns, which meant that the German pilots could initiate or break off combat at will. On the evening of 28 September, Captain Ball shot down one German aircraft and forced down two others, and Foot also got his first confirmed victory in a new French Spad S.VIIC.1, which was on loan to the squadron for evaluation trials. Foot had found himself looking down on four Albatros two-seaters, and dived down, firing on one, which crashed near Avesnes. On the afternoon of 26 October, he was not so fortunate. Leading a patrol over Ancre, he found eight enemy scouts attacking four B.E.2cs.

In the ensuing dogfight, three of the B.E.2cs were shot down and Foot's Lewis gun on his Nieuport was disabled by a burst of enemy fire. With an Albatros on his tail, he dived away at speed. However, he was still pursued by the Albatros, who with another burst set Foot's petrol tank alight. Foot side-slipped to keep the flames away from his cockpit and managed to land safely near Serre without serious injury. Five days later, after eight months on active service, he was sent home for a period as an instructor.

His place as flight commander was taken by a Canadian, A.D. Bell-Irving, one of three brothers, who had an aunt living in Mayfield, Sussex. Bell-Irving, on patrol in early November, drove down one enemy aircraft before he was hit by fire from another and wounded in the thigh, forcing him to land at Gueudecourt. His aircraft was badly damaged and overturned on landing. He was posted back to the UK for hospitalisation and was later awarded the MC and Bar for his work with No. 60 Squadron.

Harold Balfour, who learned to fly at Shoreham, joined the squadron in May 1916, followed by S.F. Vincent in June. Balfour was a member of 'A' Flight, whose commander was Captain Smith-Barry, and on one patrol saw their commanding officer, Major 'Ferdie' Waldron, shot down and killed. His stint with the squadron was short as he crushed his fingertips in an accident with a deckchair and was sent home, on his recovery becoming a test pilot. In August, Roderic Hill was posted to the squadron. His brother, Geoffrey, came out a month later with No. 29 Squadron. Smith-Barry replaced Waldron as the new CO of No. 60 Squadron. An old Etonian, and of independent means, he was described by a friend as 'not giving a damn for anyone'. He was one of the first pilots to graduate from Upavon late in 1913. He went to France with No. 5 Squadron and was in the retreat from Mons when he had a serious accident, crashing his B.E.8 and killing his observer. Taken to a French hospital, he was told German cavalry were in the neighbourhood. Despite two broken legs, he got a cab and went to Amiens. Here he caught a train to the coast and the following day he was comfortably settled in a private nursing home in London. By 1915 he was hobbling about on two sticks and persuaded a Medical Board to let him become a flying instructor, where he became very aware of the lack of any organised training programme for new pilots. Then he got a posting to the Western Front.

His experiences at No. 60 Squadron reinforced his strong views on the need for proper training, as young pilots were being posted to France with only seven or eight hours of solo flying to face well-trained German pilots with superior machines. He refused to let them go over the line until they had a period of initiation on flying on active service. Both Vincent and Hill showed an offensive spirit in combat and worked well together. Vincent shot down three German aircraft, while Hill downed two enemy aircraft and a balloon and in December was made flight commander of 'A' Flight. While escorting some twelve F.E.s from No. 11 Squadron, they got into a dogfight with some Albatros scouts. Vincent made a head-on attack on one all-red Albatros and they circled one another looking for an opening. Hill, seeing the situation, dived down to help his comrade, whereupon the red Albatros made off. It was it seems, the Red Baron himself, Manfred von Richthofen. Roderic Hill soon gained a reputation as an excellent pilot and spent most of his time testing aircraft in the squadron. Returning from home leave, he stopped off at Farnborough to pick up a new Nieuport for his unit. He mentioned he had flown the Spad and was offered an opportunity to test fly a new S.E.5 fighter for comparison. He gave an excellent display but to his chagrin damaged the undercarriage on landing. The S.E.5 prototype was taken over to St Omer by Frank Goodden in late December and demonstrated to General Trenchard. Hill was sent for to test it from the active service pilot's point of view. He gave a convincing display with an excellent landing.

Smith-Barry, in the meanwhile, had continued to put his views on the inadequacy of flying training to senior officers, including Trenchard. He submitted a number of papers on the need for a drastic re-organization, root and branch, of the pilot training system. The high casualties the RFC suffered in 1915–16 meant there was enormous pressure on flying schools to train pilots quickly for overseas posting. Their lack of experience then led them to become casualties, so more pilots were needed, causing a vicious circle. Finally, Trenchard in his eternal credit, succumbed to Smith-Barry's entreaties and posted him back to England at the end of December 1916, telling him to recruit his own staff and put his theories on training into practice.

It was in this period that Wingfield and the Brighton Shoreham Aerodrome Company battled with the War Office to get financial compensation for the requisition of their airfield. The Crown's view was that, under the Defence Regulations, they were not obligated to pay compensation except as a matter of grace. Wingfield refused to accept this situation, arguing that he would have no redress if any award was, in his view, insufficient. The company finally filed a Petition of Right, which was heard in the High Court and dismissed, as it was when it went to the Court of Appeal, before finally going to the House of Lords.

The holder of half of the company's debentures that had been guaranteed by Wingfield was a Mrs Blew, a sister-in-law of one of his law partners. As the company assets had been seized there was no money to meet interest payments, and a judgement of £3,700 was made against the company with a petition of bankruptcy against Wingfield. At this time the appeal was being heard in the Lords, the Attorney General being the famous F.E. Smith. After four days of protracted argument, the House of Lords decided to allow the appellants to withdraw their appeal, as the Crown agreed in the special circumstances of the case to pay them compensation to be assessed by an independent arbitrator. F.E. Smith, made aware of Wingfield's situation, arranged for a cheque to be sent to him next morning to extricate him from bankruptcy. A delay arose in going to arbitration, as the War Office announced it wanted to purchase the freehold of the site, which needed Treasury sanction. Wingfield therefore proposed a scheme to use the foreshore and river bank, which was still owned by the company. He drew up a plan to construct a lock gate over the River Adur, make a lake and build hangars on the foreshore that could be hired out to manufacturers of seaplanes and flying boats. This seemed to have concentrated the minds of officialdom wonderfully. In late 1917, a compensation payment of £25,700 was agreed that enabled Wingfield to clear outstanding debts and become solvent once more.

Chapter 12

Learning to Fly in Wartime

The transfer of practically the whole strength of the RFC to France, both in men and machines, in support of the BEF in August 1914, may have been a triumph of improvisation but it was also a disaster as far as the setting up of a cohesive and effective flying training programme was concerned. There were only a couple of dozen of airworthy machines still left in the country, and these were depleted still further when it became necessary to form No. 6 Squadron and withdraw more men and machines from the scant resources of the Central Flying School. Thus, civilian flying schools were encouraged to plug the gap, and this is perhaps why the Shoreham Pashley Brothers and Hale School kept going until the end of December 1914, when the airfield was finally taken over by the RFC. The Shoreham Flying School seems to have ceased operation after the outbreak of war. The RNAS were in a better position than the RFC as regards equipment and by mid-October the first batch of flight sub-lieutenants had arrived at Eastbourne for instruction by Fowler, who was left as a pro tem civilian instructor.

On 15 January 1915 the first contingent of RFC personnel and machines arrived at Shoreham airfield to set up No. 3 Reserve Squadron. Their task was to teach pupils the basics of flying up to the level of the RAeC brevet tests. After this they would move to new squadrons that were being formed and take their service wings at the Central Flying School at Upavon.

One of the first instructors to arrive at Shoreham was Horatio Barber, who spent three months there before moving on to Brooklands. He soon became well known for having such a loud voice that he could be heard instructing his pupils in the air even above the noise of the 70hp engine of the Maurice Farman. Among the observers who came to Shoreham to learn to fly was Robert Loraine, a pre-war flyer and well-known actor who had considerable success in the plays of Bernard Shaw. He even made a balloon ascent with the famous playwright. Loraine had got his brevet in October 1910, but although he possessed great courage, he was not a very good pilot. At one time his personal mechanic was Vedrines, who visited Shoreham pre-war during the British and European Circuit races. Loraine volunteered for flying duties at the outbreak of war, but after crashing two valuable aircraft, was told he would only be accepted as an observer. After being wounded flying with Corbett Wilson with No. 3 Squadron, the RFC relented, and he was offered pilot training, which he accepted with alacrity. He later commanded a squadron in France and then a wing. Another observer who came to Shoreham was Second Lieutenant Sholto Douglas. He had spent the previous week at the RFC flying school at Le Crotoy in France, where he had already passed his brevet tests. At Shoreham he managed to get another six hours solo flying before being posted to No. 14 Squadron, which had been formed at Shoreham and then moved to Hounslow. He achieved high command in the Second World War and became a Marshal of the Royal Air Force.

Another would-be aviator who found himself at Shoreham in early 1916 was Harold Balfour, who had joined the Army, borrowed £75 from his father and weedled three weeks leave from his CO to go to Brooklands and gain his RAeC brevet. He had volunteered for the RFC but was sent to France in the meantime, which he described as 'Most dangerous, uncomfortable, dirty and insanitary', so he was relieved when he was posted to Shoreham. Balfour found there was a vast difference between gaining a brevet and service flying, although he was not impressed with the level of training. He divided instructors between those who were afraid to let pupils get hold of the controls and those who were making sincere efforts to impart instruction but were ignorant of the basic principles of flight and had no properly laid down instructions to follow. Balfour had brought his 40hp car with him, which had two bucket seats, a loud exhaust and an enormous strap holding down the bonnet. He soon got on the wrong side of the local police. A summons for driving without lights at an excessive speed and failure to licence his vehicle was issued after one joyride to Brighton. By now Balfour had moved on to Gosport, and when a constable appeared with the summons and asked for Balfour, he was shown a crashed aircraft and told Balfour had given his life for his country. It seems this was checked because the constable reappeared the following week and presented Balfour with the summons. As he was due to fly to France the following day, he ignored the matter. In the 1930s Balfour wrote of his experiences in the RFC and RAF and mentioned this incident. He was somewhat taken aback to receive a letter from a Shoreham magistrate, who clearly had a sense of humour, saying he had thoroughly enjoyed his book and found his summons was still outstanding and sent him a bill for £3 10s. This time it was paid, with an additional contribution for the Poor Box! Later becoming an MP for Thanet, Balfour was Under Secretary for Air during the Second World War.

One person who has left his impression of being a pupil at Shoreham was the then Second Lieutenant Duncan Grinnell-Milne. He travelled down to the aerodrome by train and met another officer returning from leave, who reassured him that there were few parades, little drill and no compulsory church parades on Sunday. On the other hand, he was told that not much flying was done at the airfield either, and his informant said that many officers who had volunteered for flying duties had returned to their units after only a few days' trial. Most of the instructors and pupils lived on Shoreham Beach, where one large bungalow, mostly constructed from old railway carriages and called 'Pandora', was used as the officers' mess. On the next Sunday, there was a stiff breeze and massed cloud and Grinnell-Milne and half a dozen other pupils were taken to the aerodrome after breakfast. Here they visited the hangars and saw the Maurice Farmans on which they would train and two Martinsyde S.1 single-seaters, which were flown by instructors as the Shoreham contribution towards air defence against marauding Zeppelins.

On the airfield, having landed to await an improvement in the weather, was a brand new B.E.2c. At that time the machine was considered to be the ultimate in modern design by the pupils. A tractor biplane with a 90hp Royal Aircraft Factory engine, it had a dashboard with instruments in the pilot's cockpit and a stick and rudder control, rather than the handlebars and foot pedals used in the Farman. The test pilot who had flown it from Farnborough was Frank Goodden, now a second lieutenant in the RFC, with a civilian passenger, Mr Henry Lilley.

After lunch there was a slackening in the wind and a general improvement in the weather so Goodden decided to continue his journey. In the late afternoon he and his companion attired themselves in leather flying gear and climbed aboard their aircraft. The engine was started, the chocks were removed from the wheels and the aircraft taxied out and was given full throttle, taking off to climb steeply into the wind. As it reached about 150ft and crossed the airfield boundary, the engine suddenly spluttered and stopped. Beneath the aircraft was a road and numerous small meadows intersected by drainage ditches. This was not ideal for a forced landing, but the wind was still strong enough to help reduce the landing run. All of those who had been watching had already had the golden rule drummed into them. In such a situation a pilot should maintain his flying speed as far as possible, pick a landing space in front of him and land as best he could. Goodden, however, turned back to the airfield quickly and made a sharp turn over the hangars, bringing him back into the wind and allowing some 50 to 60 yards to land. The machine was handled brilliantly, but he failed to achieve his objective by a small margin. The aircraft stalled over the hangars, missed the roof by inches and disappeared behind the sheds, to be followed by a rending crash as it struck the ground. There was an immediate rush to the scene of the crash, where there was a mangled pile of wreckage with both Goodden and Lilley still slumped motionless in their seats. Before the first arrival could rush forward to pull them free, there was a flicker of flame from under the fuselage and then the roar as 30 gallons of petrol burst into flames from the ruptured petrol tank. Fanned by the wind it swept over both pilot and passenger. The former suddenly moved and fumbled with his belt and then, with a convulsive movement, staggered clear with his clothing on fire. He was seized and rolled over on the ground until the flames had been extinguished. By now the heat was so intense that the onlookers had to move back and it was impossible to get near Lilley. Fire extinguishers seemed to have little effect on the conflagration, and the motionless body was burnt to death before the eye of horrified onlookers. The whole episode only took a few minutes, but seemed to last forever. Then the wind dropped and the flames gradually died away, and the pupils were ordered back to their billets.

Next morning, the commanding officer called all the instructors and pupils together in the company office. He told them an official enquiry would be held to establish the cause of the accident and repeated the notion that pilots should never turn downwind at a low altitude when a forced landing was necessary, and always try to maintain flying speed. He emphasised that an aircraft was expendable in such a situation but a pilot or passenger were not. It was better to lose an aircraft than burn to death. Fortunately, Goodden's injuries were not serious, although he was not well enough to attend the inquest. Evidence called by the coroner revealed that Lilley, who was twenty-seven years old, had suffered a fractured skull and was dead before the aircraft caught fire. A verdict of accidental death was returned by the jury.

A fortnight after this tragic event, Grinnell-Milne suddenly found that his luck had changed. One evening an instructor took him up for a half hour flight, and from then on he started to go up daily. Meaning and order suddenly started to appear in the use of controls, and he felt at last he was making progress.

One miserable morning the pupils were gathered outside the hangars to watch one of their group go solo when an instructor asked Grinnell-Milne how much time he had in the air. His answer of three hours and twenty minutes seemed to satisfy the instructor, who then asked him if he thought he could go solo. While Grinnell-Milne was thinking of all the reasons he felt this was unwise, he heard himself say 'yes'. He was assigned an aircraft, climbed in, and the instructor gave him last-minute instructions to get well out on the airfield before taking off and not to taxi too fast. Once the aircraft started to move, all the lessons that had been drummed into him started to come back, and he began to feel his spirits rise. Then he was 400ft up and found he could see Worthing Pier coming up under one wing. He essayed a gentle but wide turn, and in no time at all Shoreham Beach came into view and he was passing over the airfield and could see the group of his fellow pupils looking up at him. Leaving them behind, he turned towards Brighton and then made a second turn back into the wind to come back over Shoreham. Putting the nose down, he pulled back on the throttle so that the glide towards the airfield was at a speed of 42mph. He crossed the River Adur on the airfield boundary and the ground began to come up. Pulling very gently on the handlebars and putting pressure on the pedals at the same time brought the nose directly into the wind. There was a gentle rumble, the machine shook, gave a lurch and he was down all in one piece. He taxied back to the sheds, bore the congratulations of his fellow pupils with a careless air, then went back to the mess and ate an enormous breakfast. He passed his brevet tests by the middle of August, and was shortly afterwards posted to Gosport for advanced flying training before getting his wings at Upavon.

The first Canadian airman to be killed at Shoreham was Lieutenant William Sharpe of Prescott, Ontario. He had been one of a party of three airmen who had come over with the 1st Battalion Canadian Contingent with a Dunne swept-wing pusher aircraft that had been built under licence in Canada by the Burgess Company. The aircraft was damaged in transit, and eventually ended up at Upavon. The three-man unit was disbanded and Sharpe was sent at his own request to Shoreham to brush up on his flying. It seems he had passed all his flying tests at the Curtiss Flying School in San Diego in January 1914, although he had received no formal certificate. On a windy morning of 4 February 1915 he went up in a Maurice Farman with Captain Ross Hulme, the CO of Shoreham, at the controls. After coming down, Sharpe took over the controls and, in the afternoon, went solo. The captain said he saw him complete two well-flown circuits and was then called away, and was afterwards told that Sharpe had crashed, some twenty minutes after take-off. At the inquest another pupil said Sharpe had been flying at about 1,000ft when he made a sharp turn, the machine side-slipped and then nose-dived into the ground. Police Constable Pateman, who was quickly on the scene, said the aircraft had dived into the ground in a field close to the Sussex Pad Inn and Lancing College. The wreckage had to be lifted manually by onlookers to enable him to drag out the dead pilot from underneath, the corpse being saturated in petrol from a split tank. The coroner's jury returned the usual verdict of accidental death.

165

This crash may well have been the one that, according to a pupil at Lancing College at the time, set the headmaster even more against flying. In consequence the out of bounds order on the airfield was even more strictly enforced on the boys. But this did not stop the aviation enthusiasts among them taking their canings as a price they had to pay for aircraft spotting. S.F. Vincent, who used to watch Piffard, and was an old boy of the college, joined the RFC and went to Beaulieu for his flying training. Having to undertake a cross-country flight as part of his course, he naturally decided to fly to Shoreham. On arrival over Lancing College, he did some acrobatics in his B.E.2c for the edification of his old college chums, which was much appreciated. The need to recruit more pilots for the RFC led the aerodrome CO to invite the headmaster over for lunch and a decorous flight over the Sussex landscape, which it appeared was much enjoyed by the academic and improved relations between the college and the aerodrome. Boys who expressed an interest in joining the RFC when they left college were able to visit the airfield in small parties and were often taken up for a flight. One pupil at Lancing was Christopher Clarkson, who lived at Littlehampton. He started at the college in September 1914, and had his nose glued to the nearest window overlooking the airfield when any aircraft could be seen. With the relaxation of the prohibition of going near the airfield, Clarkson spent all of his spare time on the side of the airfield road watching the aircraft. It was not long before he became so well known to the officers and men that he was allowed, unofficially at least, to go on the airfield. Eventually, with the consent of the headmaster and the then commanding officer, Major Powell, he spent all of his school holidays working on the aircraft, dressed in his OTC uniform. The major, whom he remembered as a most charming man, expressed his worries to Clarkson about the coarse language he could encounter from the ground staff, but Clarkson was able to assure him that his time in a public school had already amply covered this part of his education!

Clarkson commented in later years, 'I must say that everyone was not only long suffering but very kind, and by 1916 I was being taken up at odd times and being allowed to handle the controls, and a year later I was ready to go solo.' Clarkson was involved in a number of scrapes, on one occasion persuading an RNAS pilot who was ferrying a de Havilland DH.4 bomber to France to take him along. Landing at Dover to refuel, the adjutant in charge of the airfield made quite a fuss about issuing a travel warrant to an itinerant OTC cadet who possessed no travel instructions. When they finally crossed the Channel and landed at an airfield near Calais he was sent back post haste. His last escapade was as a result of a bet with an RFC officer who was only a little older than Clarkson. This resulted in him and a companion creeping out of the school dormitory at 10pm and walking over to the aerodrome, where they were holding a dance. After a snack they went back to bed at about 2am. The story was all round the school next morning, and the two boys were taken to the headmaster and birched and threatened with expulsion. Clarkson said it was largely due to the then aerodrome CO, Major Van de Byle, a South African and the adjutant, Captain Davies, who pleaded his case to the head, that the matter was allowed to drop. Clarkson, was however, forbidden to go near the airfield again and he said he never did get the chance to thank his advocates personally. Clarkson volunteered for the RFC while he was still at Lancing, and was to have gone to the Cadet School at Hastings in 1918, where his uncle was an instructor, when the war ended. He did achieve his ambition to fly when he joined the RAF in 1924, having a distinguished career, among other things being an instructor at the Central Flying School.

When Smith-Barry arrived at Gosport in early 1917 he took over No. 1 (Reserve) Squadron, and rented a nearby country house for his officers at his own expense. In a very short time, he gathered round him many of his ex-comrades from No. 60 Squadron and they sat down each morning to formulate the principles of the new training methods and made decisions on a detailed programme and their first course. It had been agreed that the main thrust of their training would be for instructors to spread their methods quickly over the many flying schools.

Smith-Barry had been particularly struck by the lack of interest shown in flying by the new young pilots who came to France. He attributed this to a failure in current training methods to motivate their pupils. The dangers of flying were overstressed and there was a prohibition on acrobatics or stunting. so the majority of pilots to arrive in France were ill-equipped for aerial combat.

167

In a very short time, the basics of the new programme began to emerge and the Avro 504J was selected for tuition as the standard training aircraft. With its 100hp Monosoupe engine, it enabled training to continue in all but very bad weather, unlike the Farman, so more time could be spent in the air. The later invention of the 'Gosport Tube', which consisted of rubber tubes with funnels, enabled the instructor to talk to the pupil in flight and comment on his progress. From the start the pupil sat in the pilot's seat with the instruments, Smith-Barry taking the robust view that any instructor who could not fly by the 'seat of his pants' was not worth keeping anyway. A standardised 'patter' was introduced from the first flight, so even if the instructor changed the instruction, it would be to a programme. Even after his first solo, the pupil would continue to fly with an instructor to be shown how to deal with emergencies. Finally, when adjudged competent by the instructor, he was sent up on his own to practise what he had been taught and build up his confidence in his own flying ability.

The first Gosport pupils soloed in about four to five hours, and quickly took to formation flying and stunting. When the 'brass hats' paid a visit, the new pilots went up in a selection of first-line aircraft that they had never flown before. They handled them so well that General Salmond, now Commander of the Training Division in Britain, gave Smith-Barry command of two more training squadrons, 27 and 55, to merge with No. 1 into a special unit. It was called the School of Special Flying or 'Some Sticky Fingers' by the wags. Six flights were formed, five to train instructors in a three-week intensive course, while the sixth flight, based at Fort Rowner, was to train new pupils and test out any new training ideas that might emerge.

The decentralisation of the RFC Training Branch in January 1917 meant that No. 3 Reserve Squadron at Shoreham was transferred to Eastern Command Group and renamed, perhaps more appropriately, No. 3 Training Squadron. From May onwards it gave new pilots a six-week basic course of flying training with a minimum of three hours dual and three hours solo. By mid-summer it had converted to Avro 504Ks and was using the new methods of training advocated by Smith-Barry. Even so, Shoreham struck a bad patch for the six weeks from late August to September, when four trainees were killed in flying accidents, three of whom were South African and one a French Canadian.

The first was Second Lieutenant W.T. Harries, who crashed at Ecclesden Farm near Angmering at six o'clock on the evening of 21 August. Three women on the Downs saw him flying low, but did not realise he was in difficulty. Then he managed to clear some trees when the nose of the aircraft dropped and the aircraft crashed – the pilot apparently jumping clear of the machine. The aircraft fell 20 yards away from the women, who discovered the pilot lying on his side. He died within a few minutes. Flight Commander T.S. Stewart, an instructor with 'A' Flight, told the coroner that the deceased had been at Shoreham for three weeks. He had made excellent progress, making nineteen solo flights and landings, and was one of the best pupils he had had for some time. When the aircraft dived, the deceased would have been thrown out if he was not strapped in. No defect could be found with the machine and it had been checked before flight. A verdict of accidental death was returned by the coroner's jury.

The second fatal accident occurred early on the morning of Monday, 3 September, T.C. Kinkead crashing at Ham Bridge, Worthing. Flight Commander Stewart was again at the inquest, and said that he was flying with a pupil at 2,000ft when he saw an aircraft some 1,000ft above them. The machine started to spiral round at about their height and then made a number of vertical banks, reducing his height to about 1,000ft and making for the airfield. Stewart said he followed him and by now Kinkead's aircraft was at about 250ft and was obviously looking for a place to land. Stewart said he thought Kinkead had throttled back his engine and in consequence lost flying speed. This was his second solo flight; he had done four hours' dual flight previously. Kinkead had, in Stewart's view, made an excellent descent and kept his head well when the engine had failed. If he had been nearer Shoreham or open fields, he would probably have made a safe landing. Another verdict of accidental death was returned.

The third accident happened to the French Canadian Lieutenant A.A. Leger on 11 September. A visitor to Rustington said that on 6.30pm on Tuesday evening he saw an aircraft flying inland at about 1,000ft. The machine then came towards the beach and he heard two cracks and saw something fall from the machine. The aircraft flew on for a minute or two, then turned on its left side, straightened out, and finally came down in the water. The crashed aircraft was about a quarter of a mile from the shore when it struck the water and turned over. A student on holiday in the area said he swam to the scene, but despite numerous dives around the aircraft he could not find the pilot, whose body was recovered on the Wednesday morning.

Flight Commander Stewart again appeared at the third inquest, although Leger was not in his flight. He told the coroner that Leger was twenty-two years old, had ten hours in the air and was thoroughly competent. In his view the accident had been caused by the exhaust manifold fouling the propeller, and he thought that when Leger realised what had happened, he was looking for a place to land when the crash occurred. Another accidental death verdict was returned.

The fourth and final accident happened on 6 September, when V.S. Edmunds, who was on his third solo flight, side-slipped and crashed. This time his instructor, Lieutenant H.V. Jerrard, appeared saying the airman had been an exceptionally good pupil and quite capable of going up on his own. The accident was purely an error of judgement through inexperience and another verdict of accidental death was returned. All four of these men were buried at the Old Shoreham Cemetery by St Nicholas Church across the River Adur from Shoreham airfield.

When Foot came back to England, he was recruited to join a number of other experienced fighter pilots, including Albert Ball, to form a new elite Squadron, No. 56, which was to be equipped with the S.E.5. Foot was selected to lead the squadron on its flight to France on 7 April, taking off from London Colney airfield. Unfortunately, Foot, who had attended the previous night's farewell party at the Black Swan at Radlett, crashed his car, a Métallurgique, on the way back to the camp and was injured. He was, therefore, somewhat under a cloud and was relieved when, on his recovery, he was asked by Smith-Barry to join him at Gosport. Given command of the sixth flight to train new pilots – thirteen of them – training commenced on 3 September, and they gave an impressive demonstration on 14 September to a visiting party from the Training Division of solo acrobatics and formation flying that took them aback. A report was called for by Smith-Barry on his methods of tuition so that they could be standardised throughout the division.

But Foot was incapable of keeping out of trouble; a month later he started to chase a hare across the airfield in his Avro with a pupil. The hare soon started to zig-zag, so Foot jammed on full rudder, forgetting how light the Avro was on its tail control. A wingtip hit the ground and the aircraft piled up into a mass of wreckage. His pupil, although uninjured, was unconscious, while Foot had multiple fractures of the leg. However, he insisted on having his photograph taken before he was removed from the wreckage. When his pupil awoke, he had no recollection of the crash and Foot reprimanded him for falling asleep under instruction. The episode that was to crown Foot's reputation among his fellow pilots happened when his mother visited him in hospital and he was on the mend. His mother suggested they might go out for a drive, but Foot insisted on driving despite her protests, crashed and she broke her leg.

Stanley Vincent was also asked by Smith-Barry to join him at Gosport, and he became a flight commander. However, his pleasure was rather short-lived when he crashed and his ageing Avro broke up in the air, an interplane strut falling off. He was in a coma for five days, but his parents were cheered up by a visit to the hospital by Smith-Barry, who typically told them that if there was anything the doctor said he ought not have, he would get it for him without delay. It was several months before Vincent was back on his feet. He paid a visit on Smith-Barry, who welcomed him back and told him to take up any aircraft for a flight. Vincent flew back to the scene of the crash and found his nerve had not been affected by the incident. Smith-Barry was satisfied Vincent had recovered and put him in charge of a Special Instructors Flight, which was set up at Shoreham early in 1918. This was later expanded into the South Eastern Area Flying Instructors School, where the CO was Major Dirk Cloete, a South African.

In August, Harold Balfour also re-joined Smith-Barry and his old comrades from No. 60 Squadron. He related how Smith-Barry would emerge from his office at 9.30am to ensure all his aircraft were in the air. His flight commanders were all waiting with their engines running up in the hangars, so when he neared the first shed, they would open up their engines and roar out of the hangars at top speed to climb away before he reached the edge of the tarmac, to their mutual delight. There is also a story of one ex-No. 60 Squadron pilot, Captain E.O. Grenfell, who came on the course and celebrated his passing out with an uproarious party. Next morning, he had to be carried out to his aircraft for the flight back to his home station. On his return his commanding officer sent a telegram to Smith-Barry asking plaintively, 'What have you done to him? He landed in the hangar without taxying or crashing!'

Vincent said that all the instructors at Shoreham worked hard but relaxed in the summer evenings by flying off after tea to look for country houses with parklands. Here a 'forced landing' was contrived so fellow pilots would have to land to render assistance. Depending on whether or not charming females appeared, repairs could be extended or completed in a few minutes for the next visit.

Vincent also tells how, in returning by air from Eastchurch with a fellow instructor, there was a loud bang and a complete cylinder head blew off, going straight through the cowling before disappearing into space. This caused a terrifying unbalance in the engine, so Vincent had to shut it down and managed to glide into a nearby field. They contacted Shoreham by telephone and then borrowed a bicycle tool kit from a passing girl cyclist and dismantled the aircraft for transport back to the airfield. This incident had an amusing sequence a while later when Vincent was flying over Lancing College with an instructor under training, and another cylinder parted company from the engine. Without batting an eyelid, Vincent told the pupil via his Gosport Tube that as he could see a cylinder head had blown off, the first thing to do was etc etc. When they landed, the instructor asked if this was what the cylinder head always did? If it was part of the course, he was highly impressed!

The School at Shoreham was in operation for about a year without any serious accident, the only injury occurring when another instructor under training, who was due to take up an Avro for a solo flight, decided not to run up the engine before take-off as it had only just landed. In the meantime, a mechanic arrived who was unaware of the situation and lay across the tailplane to keep it down for the normal engine run-up. The airman, therefore, took off with the mechanic clinging to the tail for dear life. His weight on the tail meant the aircraft was climbing steeply, despite the pilot's efforts to level off. Looking back, the pilot realised why. He managed a circuit of the airfield, hotly pursued by the station ambulance and the fire tender. By switching his engine on and off, the pilot managed to lose height, stall and make a flat spin into the soft mud alongside the River Adur on the airfield boundary. The mechanic succeeded in jumping off before impact and falling into the mud without injury. The pilot was not so lucky – he was gripping the fuselage sides so tightly the shock of landing broke one of his wrists.

Chapter 13

New Aspects of War – The Submarine Zeppelin and the Bomber

The First World War brought into play two new forms of warfare, aircraft and submarines; the latter leading the development of the British non-rigid airship and the flying boat. The submarine in particular, as the conflict progressed, came close to inducing the defeat of Britain by cutting off its supply of food and war materials from overseas. Indeed, it was only by the use of aircraft and airships over the shipping lanes – with the eventual introduction of the convoy system – that the menace was overcome.

The long-heralded and feared air raids by Zeppelins and Gotha aircraft on this country caused more psychological trauma than actual destruction. However, it did result in a large number of men, guns and aircraft being retained on the Home Front that could otherwise have been deployed on the various war fronts.

By 1915 the blockade established by the Allies on Germany was well into its stride, denying the enemy food and war material. At this time international maritime law did not permit a merchant ship to be sunk without at first being inspected for prohibited cargo, which inhibited submarine warfare by the German Navy. Even then, a U-Boat commander was held responsible for the safety of any captured crew. This effectively shackled the offensive capacity of the German submarine service, so it came as no surprise when the Kaiser issued a proclamation in February 1915, authorising U-Boat commanders to sink any ship encountered in the war zone around the British Isles. In just three months, over 100,000 tons of Allied shipping was lost.

At a hastily convened meeting at the Admiralty at the end of February, the First Sea Lord, Admiral Fisher, met with his foremost airship experts in an effort to counter this threat. At this stage in the war the Royal Navy had only about 180 aircraft and a lesser number of seaplanes. The latter had a range of only about 100 miles and could take off only from calm water. Their engines were unreliable, and their disposable load for carrying bombs and ammunition was small, so they could not really sustain any continuous anti-submarine patrols. It was therefore decided that some sort of airship would have to be developed and put into production without delay, as at that time the Navy had only three serviceable airships. Fisher estimated that some forty to fifty airships would be needed initially, and amazingly they built the prototype in three weeks. They did this by using a spare envelope from Farnborough and suspending beneath it a B.E.2c aircraft fuselage, minus its tail and wings but with the standard 70hp Renault engine. The prototype was passed to the first of the proposed airship stations at Capel, Kent for tests, and was approved for operational use. These airships were non-rigid (there was no supporting structure inside the envelope) and they became better known as blimps. There are a number of stories as to where this nickname came from, the best concerned the Short Brothers. Their firm was now busily designing and building seaplanes for the Navy but they did receive a tender to build a prototype airship like other firms. Oswald and Eustace Short were anxious to demonstrate their expertise in this field and showed off the result proudly to Horace. At that stage it was only partially inflated. Horace looked at it and, turning to his two brothers, said, 'You call that an airship, Eustace? It's too b***** limp!' Although the Short tender was not accepted, probably because of their other commitments, they did supply valves and other items needed for their construction. But the name stuck and the blimp it would be.

On 8 May 1915 the first of the non-rigid airship stations was set up at Capel, and the second was located at Polegate, near Eastbourne, which had been earmarked as a possible airfield in 1914. The situation turned out to be less than ideal since it was in the lee of the Downs, the sheds and landing ground being backed by a series of 600ft hills. Pilots, therefore, often had difficulty in landing due to the vicinity of the surrounding hills. Once work started, the conditions on the site became atrocious, the ground turning into a morass of heavy clay.

The first airship shed, which was erected by Messrs Arrol Ltd, was 300ft long, 70ft wide and 50ft high, and was waterlogged for months. The officers posted to the unit were billeted in two thatched cottages at Wannock, and the ratings were billeted at Polegate, Wannock and Willingdon. The most urgent need was to get the station operational by putting down paths and roads, and the servicemen had to undertake most of this work themselves. Perhaps not unnaturally, this was the subject of many grumbles, the general complaint being they had joined the Navy not the Navvies! On 6 July the first of the new SS (Submarine Scout) airships was commissioned at Polegate and started patrols along the Channel, and by the end of the year three blimps were in use.

In September the Kaiser, who had been taken aback by the strong reaction of the neutral nations, and in particular America, withdrew his order to allow unrestricted submarine warfare. However, with only twenty submarines, the Germans had sunk over a quarter of a million tons of shipping and it was clear that their threat was only postponed. In the meantime, the Germans were building up their U-Boat fleet with larger and longer-range boats. By March 1916 the attacks on Allied ships increased, although they were still not allowed to attack unarmed merchantmen without prior warning. By the middle of 1916 the German submarine fleet had expanded, and by the end of the year, 100 submarines were in action.

At Polegate the crews on the SS airships were gaining experience in handling their vessels. The Renault engine was constantly overheating as it had been designed for use in an aircraft with twice the speed of the airships, so its cooling was inadequate. One crew at Polegate, Lieutenant McConnel and his wireless operator/mechanic Parkinson, soon became expert at climbing out of the blimp while on patrol at 3,000ft to locate an engine fault, fixing it and then restarting the engine by swinging the propeller from behind while retaining a hold by gripping the skid undercarriage between their knees. In time they became so good at it that, should the engine misfire, they would stop it and then one of them would climb out and clean and replace the plugs before swinging the propeller and resuming patrol. It was not long before this practice became standard on the station.

On one occasion early on, the SS13 suffered engine failure some 30 miles south of Beachy Head and all attempts to restart the engine failed. The crew wirelessed for help and Lieutenant McConnel took off in SS9, met the stricken blimp over the sea, secured its trail rope and passed it down to a destroyer, which towed the SS13 back to Newhaven. At about this time, Polegate erected and tested some four SS airships, which were sent to the Italians for their use. Another blimp originally allocated to Polegate was the SS40. This was later painted black and sent to France, where it was used for night reconnaissance, which included dropping Allied agents behind German lines, before this work was transferred to the aircraft of the RFC.

On 16 June the complement at Polegate was fourteen officers and 137 ratings. The initial training for airship crews took place at Wormwood Scrubs, now better known for its prison. Here the young naval officers received basic naval training and were initiated into the mysteries of airships. Free-balloon flights were undertaken from Hurlingham Polo Grounds where, pre-war, the Royal Aero Club held its balloon races and competitions. Their training included laying out and filling balloons with coal gas from the nearby gasworks and untethered flights over the surrounding countryside. One trainee recollected a flight with Lieutenant Colonel Pollack (of Eastbourne crossing fame), who had to reprove one young and less serious-minded cadet who was bombarding the bus at Marble Arch with currant buns. Each would-be aeronaut had to make two solo balloon flights, one in daylight and one at night. One pupil got as far as Crowborough Beacon and then decided to land, as the wind was blowing him seawards. After valving the gas, he made quite a respectable landing at Mill Hill Farm at Hellingly, near Eastbourne. Here he was welcomed by the farmer, his four pretty daughters and their cousin Sue. After a very enjoyable tea, he was finally rushed to the nearby station, just in time to catch the last train after a struggle to load his deflated balloon and basket into the guard's van.

Cadets who passed their tests were sent to operational units to complete their training on blimps, with some thirty officers being given instruction at Polegate in 1916. The hands-on training involved maintaining height, course, gas pressure, engine speed and equilibrium. The speed and duration of the wind had to be

177

gauged and combined with the airship speed to calculate ground speed to enable position to be plotted. The pilot also had to remember to pump petrol from the main tank to the gravity tank every half hour. Then every two hours, the oil had to be pumped up as well. There was no means of knowing how much oil was in the sump, so the rule of thumb method was to put the blimp in a short pitching motion, and if this resulted in a blueish white smoke coming from the exhausts that was said to indicate that there was sufficient oil.

By the middle of 1916 the building work had been completed at Polegate and officers and ratings were living in huts and feeding in their own messes. One local market gardener laid out flower beds, and life took on a more agreeable and civilised aspect. The station was only a few miles from Eastbourne, with its many attractions that could be sampled on 'shore leave'. There were two swimming baths, a roller-skating rink, theatres, a music hall, cinemas and many public houses. By now the camp had its own football and rugby teams, which played other service camps in the area.

Thought was now being given to the design of a new and larger airship, with a longer range and an increased crew, to be mainly used for patrols in the North Sea and Western Approaches. The chosen envelope capacity was 150,000 cubic feet, and the prototype again used the existing envelope that had originally been supplied for the Asta Torres airship. One of these airships had made a flight from Kingsnorth to Pevensey Bay and back in 1915, a journey lasting some nine hours. The new airship was to have two engines, one a tractor and the other a pusher, which caused problems in the design of the car to hold the crew. In the end two Avro 510 fuselages were fixed together, although the later production models had special cars built for them. These were made by the Frederick Sage Company Ltd, whose manager was now Eric Gordon England, assisted by Herman Volk. The engines gave the airship a top speed of around 50mph with a crew of four consisting of a pilot, coxswain, observer and a wireless operator/mechanic. To increase the range, one of the crew was left out.

The first of these Coastal-class airships entered service in June 1916, and some two weeks later the C12 was delivered to

Polegate. It was never very popular with the Polegate crews or the senior staff. It was basically unstable and this meant it was unpleasant to fly in bad weather. This, of course, made it difficult to land and – although experience improved this somewhat – the basic instability problem was never overcome. The senior officers at Polegate railed against the retention of the C12 because it not only needed an augmented handling party for take-off and landing, but also needed much more maintenance. Less than twelve months later they finally convinced the Admiralty, and it was withdrawn to be replaced by two of the new SS Zero airships. These blimps were probably the most successful of all the various models of airships produced. Some seventy-six were in service in all, this time powered by the well-tried 75hp Rolls-Royce Hawk engine, which proved much more reliable. Even so, they were only marginally faster than the old SS airships. The envelope was 143ft long, 39ft wide and 47ft deep, with gas capacity 70,000 cubic ft. The boat-shaped car accommodated three crew: an observer in the front with a Lewis gun, a pilot and then the mechanic in the rear with the engine behind him. The new car was not only more robust but much more comfortable for long patrols. The main advantage of the Zero airships were that they had a duration of seventeen hours, which in practice could be much extended. By September 1917 Polegate had six SS Zeros in service.

Polegate was also selected for trials involving the testing of methods of mooring an airship at sea, including the use of canvas bucket drogues. The SS10 took part in this experiment, which was carried out in the Channel with a 16mph wind blowing WSW, the grapnel lines being used for the drogue, which replaced the grapnel. This was lowered from 100ft and the airship was trimmed and the engine throttled back. When the engine stopped, the ship rode steadily into the wind. Breeze was slight after thirty minutes, and the trial was adjudged a success. Another trial took place with two Calthrop parachutes on 16 July 1916. These parachutes, which were known by the rather cloying name of 'Guardian Angels', were fitted to the SS13 and a static line was used to open them. Released from 2,000 and 1,100ft with weights equivalent to a 12st man, both descended successfully. In August three more experiments were carried out with the same type of parachute. Two carried dummies, while the third had Sir Bryan Leighton attached. The three descents were made from 900ft and were also successful. They were said at the time to be the first descent from an airship, which it may have been from this particular type.

It was near the end of 1916 that the Polegate Station was visited by the then Prime Minister, Lord Herbert Henry Asquith. By February 1917 the Kaiser had again ordered his submarine crews to sink any merchant ships in the war zone. The Germans now had over 100 U-Boats in action and in the first month of this order 450,000 tons of shipping were lost, in the second 500,000 tons, and in April 850,000 tons. Although this was the month in which the United States entered the war, the Germans were becoming increasingly confident that they could starve Britain into surrender before any substantial aid could get through from America. At long last, in May 1917 the convoy system was introduced, and it was also decided that, while the airships had proved their worth in discouraging U-Boats, some more direct offensive action was needed that could only come from the more extensive use of aircraft. Initially this meant using seaplanes, although it eventually emerged that with the gradual increase of reliability in engines, land planes often had a greater range and increased bomb-carrying capacity.

As part of this new offensive drive, the 5-acre shingle foreshore at Newhaven, on the eastern side of the harbour, was selected as an RNAS seaplane base, which opened in May 1917. Four Short 184 seaplanes were used for the four to five-hour patrols in the Channel from dawn to dusk, covering Dungeness to the Isle of Wight. The station billets were at Bishopstone, which had a farmhouse, a farm and a few cottages, the officers' mess being in a long building known as the 'Tidemill'. The village was only just above sea level at high tide, and two large hangars were built on a shingle bank, where maintenance was undertaken. The base was about half a mile from the harbour wall, which gave some shelter from the south-westerly and west winds. The Short 184 seaplane, with its 260hp engine, was theoretically capable of carrying a 112lb bomb and two 50-pounders, a Lewis gun for the observer and a wireless with a Morse key, although the latter was rarely used.

In fact, if the seaplane was new or had been overhauled recently it could just about struggle off the water with such a load, but the continually damp conditions in which it operated caused the fabric covering to slacken and then absorb even more moisture. Thus, it would eventually be necessary to remove one bomb, two or, in extremis, all of the armament. The current view of the pilots was that even if a submarine was sighted it would probably submerge before the seaplane could get into a position to attack it, so that it was not all that important anyway.

Handling, starting and launching a large seaplane was an art in itself. In front of the hangar on the flat, the tail float was 5ft off the ground. To get the seaplane in the water it had to be mounted on a two-wheeled trolley by the handling crew. They pulled down the tail and rocked the seaplane backwards and forwards on to the heel of the two floats so that the trolley could be more easily eased underneath, then the tail would be lifted from the trestle and balanced so that the aircraft was slightly tail-heavy on the trolley. The trestle would then be replaced under the tail and the bombs and guns, plus any other gear, loaded aboard. The tail would next be lifted away from the trestle and the seaplane slowly pushed to the head of the slipway with a cable hitched to the trolley. It was then gently lowered down the slipway and two chocks held ready, as the seaplane had to be stopped at the slipway just before the floats entered the water. The pilot and observer then clambered into their cockpits and the safety pins of the bombs removed and given to the observer to retain so that he could prove if the bombs were released and failed to explode that they had been armed before take-off.

The pilot would use a system of compressed air from two air bottles to start the engine as the propellers were too large to start by hand swinging. He then signalled to the handling crew to hold the tail while the seaplane was slowly winched down until the floats took the weight. The cable was then released and the handling crew lowered the seaplane into the water. A quick burst of the engine with the joystick fully forward took the floats clear of the trolley, and the engine then had to be throttled back to stop the seaplane nose diving. Finally, the seaplane was taxied out to its position for take-off. When the wind was between south and south-west, the seaplane could be headed into the wind for take-off, but in flat calm conditions it would be almost impossible to get off as the floats often refused to 'unstick' from the water.

There was an area of smooth water at Newhaven, provided by the harbour arm, and with an offshore wind it was possible, but only just, to taxi out far enough to take off towards the beach. Even if the pilot got the seaplane off the water, he then had to gain sufficient height to clear the beach and then turn seawards again. One pilot tried this, found he had insufficient height and in his situation turned to starboard to try and gain the open sea. With an underpowered and overladen aircraft (they had to remove a 50lb bomb before starting to get off at all), the machine failed to climb and the aircraft hit the sea at 60mph. This was a third faster than their normal landing speed and the float undercarriage collapsed, the nose dipped, and the seaplane turned over in the water. The observer, who was not strapped in, flew out of the aircraft and struck the pilot's head as he whizzed past before plunging into the sea. The pilot, on the other hand, was so securely strapped in that he was trapped under the sea until he managed to release himself and swim to the surface. The observer, meanwhile, had managed to scramble on to the wing, where he found that the arming vane on the 112lb bomb had become unwound, leaving the striker free to hit the detonator and explode the bomb. He hastily rifled his pockets to find the arming pin and fit it back to make the bomb safe. The pilot then surfaced, was hauled aboard and they waited for the rescue boat to appear. Both men were saved.

On the following day another pilot attempted to take off in a south-west wind in the lee of the harbour wall with fatal results. After two unsuccessful attempts to rise, he yanked on the stick when he got close to the wall. The Short refused to take off, the tail dropped, and the seaplane hit the wall at about 40mph, this time killing both the pilot and observer.

One of the worst airship accidents occurred near Polegate on 20 December 1917. Four airships, SSZ6, 7, 10 and 19, took off on patrol, but deterioration of the weather led to them being recalled. By then, snow flurries and thick stratus cloud made it impossible for them to reach base safely. They were, therefore, ordered to scatter in open country and make independent landings. The crew of SSZ6 were lucky as they landed near a country house and were soon enjoying roast pheasant and vintage port. SSZ7 and 19 descended near a Coastguard hut at Beachy Head, and were secured and told to stop there. SSZ10, with a transmitter out of action, landed on farmland between Jevington and Willingdon. By 8pm forecasts of gale winds resulted in instructions for SSZ7 and 19 to return to Polegate, and SSZ19 reached the base safely. SSZ7 was going northwards towards East Dean with the observer using his Aldis lamp to try and recognise landmarks. Suddenly and unexpectedly, they came on SSZ10 fogbound on the ground. Lieutenant Swallow, in charge of SSZ7, at once applied the elevator, but it caught on the fabric of the grounded airship, tearing it, and the exhaust of the SSZ7's engine ignited the escaping gas. The two air mechanics on the SSZ7 jumped clear but suffered severe internal injuries. The SSZ7 then shot into the air, blazing from stem to stern, and fell to earth, Lieutenant Swallow dying in the burning wreckage, which fell close to the two injured men. By then a ground party had arrived, and two air mechanics, Steere and Robinson, removed and carried away two red hot bombs from the SSZ10 before they could explode. Lieutenant Waters – who was in charge – suffered a shattered arm when another bomb exploded and it had to be amputated later. The two air mechanics were subsequently awarded the Albert Medal in gold for their bravery, and the officer got the medal in bronze. An inquiry into the tragedy concluded that the accident was the result of sheer bad luck in the appalling weather conditions.

The seaplane patrols that were flown east to Dungeness or west to the Isle of Wight gave a wide berth to Portsmouth and usually kept a height of 1,000ft as the naval anti-aircraft gunners were perfectly happy to fire on both friend and foe. One observer prided himself that in the case of engine failure he could sent out an SOS call with his call sign before the seaplane came down in the water. The alternative was to scribble a message on special paper, which could be clipped to a pigeon's leg. To release the pigeon in flight involved holding it in both hands and throwing it downwards and forwards to avoid it hitting the tail and falling in the water. Two pigeons were provided for a further try if the first was unsuccessful.

In fine weather the seaplane crews would fly along the coast, especially in summer, and wave to the girls on the beach, and those walking along the promenade. This led to the commanding officer calling all the crews to his office to read them a message from the area commander pointing out that there were no submarines in the Brighton Aquarium! Early morning patrols were not very popular, crews had to get up at 3.45am, when they were given a mug of lukewarm cocoa and a biscuit before making their way to the slipway and their waiting seaplane. It was normal practice to maintain one aircraft on patrol in daylight, weather permitting and subject to the availability of serviceable machines, aircrew and mechanics. One pilot who was forced to return home with engine trouble had been escorting a merchant ship from Dungeness to Beachy Head. He was just pointing out the ship, on landing, to a fellow pilot, which was now rounding the head of the Seven Sisters cliffs, when they saw a column of water shoot some 30ft high abaft the bow and the ship started to sink. She had been torpedoed, but as she was so close to shore rescue boats soon saved the crew. This part of the coast was always clouded, so it was not easy to spot U-Boats.

On 7 July 1918 Lieutenant Ackery took off from Newhaven with his new observer, Lieutenant Dangerfield, to escort a convoy up the Channel to Dungeness. The ships were soon sighted off Hastings, and the wearisome task of circling the convoy began. Suddenly the two airmen saw a line of foam streaking seaward and south, heading for the lead ship. They at once realised that it was a torpedo track but at the very last moment it seemed to veer off course and just pass in front of the ship. Ackery was upwind and quickly turned and headed in the direction of the wake of the torpedo. To his astonishment, he saw the submarine surfacing, seemingly oblivious to the approaching aircraft. First the conning tower appeared and then the hull, streaming with water. The bomb sight of those days was pretty rudimentary, consisting of a fixed sight with a moveable cross wire. As neither Ackery nor Dangerfield had had any chance to practise their bombing as a team, the actual bombing run became rather a frenzied affair. The drill they had been taught was for the observer to stand up in the cockpit and place his hands on the pilot's head and move it either left or right to direct him to the target. Dangerfield had already dropped the camera over the side in the initial excitement at seeing the submarine, so was by now a little overwrought. In consequence, Ackery found his head was being wrenched rather than positioned, but they both felt the bump of their 112lb bomb leaving the bomb rack and looked over the side. To their delight they saw the bomb had struck the water 6ft away from the submarine on the midships of the rapidly diving boat. When the spray from the explosion cleared, the submarine had disappeared, but they saw oil coming to the surface. They signalled their base and continued to circle the area. Meanwhile the convoy, which seemed oblivious to all the excitement, had moved off into the distance. In a short time, naval vessels came on the scene, followed at a more stately pace by a blimp from Polegate.

The pair received a hero's welcome on their return to Newhaven, as this was the first time that No. 242 Squadron, which had taken over from the RNAS in April 1918, had actually attacked a submarine. Although a 'kill' could not be claimed, an oil slick was seen in the area of the bombing for several days afterwards. At that time ship's crews were paid prize money for sunken ships, so an aircraft with a two-man crew could gain quite a substantial sum if they sunk a submarine.

A few days later there was another fatal accident at Newhaven when a newcomer took off close to the shore towards the beach, which he just cleared, although for some reason he did not turn back towards the sea. When he did come back low down and very wide, onlookers relaxed, convinced he was now alright. Suddenly the aircraft dipped and crashed into the brickwork of the Tide Mill sluices on the camp, both airmen being killed instantly. Although such incidents could not be forgotten, especially the total silence after the horrifying sound of the impact of splintering wood and tearing fabric, life had to go on. In the evenings, crews would visit Brighton or Eastbourne for their entertainment. Brighton was preferred because it was more lively. One group of pilots and observers had a box in the music hall, and took some dried peas with them, which they flicked at the kettle drum in the orchestra pit. When the magician came on and brought out his pigeons, a shower of peas descended on the stage and the group

185

had to leave rather hurriedly. The pigeons – which had enjoyed the unexpected provender – had in the meantime given up any interest in their role in the performance.

In the House of Commons debate on the Army Vote in 1909, the question of air raids had been raised and one MP ridiculed the idea that a town like Brighton would be bombed in any future conflict. Another admitted that it was in the bounds of probability that a naval base such as Portsmouth might be attacked from the air. The transfer of practically all of the RFC to France led the Admiralty with some reluctance to take over the task of air defence of the British Isles. Fortunately, the Germans lost several airships early in the war and initially had no arsenal of aerial bombs for attacks on this country.

Reginald John Bone, a former pupil at Eastbourne Flying School, who had served for a while with Commander Samson in Dunkirk, returned to this country early in 1916 to be given the command of a small unit at Detling in Kent. By now the Germans were sending over seaplanes to attack east coast towns, particularly on Sundays when they thought the British would be off guard and having their Sunday lunch. Bone, anticipating a raid on 19 March, put sandwiches and a flask of coffee in his Nieuport on the runway and awaited events. There was a raid at Margate and Bone soon got into the air, but it took him all of his time to try and catch up with the raider, who by then was making for home. He did eventually succeed and managed to get in a good burst of machine gun fire. The German seaplane went into a steep dive but flattened out to land on the water, the pilot – it would seem – having been shot in the ankle. As this was the first 'hit and run' raider shot down, Flight Commander Bone was awarded an immediate DSO.

The first Zeppelin attack on London took place in May 1915, and on the night of 26 September 1916 the greatest of all the Zeppelin commanders, Captain Mathy, made landfall at Dungeness, Kent, at 9.30pm in his craft, L31. Because of the excellent visibility, he decided to go for a target off the normal defence patrol area. Mathy turned out to sea again north of the Isle of Wight and approached Portsmouth at about ten minutes to midnight. His airship was soon picked up by the searchlights over the city, and Mathy later reported that he dropped his bombs on Portsmouth and the dockyard. No reports of any explosions in the area were ever received, so it must be assumed the bombs were either not fused or perhaps even 'duds'. The airship then turned and passed over St Leonards at 1.15am on the way back to its base. The only aircraft that attempted to intercept L31 were two seaplanes from Calshot, but they failed to make contact.

The apparent gap in the air defence system was deemed serious enough for the War Office, which had now taken over air defence, to redeploy No. 37 Squadron, which was forming at Chelmsford. In the event this did not prove necessary, because No. 78 Squadron was due to form on 1 November with its HQ at Hove and airfields at Telscombe Cliffs (between Peacehaven and Newhaven) and the Chiddingly Causeway near Tonbridge in Kent. The Telscombe airfield was ready by September, but it was not until a month or so later that No. 78 Squadron took up occupation, although No. 50 Squadron did use it occasionally in the interim, to plug the gap.

The Telscombe Cliff airfield was 120ft above sea level on the chalk downs, covering 1,500ft × 1,500ft. Two canvas Bessoneau hangars were used to house No. 78's six aircraft, a mixture of B.E.2c and B.E.12 biplanes. Living conditions during the winter were particularly spartan for the men, who mostly lived in tents, the officers being billeted in the area. Regular patrols were made, but in February 1917 it was decided that the end of the Zeppelin raids meant that the ever-increasing demands of the Western Front should be met from Home Defence squadrons, which could be run down accordingly. On 7 March, No. 78 Squadron, which had an establishment of twenty-four pilots and eighteen aircraft for the two airfields, actually had only five pilots and four aircraft, and also had a unit at Gosport.

On the night of 16/17 March, five Zeppelins, four of which had been modified to increase their height ceiling and one new airship, made an attack on London, but this was badly affected by the weather and was not a success. Neither was the first operational sortie on that night by No. 78 Squadron from Telscombe Cliffs. Second Lieutenant D.D. Fowler, who took off in a B.E.2c at one minute past midnight, crashed nine minutes later, a mile and a half from the airfield.

The aircraft was almost completely burnt out when found and the pilot dead. It was thought Fowler might have had some sort of mechanical trouble and was returning to the airfield when he crashed. This was only ever surmised, as examination of the burnt wreckage failed to produce a firm conclusion. Fowler was buried in the cemetery at Rottingdean Church.

Nevertheless, the official view that the Zeppelin attacks were diminishing proved correct, but a new menace was provided by the Gotha bombers. These machines were twin-engined biplanes with a wingspan of 72ft and were powered by two 260hp Mercedes engines. They cruised at 70mph, had a ceiling of 17,000ft, and could carry seven 100lb bombs and six 25-pounders. Most of the obsolete aircraft used by the RFC for air defence did not have this performance, and operating individually, rather than in squadrons, found the Gotha formations formidable opposition. On their first daylight raid on London on 13 June 1917, one of the seventy-odd bombs they dropped fell upon an infant school, killing sixteen children (only two of whom were over five years old) and injured another thirty. The public outcry over this, and the sight of German bombers seemingly dropping their bombs at will over the capital, was not easily placated. Urgent Cabinet meetings were held, and it was agreed to double the strength of the fighters, and a squadron was brought back from France. After a further daylight raid on 7 July there was even more public dismay and a demand for action, with yet more Cabinet meetings. Four days later, a committee was set up, nominally under the Prime Minister Lloyd George, to examine air defence and the organization of the RFC, but the actual work was done by Lieutenant Colonel J.C. Smuts. An interim report was made, recommending that air defence should be under the control of one man, which was adopted. This led to a steady improvement in interception and destruction of a fleet of German bombers. In the main report, Smuts recommended that an Independent Air Arm should be formed, and the Royal Air Force came into being on 1 April 1918, despite some opposition.

There is little doubt that the raids on London, which were not particularly effective from a military point of view, roused the public and pressurised the authorities into shaking up and drastically re-thinking the air defence of Great Britain. The lessons learned were still very much in the minds of the senior officers in the RAF between the two wars, with the result that, although the Battle of Britain in 1940 was a close-run thing, it showed that those early lessons had been heeded.

From May to August 1917 the aircraft at Telscombe Cliffs made a number of sorties as a result of warnings of Gotha raids. The highest number of aircraft put up at one time was four, but as most of the raids were directed at the coastal towns in Kent, their efforts were largely wasted. At the end of that period it was decided to close down the airfield and by the end of September 1917, No. 78 Squadron had moved to Sutton's Farm in Essex.

At sea, the introduction of the convoy system, combined with the use of more aircraft, meant that U-Boats were now shifting their attacks to coastal waters. Most ships were now sunk within 10 miles of the coast, and one suggestion was that aircraft patrols over the Channel should be increased to twenty-minute intervals to keep the U-Boats away from coastal shipping channels. By the beginning of 1918 the RFC had a substantial number of surplus training aircraft, now that the Avro 504K had been made the standard trainer. The de Havilland DH.6, designed by one of Britain's most prolific and effective designers, had not been a success. Some 300 were now surplus to requirements, a most unusual situation. The engine was not particularly reliable, and the aircraft was underpowered, so only a 100lb bomb and a lightweight wireless could be carried without an observer. Telscombe Cliffs airfield was reactivated, as were many others around the coast and Special Duty Flights formed. The one at Telscombe was first named A Flight of No. 253 Squadron, but subsequently renumbered 514 Flight, becoming part of No. 242 Squadron, which had two other flights located at Newhaven.

There were six DH.6s, and a complement of twelve officers, five warrant Officers and NCOs and thirty airmen at Telscombe Cliffs. Most of the units operated in makeshift and difficult conditions, and forced landings at sea were by no means uncommon. It was found, however, that the DH.6 had one great virtue; whatever its other faults, it was not only stable but floated for several hours when ditched. As far as is known, no DH.6 actually sank a submarine, in fact very few pilots actually saw one. They did, however, help to reduce the number of ships sunk in coastal waters. A memo from the CO of No. 18 Group said:

> It is considered considerable credit is due to the pilots who first undertook anti-submarine work, flying land machine over the sea, particularly in cases of those using the DH6 type, a training machine of poor performance, by no means suited to the work. It is to be remembered that these flights had to work under difficult conditions, in squadrons hastily organised with personnel under canvas, no repair facilities and in all cases a serious shortage of non-commissioned airmen in the technical grades.

Chapter 14

1917

The entry of the Americans into the war gave the Allies new hope, although it would take time for their fighting men to take their place in the line in France. It was accepted that, as far as aircraft were concerned, the US Air Service would have to rely on Britain and France for its supply until the American factories got production under way.

The Russian Revolution meant that the pressure on the Germans from the Eastern Front was waning, and the introduction of a new defence in depth system on the Western Front in the Hindenburg Line resulted in the Germans being able to withdraw some fifteen divisions to their reserve for future offensives.

It was now clear to both the Allies and Germany that if air superiority was to be achieved it was vital to have sufficient up-to-date aircraft and an effective organization for aircraft production and the right battle tactics. The German Air Service had been the first to grasp this nettle and had also organised its scout aircraft into fighter squadrons, or Jagdstaffeln, with fourteen aircraft each. These machines were flown by handpicked pilots, all experienced in aerial combat, and the sole purpose was to destroy Allied aircraft. They now had the new Albatross D biplane fighter with twin machine guns and a superior performance over any Allied aircraft, so they were, in fact, an even greater menace than the Fokker monoplane. Although new aircraft were in the pipeline for delivery to the RFC, only a trickle arrived in the early months of 1917. Even these suffered from teething troubles, inevitable with new designs, and often proved more trouble than they were worth, when the RFC was fighting for its life.

So it was that April 1917 became known as 'Bloody April' throughout the RFC, the Trenchard dictum of continuous offensive with inferior machines resulting in over a third of the flying personnel of the RFC being posted as killed or missing in that thirty-day period.

The long-awaited replacement for the B.E.2c and its variants started to appear early in 1917. Designed at the Royal Aircraft Factory at Farnborough, the R.E.8, or 'Harry Tate' as it was called, had the same wings and tailplane as the B.E., with a new fuselage. Only slightly faster than the B.E., it was no more manoeuvrable, although the pilot did have a forward-firing gun with interrupter gear and the observer a Lewis gun mounted on the new Scarff ring improving his field of fire. The other new machine from the factory was the S.E.5 single-seat fighter. The second prototype suffered a setback when Frank Goodden, the chief test pilot at Farnborough, took it up on 28 January. At 1,500ft, the port wing folded and Goodden was killed in the ensuing crash. An investigation showed that the failure was due to the inadequate strengthening of the compression ribs. These were redesigned and all earlier production aircraft modified, which eliminated the problem, Roderic Hill taking over the job of chief test pilot at Farnborough.

At this time the Bristol Aeroplane Company was also contemplating a replacement for the B.E. type. The outcome after the production of two prototypes was the Bristol F.2A, which was designed as a fighting aeroplane. It was a two-seater biplane, somewhat unusual in that there was a gap between the lower wing and the fuselage. This was reminiscent of the GE3 designed by Eric Gordon England for Bristol in 1912. The best version of the Bristol Fighter was the F.2B with the Rolls-Royce Falcon engine of 275hp. As the supply of these engines was limited, other powerplants were fitted with some loss of performance and reliability. The aircraft had a forward-firing Vickers with Constantinesco interrupter gear and one or two Lewis guns on a Scarff ring in the rear cockpit. Like the R.E.8, its first appearance over German lines was a disaster, six aircraft from No. 48 Squadron meeting up with five Albatros D.IIIs, one being piloted by the Red Baron, Richthofen, himself. Four Bristol Fighters were shot down, only two machines escaping, one of which was a write-off. At this time the pilots were using the aircraft like a two-seater and trying to give their gunners the opportunity to fire at the scouts. It was not long before the more offensively minded pilots, and particularly the Canadians, realised that the 'Brisfit', as it was now called, should be handled as a fighter, leaving the gunner to protect the tail. The prime exponent of this tactic was Lieutenant McKeever, a Canadian pilot who shot down thirty enemy aircraft, while his regular observer destroyed eight.

Major Evelyn Graves, who was educated at Brighton and was a pupil at Lancing College (1905–08), was a peacetime soldier and gunner. He served for four years with the 25th Battery in India, and returned to this country before transferring to the RFC in October 1914. A serious flying accident during training in February 1915 left him lame. After a period on the HQ Staff of the now Brigadier General J.F.A. Higgens, he returned to flying in December 1915, and was posted to No. 20 Squadron flying the F.E.2b. A report in the RFC Communique for the period 13–30 April 1916 refers to a five-aircraft reconnaissance, in which he participated, and which came under continuous enemy attack as soon as they crossed the line. The F.E.2b observers shot down two enemy scouts without any loss to themselves. Graves was later promoted to flight commander and then posted to No. 60 Squadron as CO when Smith-Barry left. At this time, early in 1917, the squadron had moved back to Le Hameau airfield. The weather at this time was exceptionally cold, guns froze in the air, and the pilots had to apply liberal amounts of whale oil to their faces to prevent frostbite.

On his sixth patrol, on 6 March, Major Graves saw eight enemy fighters attacking a lone F.E.2b and led his patrol into a dive to join the unequal combat. They were too late to save the F.E.2b and Graves himself was immediately attacked by a German fighter, which set his machine on fire. He crashed north of Riviere and his body, with a bullet through an eye, was found among the wreckage. Two of his patrol who had their guns jammed were damaged by enemy fire but managed to shake off their pursuers and get back to their airfield.

Artillery dominated the Western Front in 1917, Britain having overcome the shell shortage of the early war years. Millions of shells were now fired in preliminary bombardments and at the third battle of Ypres, 4.4 million shells were fired at a cost of £22 million. With the aid of aerial photography, which enabled detailed maps to be produced, and new methods of fire control, precision fire was now possible, eliminating the old area barrage.

This massive use of artillery increased the possibility of artillery observation aircraft being hit by shells fired by their own side. Second Lieutenant Oswald Ball – the son of the headmaster of the Shoreham Council Schools – was twenty-two years old when he joined the Royal Sussex Regiment on the outbreak of war. He later transferred to the RFC and learnt to fly. On 5 April 1917 he had been in France for seven months and was making an artillery spotting flight when heavy cloud forced him to descend and he came directly in the path of Allied shellfire. His aircraft received a direct hit and disintegrated. Second Lieutenant Denys Greenhow, another Lancing College boy, was not as fortunate as his brother, who was made a PoW late in 1915. Denys Greenhow had spent three months in France as an observer, when on 6 March, his aircraft was attacked by five enemy scouts. Although the pilot managed to land the aircraft, Greenhow subsequently died from his injuries.

The replacement for Major Graves as CO of No. 60 Squadron was Captain Alan John Lance Scott, a former flight commander with No. 43 Squadron, whose CO was Major Sholto Douglas. Scott was born in New Zealand in 1883; his father was of Irish descent but emigrated to New Zealand with his parents in the 1850s. Scott senior returned to England to complete his education and studied for the Bar, and practised for some years before returning to New Zealand to marry. His wife inherited Holbrook House, Horsham, in 1905, and the family returned to live there. Like his father, Alan Scott became a barrister, being a pupil in the chambers of the celebrated F.E. Smith pre-war, and was a keen supporter of all field sports. An officer in the Sussex Yeomanry, he later joined the RFC and, like the two previous incumbents of No. 60 Squadron, had a serious accident while learning to fly that broke both his legs, and even when mended, this resulted in him having to be lifted bodily into the cockpit of his aircraft. Through F.E. Smith he became a firm friend of Winston Churchill, who flew with him on a number of occasions. Cheerful and charming, he had friends in all strata of society. He was somewhat in the mould of Smith-Barry except he was an indifferent pilot, but had enormous courage and was always to be found in the thick of any dogfight. Unorthodox, tolerant and casual, he had a jaunty disregard for inconvenient regulations, often getting his way purely by force of character and stubbornness. One of his pilots said that his only flaw was that he thought the best of everyone, and sometimes accepted combat claims from pilots who had not proved themselves in battle when on flight patrols. By now the losses of senior officers had led the RFC HQ to confine commanding officers to 'test and recreational flying' only. Scott blithely ignored this, joining patrols as he put it, for 'recreational purposes', which made him a highly popular leader with everyone in his squadron.

Two new pilots joined the squadron in March: W.H. Gunner, who lived in Arundel, and Billy Bishop, who was to become the highest-scoring Canadian ace. Scott recognised in Bishop a combination of aggression, daring and marksmanship, and let him have free rein. Bishop was never a very skilled pilot and crashed a Nieuport after his first patrol with the squadron. Unhappily, this was seen by Brigade Commander J.F.A. Higgens, who in a later interview told Bishop he would have to return to flying school for additional instruction. As the squadron was still short of pilots, Scott still sent him up on patrol and on 25 March Bishop shot down his first Albatros D.III scout. Although he then had to force land behind Allied lines with engine failure, nothing more was said about additional training, and his score of aircraft destroyed grew gradually.

Scott and Bishop shared an enemy two-seater on a snowy morning in early April when two of their accompanying patrol were shot down, one being killed, the other made a PoW. By the middle of the month Scott had lost eight pilots and had to abandon offensive patrols until he was supplied with more pilots and machines. At the end of April, the squadron had suffered twenty pilot losses, either killed, wounded or missing, and problems were also being encountered with their replacement Nieuport Scouts. The machines were having to be built using unseasoned spruce, all the seasoned wood now being taken by the new aircraft factories the Americans were setting up in their own country. After one pilot was killed over the aerodrome while practising air-to-ground firing, Scott jumped into the nearest Nieuport and gave a flying display to boost his pilots' confidence in the aircraft.

Gunner was now getting his eye in, and on 11 May drove down an Albatros two-seater. Six days later he shot down an Albatros scout during an early morning patrol. On 28 May Gunner was in a patrol led by 'Grid' Caldwell, a New Zealander, when they encountered nine

Albatros near Lens. Gunner's Lewis gun jammed, and he had to dive away and try to get it working again. One of the patrol was killed, and Caldwell only escaped being shot down by feigning loss of control and diving to within 200ft of the ground.

This was also the day that Major Scott decided to take one of his recreational flights on his own, although he was anticipating a visit by General Allenby for an inspection at 9am.

Finding a group of enemy scouts below him when he crossed the line, Scott dived through them, scattering the formation to the four winds. As a patrol of No. 56 Squadron had been stalking them in preparation for a surprise attack, they were not at all pleased at his appearance. In the general melee that followed, Scott had his petrol tank pierced by a stray bullet and he was forced to land behind Allied lines, fortunately without damage to his machine or himself. In a short time, he had organised a message through to his squadron office to arrange for a car to pick him up on a main road, and then borrowed a horse from a nearby ammunition column and galloped off to his rendezvous to be picked up. He arrived back at camp just a few minutes before the appearance of General Allenby. The Brigade Commander John Higgens, as was his wont on these occasions, took a pretty dim view of the whole episode.

On 3 June, Gunner gained the Military Cross for an action that occurred while he was on patrol with A Flight over Vitre. *The London Gazette* of 18 July 1917 gives details:

> When on offensive patrol he engaged and attacked nine hostile aircraft, two of which were attacking the rear machine of his patrol. Having conveyed the other machine back to the aerodrome, he again returned with his patrol in response to an urgent call for aeroplanes to drive off hostile aircraft. He had been wounded in his previous encounter, but insisted in carrying on, and on numerous occasions has shown great skill and courage in offensive work.

On 10 July the klaxon sounded on the airfield, after a wireless report that enemy aircraft were attacking Allied trenches near

Monchy-le-Preux. All available pilots, including Scott and Bishop, rushed to their machines and, reaching the Allied lines, found a dozen enemy fighters at about 1,000ft, just about to return to their lines. Bishop was caught between two scouts, who were shooting at him from both sides. Fortunately, Scott saw his predicament and fired at one aircraft, setting it alight and allowing Bishop to deal with the other. Bishop returned home and rushed to find Scott and thank him for his help. He found that Scott's machine had been badly shot and he'd gone to hospital with an arm wound. This was his last appearance as a squadron commander, for he had been notified earlier that he was in line for promotion to command a wing. He was, therefore, ordered to take up his new command immediately upon leaving hospital.

By July the squadron was starting to be re-equipped with the new S.E.5a; although it was only a little faster than the Nieuport, it was a sturdy machine, which could be dived without fear of the wings failing. It also had two guns, a synchronised Vickers firing through the propeller and a Lewis gun fitted above the top wing. The Wolseley engine then installed was unreliable, and at one stage pilots were ordered not to cross enemy lines, a command Bishop ignored if he was in pursuit of a German aircraft.

On 29 July at 7am, Bishop, Caldwell and Gunner were on patrol in their new machines over Beaumont when they found a two-seater that looked suspiciously like a decoy. As they approached it, four Albatross aircraft dived on them out of the sun. The dogfight was fast and furious, when suddenly Gunner's engine failed and he put his nose down to try and glide towards his lines. A black Albatros fastened on his tail and shot him down in flames. Neither Caldwell nor Bishop were able to help as they were also fighting for their lives. Bishop did shoot down one German but both Caldwell's guns jammed. Although badly shot up, they both managed to get back to their airfield.

The circumstances of Gunner's death led to a reluctance on the part of the pilots to change over to the S.E.5a. An award of posthumous MC was made to Gunner's father at Chichester Barracks on 26 March 1918, where the officers and men of the Royal Sussex Regiment were on parade. Gunner's replacement was Alex Beck, who, like Eric Gordon England, was born of British parents living in Argentina and was educated at Eastbourne College. At the time he had forty-three hours solo, but was still only seventeen years old. When his parents discovered he was in France, they protested and after only three weeks he was recalled to England. However, even in that short period of time he flew a number of patrols and was hit by anti-aircraft fire and had to make a forced landing. He was to re-join No. 60 Squadron early in 1918, proving to be a doughty fighter pilot.

A report in the 'Sussex at War' column of the local paper on 29 October revealed that Lieutenant Lawrence Wingfield, who had been shot down on the first day of the Battle of Somme, had escaped from his prisoner-of-war camp after some fifteen months behind the wire. He was reunited with his parents on Sunday, 28 October.

After his capture, Wingfield had been incarcerated in three different prison camps. The first was at Rosenbad Kronad in Bavaria, which was a Napoleonic fortress. Then in April 1917 he was moved to Crefeld, which was only 15 miles from the Dutch border, but the Germans, fearing a mass breakout, then dispersed the prisoners, and he ended up at Strohen, some 40 miles from Bremen and over 90 miles from the Dutch frontier.

Eschewing the standard practice of tunnelling to freedom, Wingfield planned with a fellow officer to take advantage of an old disused gully that ran across the camp and joined a ditch, which, although protected with barbed wire, gave access to the outside world. A suitable night for the escape occurred, but it was pitch black and pouring with rain. Crawling along the gulley, which was now full of water, proved to be extremely exhausting, and after cutting the wire, Wingfield found he was stuck tight, with little energy to extricate himself. By then his companion had joined him, and was so anxious to get through that he seized Wingfield's legs and thrust him so hard that he shot out like a cork from a champagne bottle. By now the guards were aware that an escape was taking place, and bullets were flying everywhere. Wingfield, deciding that it would be wise to keep his head down, took refuge in a water-filled ditch for three-quarters of an hour until the commotion died down and then decamped.

Now soaking wet, Wingfield found his home-made compass was useless, so he decided to put some distance between himself and the prison camp. He soon realised that it was safer to travel at night, and chose barns full of straw in which to rest up during the day, burrowing in to sleep. One day he was found by a group of French prisoners-of-war who worked at a nearby farm. They took him back to their billet, gave him food and let him sleep to regain his strength. On the fourth day he resumed his trek, and four days later, after covering about 20 miles a day, reached the Dutch frontier, where he had to cross a wide river. Here he had a stroke of luck, meeting a man who led him to the narrowest part, just 100 yards wide. Wingfield stripped off, tied his clothes in a bundle and, placing them on a plank, swam across to the other side, pushing the plank in front of him. Clambering up the Dutch bank, he dressed again and after a long walk found a Dutch farmhouse, where he was welcomed with a hearty breakfast. His escape had taken eight days, and he returned to London in the third week in October. He was given the immediate award of the Military Cross for his escape, and like other officers, given an audience by the King. His original bombing operation of July 1916 was recognised after the forming of the RAF in April 1918, when he was awarded the Distinguished Flying Cross, which had replaced the MC.

Captain Grinnell-Milne, who learned to fly at Shoreham, was also forced down behind German lines in 1916 and taken prisoner-of-war. He too, succeeded in making his way to freedom after a number of attempts. Normally ex-prisoners-of-war were not allowed to resume active service in the same theatre of war. He managed, however, to evade this rule by devious means and flew with No. 56 Squadron until the war ended.

On 2 November 1917, Captain Henry Hall Griffith was killed in rather a bizarre flying accident. The son of Alderman and Mrs Arthur Foster Hall, he was educated at Brighton College and Christ's College, Cambridge. He took a degree in 1912, before joining his father's firm of solicitors. An accident before the outbreak of war prevented him from enlisting, so he went to Hendon and took his RAeC brevet at his own expense. He then joined the Army in June 1916, was commissioned in August and transferred to the RFC. On 16 October he went to France to join No. 45 Squadron, and on his second flight over the lines in a Sopwith 1½ Strutter, was attacked by half a dozen German scouts. His observer, despite being wounded in the head at the start of the encounter, helped to fight off the enemy aircraft. One enemy scout was driven down out of control, and they managed to escape. Although their machine was badly damaged, Griffith made a perfect landing at Fienvillers airfield.

After completing nine months' active service in France, Griffith was posted back to England as an instructor with No. 63 Training Squadron, based at Joyce Green in Kent. He took off before noon one day to test an aircraft with a sergeant as a passenger. There was low cloud, and he climbed to 800ft and then disappeared into the cloud, re-emerging in a spinning nose dive after a loop manoeuvre.

George Packham, skipper of the barge 'Whynot' of some 40 tons, called down to his solitary crew member Alf Kelsey, telling him to come up and see the aircraft. Alf was enjoying his favourite meal of streaky pork and shouted back that it was probably a learner from the training field at Joyce Green, when there was an almighty rending crash above deck. Alf rushed up and found Packham still standing at the wheel in a state of shock. The barge was a mass of smashed rigging, spars and equipment, which had been demolished as the aircraft swept over the bow and crashed on the deck. Packham rushed forward with Alf to find Griffith had been killed on impact. The barge was no longer controllable, and was now drifting across the river. Then a tug appeared and its captain, realising the situation, managed to lash his vessel to the wrecked barge and beach it in the mud by the Long Reach Tavern near Joyce Green. As the barge ground to a halt there was a movement among the wreckage, and the sergeant staggered out, badly shocked but not seriously hurt.

Packham told Alf he would have to report to the London barge owners about the accident immediately and left him in charge while he went by train to Dartford on his way to London. The survivor was soon taken away to hospital but the RFC officers who came aboard the barge insisted that Griffith's body could not be removed until the officers who were going to investigate the accident came aboard next morning. In the meanwhile, the body was covered with a blanket. Alf slept fitfully that night and woke up when he heard noises in the hold. Plucking up his courage, he took a lamp and slowly climbed the companionway. Holding the lamp in the air, he looked down into the hold. A pair of rat's eyes glistened in the dark and then the rodent scampered off, much to Alf's relief. Next morning Alf told the officers about the incident and they took pity on him and gave him a pass so that he could sleep in their camp until the enquiry was completed and the barge released. At the inquest that followed, Major Maxwell, the CO of No. 63 Training Squadron, said Griffith was an expert pilot and he could only suggest that he might have lost consciousness since the aircraft he was flying was very stable and would have righted itself normally. The RAMC doctor who examined the body said death was due to a sustained fracture at the base of the skull and other severe injuries. He said he had been talking to Griffith only an hour to two before the flight, and that he had seemed perfectly well. The coroner was told that a careful examination had been made of the wreckage, but no clue had been found as to the cause of the accident and the verdict of accidental death was returned.

Towards the end of 1917, plans were completed to set up two new aerodromes in Sussex. The first, between Yapton and Ford, was to be some 85 acres in size and was to be called Ford Junction. The other occupying 185 acres of farmland was at Tangmere, about 4 miles from Chichester. Both were to be designated Training Depot Stations and were to be built mainly using prisoner-of-war labour.

The year 1917 was also notable in that Henry Royce, the Rolls-Royce engine designer, moved to West Wittering due to ill health, and directed his staff from 'Elmstead'. This arrangement was not unacceptable to his staff because his visits to the works in the past had resulted in him dismissing workmen he felt were not doing the work as laid down. The result was that, as he left by the front door, the dismissed men came in the back door and were re-engaged.

Chapter 15

1918–19 War and Peace

The collapse of the Russian army and the success of the Peasants' Revolution left the Germans free to concentrate all their efforts in the West before the arrival of troops and war materiel from America swung the advantage to the Allies. The Germans needed a decisive victory, but even with the fifty-two divisions brought back from Russia they still did not have a great preponderance of troops over the Allies. To break the deadlock, new tactics were needed to enable a war of movement to be resumed, and they went to great lengths to prevent the Allies from finding out by aerial reconnaissance where the great offensive might take place.

It actually started on 21 March, preceded by a five-hour bombardment, and was followed by the use of specially trained stormtroopers skilled in infiltration tactics. A dense fog assisted the attack, and British lines were soon overrun and resistance started to crumble. After three and a half years of bloody war, the British Army was composed almost entirely of wartime soldiers, trained in trench warfare, rather than in the open warfare that had now burst upon them. Tactically the German offensive was very successful and made great advances, but the British fought stubbornly in retreat and German losses and fatigue gradually diminished the impetus of the attack. The need for airfields set up near the battlefields was more important for the Germans, since they had produced aircraft with high performance but short range, while the RFC, which had had to operate well inside enemy lines, did not have this problem. Some German squadrons that did move forward with the advance often lost contact with their headquarters in the rear. The concentration of German aircraft on a limited number of airfields also made them vulnerable to intensive attacks by Allied aircraft. With the emergence of open warfare, aircraft became increasingly important for attacking troops and transport now in the open and for bombing bridges.

At long last the RFC now had new aircraft in service that matched those of the Germans, and they had them in greater numbers. The S.E.5a, Sopwith Camel, Bristol Fighter and the DH.4 bomber roamed the skies with impunity. New pilots with adequate flying hours and combat training, including a substantial injection of pilots from Canada, meant there were ample reserves of both airmen and aircraft.

While the lone 'ace' might still command the attention of the popular press, the new leaders in the air led formations into battle to achieve tactical surprise and maximum losses to the enemy, rather than to build up individual scores. Air combat reached its peak on the Western Front in spring and summer 1918, but in the end, it was the ground attacks by hundreds of aircraft in the land battles that had the greatest impact on the conflict on the ground.

Although the Germans had increased their aircraft production substantially during the last year of the war, they were unable to replace pilots when they were suffering losses of 300 to 400 a month. In addition, the Allied blockade gradually cut off materials for repairs and, most vital of all, fuel for aircraft. Towards the end, German fighter squadrons had to restrict its flying to match dwindling oil supplies.

At midday on 9 January 1918, an R.E.8 of No. 21 Squadron, piloted by Captain G. Zirman, was engaged on a photographic reconnaissance in the Passchendaele area. The observer was Second Lieutenant Henry Arthur Somerville MC, an Eastbourne man who had a truly remarkable war record.

He had enlisted in the Royal Field Artillery in 1911 as a boy soldier of fifteen years. After the outbreak of war, he went to France and was in the retreat from Mons, and at the Marne and Aisne, and was in both the First and Second Battles of Ypres. In the latter, he was badly gassed and received a shrapnel wound in the arm, spending six weeks in hospital. Somerville was promoted to sergeant and volunteered for the infantry. When the Battle of the Somme began, he served for six weeks with the Royal Berkshire Regiment. By the beginning of 1917 he was commissioned in the Royal Sussex Regiment for service in the field. At the Third Battle of Ypres on 31 July and 1 and 2 August 1917 he was awarded the MC and the citation read:

> This officer showed wonderful energy and initiative in consolidating the captured position under very heavy enemy barrage. He took out a party of twenty-four men in daylight, right up to the line of the Steenbeck, and occupied four posts as an outpost line, when he came under heavy rifle and machine gun fire, having three men killed and four men wounded while getting in to this position. He held this line for twenty-four hours under very heavy artillery fire, and was much troubled by enemy snipers. He spent four hours endeavouring to establish touch with the unit on his left flank, during which time he was continually sniped at. This wonderful good spirit under most difficult conditions won for him the admiration of all ranks.

The award was presented to Second Lieutenant Somerville by King George V in November 1917 at Buckingham Palace. In August he had volunteered for training as an observer with the RFC and returned to the front late in November on active service.

It was on this, his first operational flight, that he encountered Max Mueller, who was leading six Albatros D.Vs of the Jasta Boelcke. Mueller was a Bavarian ace who had already shot down thirty-eight Allied aircraft. Sighting Zirman's R.E.8, he led his formation to cut it off. Zirman manoeuvred his aircraft to give Somerville a chance to fire at the formation leader at close range. As Mueller closed in for the kill, Somerville fired a long burst and Mueller's Albatros suddenly veered away and burst into flames, falling out of control. Horrified, Mueller's fellow pilots saw him jump from his machine and fall to his death near the town of Moorslede. In the confusion, Zirman made good his escape and returned to his airfield safely. Writing later to his parents, Somerville said, 'He (Mueller) had

38 British machines to his credit and we were nearly the 39th.' In his last letter to his parents before he was killed on 28 March on active service, Somerville wrote, 'Just a few lines to say I am OK. We are having a glorious time with the Hun: never has he had to pay the price as he is doing today.'

Another Sussex man was serving with No. 22 Squadron who had been re-equipped with the Bristol Fighter in August 1917. In May of the following year Second Lieutenant Howard Umney joined them as an observer. Umney had been educated at Charterhouse and had started a career in the pharmaceutical industry, where his father was a leading figure. Living at Yapton near Arundel, he enjoyed a great deal of success with his regular pilot, Second Lieutenant E.C. Bromley. On a fine day on 8 May the pair dived on an enemy two-seater and as they pulled out of a dive Umney gave the aircraft two short bursts from his twin Lewis guns. The enemy went into a nose dive and crashed. In the following week the two shot down two more enemy aircraft, and on 16 May they met a formation of enemy scouts and Umney shot down one, which caught fire and crashed. Almost immediately afterwards Umney fired a burst at another scout, which went into a spin before crashing. At the end of the month Umney scored one more victory with Bromley and two more with another pilot Lieutenant F.G. Gibbons, bringing his total of aircraft destroyed that month to eight. He was awarded the MC, the citation saying '... during recent operations Umney has destroyed five enemy aircraft and shown untiring energy and keenness, setting a splendid example to other observers in the squadron, in the air and on the ground and greatly helped his pilot in these encounters.'

Two old boys from Eastbourne College (1913–16) were Andrew King Cowper and Alex Beck (who was mentioned earlier). Both joined the RFC in 1917 and both became 'aces' and served with distinction on the Western Front in 1918.

Cowper now joined Eric Pashley's old squadron, No. 24, in August 1917. The squadron had by now had their DH.2 pushers replaced by a new de Havilland design, the DH.5. This aircraft was unusual in that the top wing had a back stagger to give the pilot a clear view forward. It was fitted with a forward-firing machine gun and had a top speed of 100mph at its best operational height of 10,000ft. It was undoubtedly inferior to the Sopwith Pup, which had already been at the front for six months. Although sturdily built, it was not a success, except for trench strafing. Over its seven months' service, the squadron destroyed only three enemy aircraft and forced down another fifteen out of control. Nevertheless, by November Cowper had got his eye in and, even flying the DH.5, had forced down two enemy aircraft. In the New Year the squadron started to re-equip with the S.E.5a. Both pilots and ground crew greeted the arrival of their new machines with great enthusiasm. Now capable of a speed of 130mph in level flight, the type was less streamlined than the Albatros, but was a sturdy, well-built aircraft with a stability that made it an excellent gun platform.

On 26 February, Cowper forced down a Pfalz scout on a morning patrol, and it landed on an airfield used by No. 25 Squadron at Ham. The pilot was reported to have thrown up his hands immediately on landing, confiding to his captors that he'd come down there because he was afraid had he landed on a French airfield he would have been shot.

Lieutenant Colonel F.V. Holt of No. 22 Wing heard of the captured machine and decided he would fly it back to No. 24 Squadron's airfield for the pilots to look over. He got off the ground all right and, reaching 100ft, put the aircraft into a roll. At this point he jammed the joystick against the fuel pump handle while he was upside down. Luckily the pump handle broke, and he managed to right the aircraft and land in one piece. This machine was later exhibited at the Lord Mayor's Show, and was also on display at the Agricultural Hall in London with other captured German aircraft. The same afternoon Cowper shot down another German machine, which broke up in the air. This was the day that the squadron downed six machines in all, three of which were Fokker Triplanes.

In March, Cowper was awarded the Military Cross, the first decoration for the squadron since they were re-equipped. With the start of the German March offensive, the squadron aircraft were out as soon as the fog cleared to attack German troops with machine guns and bombs. Next day the squadron had to move back to Moreui, new pilots who had arrived earlier being shepherded to their new airfield by Cowper. In the frantic days that followed, Cowper shot down another five aircraft, on one occasion having to walk back from Cachy after his machine had been shot to ribbons in ground strafing. The squadron history records show that Cowper had some extraordinary escapes after his aircraft had been riddled by ground fire on other ground-strafing missions. On 24 March Cowper was promoted to Flight Commander of B Flight, but his reign was brief, as after eighteen days his operational tour was up and he was posted back to England. He was awarded a further two bars to his MC later. The citations speak of great courage, gallantry and skill with magnificent dash and determination. On 21 April his squadron shot down their first balloon, making a total of 100 enemy aircraft shot down using the S.E.5a. This was also the day that Baron Manfred von Richthofen was shot down and killed. Lieutenant Colonel Holt was taking a pilot from the squadron who had performed some hair-raising stunts over a nearby battery to see the battery commander and apologise. On the way they came upon the Baron's red triplane being stripped for souvenirs, and Holt helped himself to some pieces of fabric and took them back to distribute among the squadron's pilots. Holt – thirteen years on and now an Air Vice Marshal in the RAF – was killed near Tangmere when his aircraft collided with a Siskin fighter of No. 43 Squadron.

After No. 60 Squadron moved to Bailleul in early March, Beck re-joined the squadron. Within two days the German offensive began and the squadron had to move back to Le Bellevue, some 6 miles from Doullens. With the return of open warfare, the squadron was soon heavily involved in strafing exposed German troops in an attempt to slow down their advance. By the end of March, they had lost ten pilots out of twenty-five, and in the middle of April the squadron had to move again back to Boffles, near Frevent, where they were to remain for six months. It was mostly tented accommodation and the aircraft had to be left out in the open, causing many maintenance problems, including a significant increase in engine failures. With the improvement in the standard of flying training, pilots were now arriving with up to one hundred hours in their log books and at least a grounding in aerial combat. Nevertheless, it was still normally three weeks before they were allowed to cross the line, and they were then told to stick closely to their flight commander, as stragglers had a very short life.

Beck's six weeks with the squadron in mid-1917, before he was sent back to Home Establishment as under age, had enabled him to get the taste and feel of squadron life. Thus, he started his second posting with some knowledge of what to expect, plus the extra flying hours he had accumulated in England. On 6 June he was flying with Captain Scholte, the Flight Commander of C Flight, when they attacked and drove down a German observation balloon near Pye in Sussanne. Although few aces on both sides specialised in destroying balloons, they were no means easy meat. It is said that the RFC/RAF regarded the actual destruction of a balloon as being equivalent of shooting down three aircraft. Balloons were normally flown at around 7,000ft, a few miles behind enemy lines, and had many advantages over aircraft for observation being a comparatively stable observation platform and in immediate contact with gun batteries by telephone line. The use of Buckingham ammunition, which only had a range of about 150 yards, meant the pilot attacking a balloon had to get really up close and, even then, it was by no means easy to ignite the gas in the balloon envelope if it was rainy or misty. It ignited very slowly, thus giving the observer the opportunity to jump clear using the parachute attached to the side of the balloon basket with a static line. A trained balloon observer was worth many times the cost of a balloon, but it was still not the done thing to shoot at an observer as he came down. In any case, with the site round the balloon covered with anti-aircraft guns, it was vital to get away quickly after the attack if you were to survive the hail of fire that came up from the ground. The winch was often fitted to a lorry and the balloon crew could wind down their craft at a rate of 150ft a minute while the lorry careered away still lowering it. Hence, surprise was an essential element in any successful balloon attack either by cloud hopping and then diving on the balloon, or by coming in very low and surprising the defences. This could be successful but the attacker had to beware of the telephone wires round the site.

Beck took part in another offensive patrol on 3 August, and a further two the next day, helping to take down another three balloons. On 8 August he shot down his first enemy aircraft. The combat took place over Folier-Rosières, the enemy machine being a two-seater, and from then on, his victories began to mount. On the 14th he claimed an Albatros D and a Hannoveraner, one in the morning and the other in the afternoon. On the 22nd he went on patrol, where he and two other pilots forced down two aircraft, and at the end of the month he shared two more shoot downs, giving him a half share in each. By September Beck was promoted to captain, made the flight commander of B Flight, and recommended for the DFC. He had now been on active service for over seven months and was due a rest. He was offered the chance to stay, which he accepted, but asked to be allowed to forego acting as flight commander so he could have a roving commission. This was agreed, but the lack of replacement flight commander meant he still acted in that role. During his tour in France he shot down nine confirmed aircraft and was, in fact, the last pilot of his squadron to shoot down an enemy aircraft, a LVG C.VI, on 2 November, and returned home on leave just before the Armistice.

Disbelief was the dominant emotion of pilots at the end of the war, particularly after being warned that anyone shooting down an enemy aircraft after 11am on 11 November would be court martialed. There was an inevitable sense of anticlimax after the continuing tension of wartime flying, and many had difficulty in grappling with the problems of adjusting to a new post-war world where unemployment was rife.

Even in these now hallowed days of peace, death was still at the elbow of the aviator, and pilots who survived the horrors of the war still faced accidental death. Lieutenant Alfred Norman, son of the Reverend Henry Norman of Palmeira Square, Hove, was one of the few pilots who was also a poet. Joining the RFC in 1917, he learned to fly in Yorkshire, and then went on a night flying and bombing course before being posted to the Independent Air Force, whose task it was to bomb Germany in retaliation for the raids on Britain. On duty during the Armistice, Norman crashed at Amiens while flying in fog on 20 November and was killed instantly. A correspondent of *The Times* newspaper described him as a boy of great literary promise when he reviewed Norman's first slender book of poetry, *Ditchling Beacon*, in March 1918. His poem 'Cocksdorp' appeared in the newspaper and read that the body of a flying officer, presumably British, had been washed up at Cocksdorp on the shores of Texel Island off the Dutch coast:

> I wonder, when the end comes and Death calls me,
> If I shall rest at Cocksdorp beside the sea,
> When the grey waves mutter and the white waves foam,
> And the wind that's calling is the wind of home.
> I wonder, when the Springtime cowslip peep,
> Through the long rich grasses where the sea folk sleep,
> I wonder if they'd let me seek once more,
> Those low red houses on the Sussex shore,
> Or hear the voices of the creeping tide,
> In Shoreham harbour where the tall ships ride.
> With night about me like a purple gown,
> And the moon a sickle over Lancing Downs.
> Cold Texel Island would soon fade away,
> And the grim tower watching over Cocksdorp Bay.

It was early in 1918 that the Air Ministry and the US Government came to an agreement that Tangmere and Ford Junction airfields, plus three more to be built in Sussex – at Rustington, Southborne and Goring – should be transferred to the new US Army Air Service. They were to be used as training depots and would provide accommodation for thirty squadrons of Handley Page 0/400 bombers, which, it was hoped, would be in France in mid-1919. By June 1918 both Tangmere and Ford Junction were nearing completion. Rustington was only half built, and Southbourne only just started. It was decided to abandon Goring as it could not be built in the time left. The Americans took over Ford Junction in August and Tangmere in September. In the interim, No. 92 Squadron used Tangmere to work up on their new S.E.5as before going to France.

The Armistice revealed that only one training course had been partially completed at Ford Junction, and the Americans soon moved to Tangmere to allow Ford Junction to be used as a demobilisation centre for the RAF. It was not long after that US troops left Tangmere and it reverted to No. 61 Training Squadron. By the end of 1919 it closed, although the Air Ministry retained the land and buildings. Ford Junction closed early the next year, but with Rustington and Southbourne nearly complete, the land was returned to agricultural use and the buildings dismantled and sold off.

Early in 1919 the Flying Instructors' School at Shoreham closed, and both Vincent and Foot were among a number of experienced pilots selected to ferry German aircraft across the Channel as part of the reparations agreed under the terms of the Armistice. On one of their first trips they each brought back a Fokker D.VII and agreed that before delivering them to their final destination at Hounslow they would show them off to their former comrades at Shoreham and Gosport. However, when Vincent was nearing Brighton, he suffered an engine failure and had to come down on the East Brighton Golf Course near Roedean School. Landing on a fairway, he ran into a bunker and upended the Fokker. Seeing the landing, a number of girls from the nearby Roedean School rushed to the scene but when they saw the black crosses on the wings, they screamed and retired hastily to the protection of their school. With the help of some farm labourers, Vincent managed to get the aircraft back on its wheels and then found he had run out of petrol. This was sent on from Shoreham and the aircraft refuelled. He then pressed on to the airfield, where he and Foot gave a first-class display of acrobatics.

At the beginning of April 1919, the newly formed No. 1 Wing of the proposed new Canadian Air Force moved down to Shoreham. There were two squadrons: No. 1 had S.E.5as, its CO being Captain A.E. McKeever, the outstanding Canadian ace on Bristol Fighters, while the CO of No. 2 Squadron was Captain Lawson, who had served with the RNAS before transferring to No. 245 Squadron of the Independent Air Force. His unit had DH.4 bombers.

Despite the RAF rank anomaly, one of the flight commanders of No. 2 Squadron was Major A.D. Carter, DSO and Bar, AFC and Croix de Guerre (Belgium). Originally in the Canadian Infantry, he had learned to fly in the summer of 1917. After four months on coastal patrol, he was posted to No. 19 Squadron in France, then equipped with French Spads. Shortly afterwards the squadron re-equipped with the new Sopwith Dolphin and, although there were those who reviled the machines, Carter seemed to find them to his taste. He shot down his first enemy aircraft on 15 March 1918, and the new type proved to be a highly successful ground strafer during the German offensives in March and April of that year. In the next four months Carter shot down thirty-one aircraft, but on 19 May was shot down himself and wounded. He spent some time in a German hospital but had recovered by the time the war ended. On 22 May 1919 he took up a Fokker D.VII at Shoreham and gave a display of acrobatics over Lancing College. At 7,000ft the top wing folded up, and Christopher Clarkson, who saw the crash, described it as the most spectacular he had ever seen at Shoreham. While the top wing gently drifted down, the rest of the machine nosedived into the earth of the 16-acre field behind Lancing College. Major Carter is buried in the Old Shoreham cemetery of St Nicholas Church across the River Adur, with the French-Canadian and three South Africans killed in training in 1917. Financial retrenchment on the part of the Canadian Government finally resulted in the units being disbanded and the equipment being dispersed.

The war years had presented the aircraft company of White and Thompson – located at Middleton near Bognor – with both an opportunity and a challenge. It had been decided in the early stages to concentrate on the design and production of flying boats but this involved many problems, including, in particular, the design of flying boat hulls. The company's designer, F.P.H. Beadle, had the advantage of being able to use the services of Saunders of Cowes, which had been building yachts and motor boats for many years. Saunders was awarded subcontracts to build the hulls, using wire-sown multi-skin hulls. These were affected by landing shocks, when the wire cut into the cedar frames and led to maintenance problems.

J.C. Porte, the British expert and advocate of the flying boat, had gone to America pre-war to join Curtiss and pilot the new machine being built for an attempt on the *Daily Mail* £10,000 prize for a transatlantic flight. He returned to England on the outbreak of war.

He was made a lieutenant commander in the RNAS, and eventually given charge of an experimental flying wing at Felixstowe, despite his earlier discharge from the Navy on health grounds. With no formal training either in boat building or designing aircraft, he progressively transformed the Curtiss design for the America flying boat, until the new machines could carry six times the load of the original aircraft. In October 1915 Dr Samuel White, Norman Thompson's partner and financial backer, left the company and joined the Royal Army Medical Corps, and the company was renamed Norman Thompson Flight Company Ltd. Its first new machine under the new name was the N.T.4, a twin-engined pusher flying boat biplane with wings of unequal span. Some fifty N.T.4s were built altogether, and used for training and patrols in home waters. Later the firm produced the N.T.2B, a two-seater flying boat trainer that proved very successful. Some 150 were ordered in total, part of the work being subcontracted to both Saunders and Supermarine. Later the firm built a two-seat flying boat fighter for which it had high hopes, which did not materialise since its performance was disappointing and gained no orders. When Beadle left the company at the end of 1917, his loss was a set back to the firm's prospects of further contracts from the Admiralty. In anticipation of continual expansion, substantial bank loans had been acquired to erect new buildings that were, in fact, never used. By 1918 the company was in financial difficulties and in April a receiver was appointed by the banks. When the war ended, like many other manufacturers, the company had its outstanding Government contracts cancelled, and had no alternative but to go into liquidation in 1919. Handley Page, which always had an eye for a bargain, subsequently bought the bulk of its stock at a knockdown price.

In 1919, Porte, now a wing commander, decided to leave the RAF and accept an offer from the Gosport Aircraft Company to join it as its chief designer. This was the company whose yacht yard was reorganised by Herman Volk earlier in the war for turning over to aircraft production. By now Porte's health, long affected by overwork and stress, declined rapidly, and on 22 November 1919 he died at Brighton at the age of thirty-five. There is no doubt that he had given his life for his country, though not on the more heroic field of battle.

His legacy to the RAF and the country was the flying boat, which played a vital role in the Second World War by protecting Allied shipping lanes and convoys.

The Eastbourne Aviation Company, first formed by Fowler, made its contribution to the war effort on perhaps less ambitious lines. During the war years it built twelve B.E.2cs, forty Farmans, 200 Avro 504Ks and six Avro 504Ls, some 258 machines in all. In 1918, seventy-five S.E.5as were also assembled at Caffyn's Motor Works at Marine Parade, Eastbourne.

During 1919 a number of the people mentioned earlier died. Lieutenant Colonel Barrington-Kennett, aged seventy-three, was buried at Tillington near Petworth, only one of his four sons surviving the conflict. B.C. Hucks, who had looped the loop at Shoreham and had spent most of the war as a test pilot, died in April after catching influenza. Vedrines, the French aviator, crashed in Lyons having survived the war and was killed.

Now the war was over, interest revived in the £10,000 prize that the *Daily Mail* had offered for a transatlantic non-stop flight. The advances in design and greater engine reliability and the increase in loads now possible made the feat seem attainable. There was general agreement that the flight would have to be made from Newfoundland to gain the advantage of the westerly winds that predominated in that part of the world. The first two contestants were Harry Hawker and F.P. Raynham, who had both been at Shoreham pre-war. Hawker, with his navigator Mackenzie Grieve, took off in a single-engine Sopwith Atlantic biplane, to be followed an hour later by the Martinsyde 'A', which had been christened the 'Raymor' after Raynham and his navigator, Captain C.W.F. Morgan. Unfortunately, the 'Raymor' was caught by a gust of wind on take-off and it struck the ground, upon which the undercarriage collapsed, shaking both pilot and navigator very severely, so the flight had to be abandoned. By this time Hawker had got halfway across the Atlantic but was in serious trouble with the overheating of his Rolls-Royce Eagle engine. He, therefore, had to accept that there was no way he would reach Ireland. He eventually found a Danish steamer after he had flown 1,400 miles and ditched beside it, so both he and Mackenzie Grieve were rescued. The aircraft was abandoned, but was still afloat ten days later when it was found by an American freighter and salvaged, being brought back and put on show at Selfridges in Oxford Street, London.

Thus, the field was clear for the third contestant, Jack Alcock, another frequent visitor to Shoreham airfield before the war. He and his observer, Arthur Whitten Brown, took off from Lister's Field, St John's, in a Vickers Vimy twin-engined bomber at 5.13 BST on 14 June 1919. Like Hawker, they had Rolls-Royce Eagle VII engines of 360hp each, and enough fuel for 2,440 miles. The Vimy managed to get airborne but lost its auxiliary propeller, which was to have powered their wireless set. Alcock told reporters afterwards that it was a terrible journey, and that they scarcely ever saw the sun, moon or stars throughout their flight. With dense fog coming up, they had to descend to 300ft, with the machine covered in ice and frozen sleet for four hours. Alcock was convinced at one point that the machine nearly looped the loop. The pair finally made landfall at Clifden, County Galway in Ireland, coming down in a bog close to a Marconi wireless station at 8.40am on 15 July. They had sufficient fuel to continue but decided a landing near the wireless station would ensure the early news of their success. Total journey time was sixteen hours twenty-seven minutes after covering 1,890 miles, at an average speed of 188mph. Both airmen were subsequently knighted, and were feted wherever they went. Alcock's triumph was, however, short-lived. On 18 December he flew a Vickers Viking amphibian to the Paris Air Show. Encountering fog at Rouen, he had to make a forced landing, and struck a tree, his body being found in the wreckage. A week earlier Jose Weiss, the Amberley glider pioneer, had died in his sleep at the age of sixty.

With the onset of peace, solicitor G.A. Wingfield decided to resume his operations in the new aeronautical world. As he still had control of the land south of the railway line at Shoreham, he decided to revive the Sussex Aero Club, although the total area would be insufficient for a flying school. At the end of 1919 an advertisement appeared in the local press announcing the proposed reopening, with details of a new luxurious club house, golf course, hard and grass tennis courts, plus hangars, a landing ground and a garage and repair shops. Those halcyon days of flying were now a thing of the past and aviation was now a very expensive hobby, while it was also becoming the subject of strict regulation by the Government. So, the plan seems to have come to nothing, with Wingfield departing from the scene, although leaving behind him an airfield that still survives today, a tribute to his acumen in selecting the site originally.

By 1919 Major Fowler had been demobilised from the RAF and returned to Eastbourne. During his career in the RNAS and RAF he had served in the Isle of Grain, flying anti-submarine patrols, and also had a spell at Dunkirk. In 1917 he returned to instructing at the Central Flying School, and then went to Cranwell as a senior instructor. He returned to Eastbourne as its commanding officer, rounding off his service career in charge of the experimental seaplane base at Hamble, near Southampton.

Fowler was not slow to restart his passenger flights at Eastbourne, recruiting a Lieutenant Loten to assist him. The free flights for readers of the *Eastbourne Gazette* were also resumed, and continued to be popular, especially with the ladies. Loten and Fowler also made a number of seaplane flights from the old site at Paston Place, Brighton, besides the beach at Eastbourne. However, Fowler soon took the view that public interest in flying was becoming sated and that passenger flights – although still marginally profitable – represented a diminishing source of income. He, therefore, turned to reviving his flying school, and being well aware of the value of publicity, decided to take up a school for female aviators. He knew this would attract press coverage, and it did, numerous photographs appearing of his young ladies in flying gear, swinging propellers in a most elegant way. The charge for a private flying licence was £125, while a commercial licence cost £300. In the event the scheme does not seem to have been successful, but by now Fowler had been approached to join a British Air Mission to Japan to help set up a flying school for Japanese Navy pilots near Tokyo, and he was later joined by Loten. The Eastbourne Aviation Company, therefore, gradually faded away, a receiver being called in the following year.

Joyriding was still a source of income for demobilised pilots, and the town council at Brighton received a number of applications for permission to fly from the town beaches and grass sites during 1919. The Avro Company now decided to launch a passenger flying service, and gained the concession to take up passengers on pleasure flights from an airfield it set up at Ladies Mile, between Patcham and the top of Stanmer Park on the outskirts of Brighton. The Tilling Bus Service ran a service every few minutes from the aquarium. The flights started on 12 July, and the mayor and mayoress were due to make their first flight, but bad weather in the morning meant this had to be cancelled. By the afternoon the skies had cleared and some 100 passengers took to the air before a crowd of 1,500 spectators. Flights were advertised as costing one guinea (£1.05), while it was possible to book a return flight for the Goodwood Races for seven guineas (£7.35) and in August one flight was made to Birmingham. A special air show took place on 25, 26 and 27 October, at which Miss Nellie Gibson made a parachute descent using the now somewhat outmoded Guardian Angel parachute. In addition, the new Avro Baby was on show, a small light biplane with a wingspan of only 28ft. Owing to the difficulty of obtaining a suitable lightweight engine, the original Green engine of 35hp, which Pixton had in the Avro D when he flew to Oakwood, was rebuilt and appears to have been a success.

So, after 136 years, the aeroplane had virtually eliminated all opposition. Airships would still hang on, but after the 1930s they were virtually relics of a bygone age. Balloons would still appear at occasional garden fetes but would only re-emerge from the shade when the gas burner was adopted to provide hot air after the Second World War, proving the Montgolfier brothers had the right idea but not the technology. The vast surpluses of aircraft, spare parts and material were now being advertised and the *Sussex Daily News* carried a full-page advertisement by the Disposal Board on 18 September 1919. At that time a Bristol Fighter was being offered for £800, a third of its production cost, but – later – even greater bargains appeared such as a fully airworthy Avro 504K in exchange for a motorcycle.

Commercial aviation, seen as a panacea by both the Government and the aircraft manufacturers to their problems in developing aviation, would take some time to become viable. Wartime aircraft adapted for passenger use were expensive to operate and most of the early airlines fell by the wayside. It became apparent over a period of time that the Government policy that an airline should 'fly by itself' without subsidy was a virtual impossibility and that our air links with the Commonwealth were important enough to justify Government help.

So Sussex aviation became a little like the sleeping princess. It was not until the late 1920s that F.G. Miles and Cecil Pashley started to use a small part of the defunct Shoreham airfield again. Tangmere was reactivated by the RAF as a fighter station and Ford came back to life in the 1930s as a new surge of flying activity began again in the county.

Index